# MARTIN LUTHER

TEXT BY PETER MANNS
PHOTOGRAPHS BY HELMUTH NILS LOOSE
INTRODUCTION BY JAROSLAV PELIKAN

# Martin Luther

## An Illustrated Biography

CROSSROAD · NEW YORK

1982
The Crossroad Publishing Company
575 Lexington Avenue, New York, N.Y. 10022

Originally published as "Martin Luther" © by Verlag Herder, Freiburg, West Germany
Translated by Michael Shaw
English translation copyright © 1982 by The Crossroad Publishing Company

Printed in West Germany


Library of Congress Cataloging in Publication Data

Manns, Peter.
    Martin Luther: an illustrated biography.

    1. Luther, Martin, 1483–1546.    2. Reformation--
Germany--Biography. I. Title.
BR325.M284  1982    284.1'092'4   [B]     82-14972
ISBN 0-8245-0510-7

# CONTENTS

# INTRODUCTION

"Martin Luther the Reformer is one of the most extraordinary persons in history and has left a deeper impression of his presence in the modern world than any other except Columbus." So spoke "America's sage," Ralph Waldo Emerson, in a lecture on Luther delivered in Boston on February 15, 1835.

Luther was born in 1483; Columbus discovered America in 1492: that coincidence has long engaged the reflection, not only of American thinkers like Emerson, but of historians and of theologians, whether Roman Catholic or Protestant; and it may well serve as the occasion for some thoughts on the publication of *Martin Luther: An Illustrated Biography* by Peter Manns in America. For it is in many ways a continuation of that reflection on the coincidence of Luther and Columbus when the author of this volume, a Roman Catholic historian and theologian, finds it possible to speak about Luther's faith "from the inside" and sometimes even to identify himself with Luther's ideas and beliefs more closely than many Protestants (including, of course, Ralph Waldo Emerson) have been able to do. Perhaps the most impressive feature of the book for American readers will be the author's repeated emphasis on the continuities between Luther's pre-Reformation Catholicism and his stance as the Reformer; for we have been accustomed to concentrate on the discontinuities, as Luther himself tended to do when, in his polemical writings, he had to deal with challenges from the right or the left. The perspective of five centuries, the careful research of the last hundred years, and the far-reaching changes in the relations between Roman Catholics and Protestants—all of these factors make it possible for such a book as this to appear at all. For it to appear in America as well means that our life and culture, as well as our faith, may have special reason to attend to a portrait of Luther that has been drawn in this new way.

None of this would have been possible without the change of spirit symbolized by the Second Vatican Council. On one question after another, the Council manifested an attitude, as well as a method of theological thought, far more congenial to the Reformation than

that of the First Vatican Council had been. To come from a study of Reformation debates about the doctrines of the Church, the ministry, and the sacraments to the decrees of the Second Vatican Council is a remarkable experience. Although the eventual outcome is, to be sure, a reaffirmation of traditional definitions of the priesthood, the seven sacraments, and papal authority, these definitions now stand in the context of a new and deeper recognition that the Church of Christ is in the first instance a body of believers, not an external institution, and that "priesthood" is a category that in the New Testament is applied either to Christ as High Priest or to all believers as kings and priests, but not to a special caste of the ordained. The arguments in support of such affirmations, moreover, have now become much more profoundly biblical, making use of the critical insights, historical research, and theological method that are characteristic of biblical theologians irrespective of confessional orientation. Conversely, it is no less remarkable an experience (as Dr. Manns shows) to come from the decrees of the Second Vatican Council to the debates of the Reformation. Many of the arguments employed by the adversaries of the Reformation—one thinks, for example, of the tortured reasoning in support of withholding the chalice from the laity in Holy Communion—cannot be defended, and no respectable theologian could get away with advancing them today.

Yet it would be an oversimplification to attribute this new picture of the Reformation principally to the "era of good feeling" represented and created by the Council. In many ways, the obverse is the case: the Council owed its reinterpretation of the Reformation, as well as its repossession of biblical theology, to the scholarly work of the two or three preceding generations, in which the distinctions between Roman Catholics and Protestants gradually became less significant for theological research. The work of several Roman Catholic historians—whose mentor was Joseph Lortz of the University of Mainz, where Peter Manns continues his work—raised up a new genre of Reformation research, which, building on the foundations of the medieval scholarship carried on by such giants as Martin Grabmann (1875–1949), sought to put Luther and the other Reformers into their late medieval setting and thus to understand both the strengths and the weaknesses of Luther in the light of the fourteenth and fifteenth centuries. These had been the very centuries that much of the "Thomist revival" had tended to denigrate in its zeal for "the thirteenth the greatest of centuries," with the result that the thinkers who came after Bonaventure and Thomas Aquinas—even the "Doctor Marianus" Duns Scotus, not to mention William of Ockham—did not receive the benefit of detailed scholarly research or even of critical editions. (The new edition of Duns Scotus, launched by the indefatigable Father Balić, still has a long way to go, while the Ockham edition, under the leadership of the Franciscan Institute at St. Bonaventure's, is moving toward completion, perhaps in time for the septicentennial of his birth in 1985.)

Out of such research has begun to come a new picture of the late Middle Ages, as well as a new picture of the Reformation. Many of the ideas for which Luther has been blamed by Roman Catholic polemics, or praised by Protestant hagiography, may now be seen as the common property of late medieval thought, shared (and often in a debased form) by his Roman Catholic opponents. One could say, therefore, that the scholarship of the twentieth century has begun to supply some of the missing quotation marks in the texts of the sixteenth century. The quotations to be identified are not, of course, only those from the late Middle Ages. The church fathers and even, *horribile dictu,* the Scriptures have not been credited as the sources for phrases and ideas that appear in Luther. It is, for example, a characteristic emphasis of Luther to regard the Virgin Birth, whose miraculous character he never doubted, as nevertheless a sign of the humility of Christ rather than of his sovereignty over the laws of nature; for, Luther said, Christ did not shrink even from being born of a Virgin. Protestant scholars, especially once they themselves had concluded that the idea of a miraculous Virgin Birth was an embarrassment, pointed to this as evidence for Luther's distinctiveness over against the patristic and medieval traditions. That distinctiveness, however, must be seen in the light of a sentence in the *Te Deum,* traditionally ascribed to Ambrose and Augustine on the occasion of Augustine's baptism and embedded in the canonical and liturgical life of medieval monasticism, especially of Luther's Augustinians: *"Tu ad liberandum suscepisti hominem non horruisti Virginis uterum,"* translated in the *Book of Common Prayer* as: "When thou tookest upon thee to deliver man, thou didst humble thyself to be born of a Virgin." It belonged to patristic and medieval Piety, then, to see the Virgin Birth as part of the humiliation of Christ, and Luther continued to stand in this piety also after his separation from Rome.

The task of identifying Luther's sources is still far from completed, and in the course of editing the American Edition of *Luther's Works* there were repeated instances where it was necessary to supplement the meager apparatus of even the best critical editions of Luther by supplying the missing references. The standard set of Luther, the so-called Weimar Edition, was launched, with considerable fanfare, to mark the four-hundredth anniversary of his birth in 1883. As is the way of most scholarly editions, it has taken modern editors longer to produce the works than it ever took the original author. Unfortunately, the state of relations between Roman Catholic and Protestant scholarship—and, for that matter, the state of Roman Catholic scholarship on the Reformation—a decade or so after the First Vatican Council did not encourage the creation of ecumenical editorial teams for the planning and production of the Weimar Edition. (Even in the editing of patristic texts there was less ecumenical cooperation than the state of scholarship did warrant.) The quality of the Weimar volumes, uneven but still indispensable, would have been vastly improved if the critical apparatus had been able to benefit from the work of medievalists, especially Roman Catholic medievalists, as is evident from a comparison of the most recent volumes, some of them revisions of earlier Weimar versions, with the first volumes.

Still the Weimar Edition deserves a large part of the credit for the Luther renaissance of the twentieth century. Every generation since the Reformation had fashioned its own picture of the Reformer: He became, successively, an orthodox confessionalist, a Pietist, an Enlightenment rationalist, a German nationalist, a Romantic, a Kantian idealist, an existentialist—and, lest we forget, a Nazi and an ecumenist. But thanks to the availability of the texts of his early lectures in the Weimar Edition, and then to the discovery and publication of his long-lost lectures on Romans (found in the Vatican Library), scholars trained in the critical philological skills of the nineteenth century could set about disentangling the historical Reformer from these later pictures. Karl Holl (1866–1926) was such a philologist, whose work on the Berlin corpus of the Greek church fathers, beginning in 1894, was responsible for a splendid edition of an enormously complicated text, the works of Epiphanius on heresy (3 vols.; Berlin, 1915–32). Bringing the same careful commitment to an examination of Luther's works, especially his early lectures, Holl produced a series of lectures and articles which, taken together (and published together), helped to turn Luther research in a new direction. His essay, "Luther's Understanding of Religion," was delivered as a lecture in wartime Berlin on October 31, 1917, for the four-hundredth anniversary of the posting of Luther's ninety-five theses. It is still a monument in the interpretation of the Reformer, to which all of us who have worked in the field are profoundly indebted.

Nevertheless, the first section of Holl's essay, which deals with Luther's Catholic background, would have to be drastically revised today, as even a cursory comparison of it with the material in this book will show. It is a measure of how far we have come during the century since the first volume of the Weimar Edition that Peter Manns is in a position to refer to Luther not only as "the Reformer" (and that without the usual invidious "socalled") but as "father in the faith." In so doing, he has been able to set the record straight, over against earlier interpreters on both sides of the confessional boundary. His treatment of penance and indulgences is a good example, also because this was the issue in Luther's public emergence as Reformer. Professor Manns uses Luther's lifelong reliance on private confession (in which Luther differed from Calvin) as evidence that penance and confession were not, as such, the sort of legalism that Protestant interpreters have been fond of describing, but could be and sometimes were a genuinely evangelical force in the life of the Church and the life of the individual believer. On the other hand, Luther's failure to "find a gracious God" by means of penance and confession does not mark him as a pathological exception to the rule, as Roman Catholic interpreters have repeatedly charged, but rather as one who took the system at its word and then found that it simply did not work. With the author's similar treatment of monasticism, vis-à-vis both groups of Luther scholars, many readers, be they monastic or Protestant in their sympathies, may find it more difficult to agree. On the other hand, the work of Protestant historians, above all the pioneering researches of Heiko Augustinus Oberman of Harvard and then of Tübingen, is visible in the author's depiction of Luther's connections with post-Thomist scholasticism, especially nominalism.

Emerson's linking of the names of Luther and Columbus, with which this Introduction opened, suggests some additional considerations of special significance for an English-speaking audience. Despite the veritable cottage industry of Luther translations in Tudor England, well described by William Clebsch in his *England's Earliest Protestants* (New Haven, 1964), the mainstreams of Protestantism in England and America have been dominated by Luther (or any other one man) as they have in Germany and Scandinavia. Consequently, the mythology of the Reformation in the Anglican, Puritan, Methodist, and Free Church traditions has acquired certain special features. It is, I think, more than a mere impression to note that English writers on the Reformation have tended to emphasize, more than their Continental colleagues have, the moral corruption of the Church against which the Reformation was directed, and proportionately to underemphasize the specifically doctrinal issues, on which so much of German theology has concentrated. Emerson's unease with Luther's dogmatism is an extreme instance, but it is not altogether atypical. Nor was the understanding of Luther made easier when his confessional descendants in America often tried to out-Luther Luther in their insistence on the purity of doctrine as a precondition for cooperation among Christians, even for prayer in common.

American Roman Catholics, for their part, brought with them from Catholic Europe many of the caricatures of Luther that had come out of the propaganda of the Counter-Reformation. It sometimes seemed that every candidate for the priesthood—and most catechumens—must have learned that Luther (a) said one should "sin boldly," (b) rejected the Epistle of James, and (c) married a nun; but meanwhile very few of them had so much as looked at, for example, the *Small Catechism* of 1529, whose "Evangelical-Catholic" exposition of the Apostles' Creed and the Our Father summarizes, without a wasted word, the consensus of the best in the tradition. Dependent as it has been on translations from French and German for so much of its scholarship, Roman Catholic theology in America has tended to lag behind the growing edge of that scholarship. Here, as in other chapters of intellectual history, it is instructive to ask what was translated and what was not, and why. To mention only one unfortunate instance, Jacques Maritain's *Three Reformers,* which even some of his disciples consider his worst book, found a translator into English, but Adolf Herte's *Das katholische Lutherbild* did not. In the past two or three decades, that situation is being ameliorated, thanks to the books of Roman Catholic scholars in the United States and Canada.

*Martin Luther: An Illustrated Biography* can serve as a corrective on the distortions of Luther and his Reformation that have marred the confessional literature in English. Above all, the Luther who emerges from these pages stands out as profoundly Catholic in his devotion to the Church, to her creeds, and to her sacraments. Even when he denounced the Church for betraying the trust given to her by Christ, he was speaking in the name of that which the Church confessed and had taught him to confess. He was, if I may be forgiven for using the phrase again, an "obedient rebel." Neither Roman Catholics nor Protestants will find such a Luther easy to handle. Things were so much simpler when Protestant celebrations of Reformation Day in October 31 could be devoted to a litany about such evils as Mariolatry, celibacy, papal tyranny, and the practice of chaining the Bible; or when the pamphlets available in the tract rack of a Roman Catholic parish church could continue to portray Luther as a foulmouth, a psychopath, or even a suicide. These caricatures, which it is all too easy to caricature in turn, have now yielded on both sides to the more complex but also more accurate picture that becomes visible in the paintings and photographs as well as in the text of this book and that will, I dare say, be visible no less in the many other books on Luther being published in this anniversary year.

Can the man who is usually blamed or credited for tearing us apart help to bring us together? That may be too much to hope, at least for the present. But the cause can only be aided by a book about this man that dares to tell the truth. For, as an authority acknowledged both by Martin Luther and by his adversaries declared, "We cannot do anything against the truth, but only for the truth." It is a pleasure to welcome this beautiful collection of pictures and this provocative collection of historical information as a major contribution in English to our common quest for that Truth.

Jaroslav Pelikan
Sterling Professor of History
Yale University

By 1516 Martin Luther had already developed from his family's coat of arms the sign of the Luther Rose, which he explained as a symbol of his theology. In a letter he says: "The first should be a cross: black at the heart [center], its natural color, that I may remind myself that faith in him who was crucified makes us blissful. Then the just man will live by faith, faith in the crucified. But such a heart should be in the middle of a white rose, to show that faith gives joy, comfort, and peace; therefore the rose should be white and not red, because the color white is the color of the spirits and all angels. Such a rose stands in a field the color of heaven, to show that such joy in the spirit and in faith is the beginning of future heavenly joy. And in such a sky-blue field a golden ring, to show that such bliss in heaven lasts forever and has no end and is also precious beyond all joys and possessions, just as gold is the highest, noblest, and most precious metal."

# I

## THE GENERAL HISTORICAL SITUATION

To provide a relatively accurate characterization of Luther's age as it affected his development and activity is a task as difficult as it is challenging. Even the ordinary observer and reader should, at the very outset, be made aware of the limits to which such an attempt is subject.

All history, but especially the history of the age to be considered here, is mysterious in its inner workings, and while such mystery can be made visible, it cannot be made wholly transparent. An overview of the most important events and personalities of the period from all spheres of life—not a mere table of facts and names—can at least convey a rough sense of the mysterious woof of history which is man's free creation, yet also subject to laws.

The question as to the significance the historical situation may have for the distinctiveness, development, and activity of Martin Luther as a concrete individual is even more difficult to answer. On the one hand, it is indisputable that a given historical situation stamps the person positively or negatively through a multitude of influences. It also provides the frame of conditions and possibilities whose totality determines the realization and effects of human insights and intentions. Yet there is a twofold reason why it becomes impossible to isolate those factors that concretely shape the individual with the requisite degree of precision. The very mysteriousness of history thwarts such a tracing of influence. And the mystery of human personality also frustrates such analysis, for it is through its uniqueness that the individual determines what influences it will allow and toward what end it will turn them. In the uniqueness of his personality and destiny, Martin Luther is more than the sum of historically discoverable influences. He is no bottle whose content can be determined by analyzing the ingredients.

The difficulty of our task and the mistakes we must avoid in its solution can be aptly clarified by comparing them with the attempt no less a figure than Philip Me-lanchthon undertook when he kept turning to the movement of the stars because he insisted that it was easy to glean the uniqueness and destiny of the reformer by simply observing it. This method has retained its seductive charm to our day, and not just for the average person. For someone who puts the sign of the archer or of scorpio around his or his friends' neck, even though he may be enlightened in other respects, basks in the unfounded confidence that he can solve at least half of life's riddles. Luther was different. While still so medieval as to believe in the devil and not to be quite certain about the date of his birth, he ridiculed the primitive attempt of his friend and the "wretched art of astrology."

These warnings should suffice. Anyone who tries to derive a kind of "horoscope" for Luther from the "historical situation" falsifies history and Luther's personality as he tries to understand it. But if we interpret it objectively and carefully, what precisely is the relevance of the historical situation?

To begin with, Emperor Maximilian I (1493–1519) reigned over the "Holy Roman Empire of the German Nation." His epithet, "the last knight," gives a fair indication of his significance: the knights had been replaced by mercenaries and foot soldiers; their splendid armor no longer afforded protection against the fire-spewing muskets, mortars, and drakes. Military service had stopped being a matter of knightly honor and loyalty, for the emperor now had to pay if he wanted to feel that he could rely on the faithfulness of his mercenaries. Any number of "new things" were being invented and discovered, or made their appearance in the hearts and minds of men. The new had not yet burst the old, magnificent frame but it was becoming clear that it could not be accommodated, that cracks were running through the structure, and that men reacted to them both in joy and in fear. The "last knight" did much for the last time and could maintain the old framework only by making the best of the provisional quality of a transition whose ambiguity could not be ignored. Typical of Maximilian's situation and attitude was his earnest, utopian endeavor to combine the papal and the imperial dignity in his person. Somewhat less seriously but certainly not without taking reality into account, the emperor believed that this simple plan would rid him at a single stroke of all the financial burdens that weighed down on him throughout his life. For in purely arithmetic terms, it was certainly true that the pope's income from the sale of indulgences would have been more than sufficient to restore the deficit-ridden imperial budget to financial soundness.

The imperial question came to affect Luther's biography directly when Maximilian died and the pope, in league with France, first promoted the candidacy of the French king Francis I and then that of the imperial administrator, the Saxon elector Frederick the Wise, in order to thwart the election of the candidate of the imperial party, the excessively powerful Charles V. For a brief moment, the political situation was more favorable to Luther and the Reformation than at any other time in his life. Out of consideration for the elector, the heresy proceedings against him were dropped. And because Frederick the Wise could not be bought off with money, the secret papal diplomacy dangled the Golden Rose before him, and the cardinalate before one of his friends, a friend who could only be Luther. A cardinal's or a heretic's hat, such was the momentary alternative in this tense situation, at least from the perspective of the papacy. Yet the real crisis of the papacy during this time was more encompassing and deeper. Ushered in by the "Babylonian exile" of the popes in Avignon, it continued in the "Great Schism" where first two and then even three popes excommunicated each other and sucked Christianity dry. It reached the height of mortal danger under popes like Sixtus IV, Innocence VIII, Alexander VI, Julius II, and Leo X. While all of these popes became patrons of the artists of the Renaissance and bibliophilic collectors of precious manuscripts and books and thus recovered the cultural leadership of Europe, and while their wars and alliances took the political and financial power of the papal state to previously unattained heights, it was precisely through these activities that the popes unfortunately compromised for a long time to come to their real task, the leadership of Church and Christianity. The moral degeneracy of an Alexander VI and his family cries to high heaven. Yet far worse is the ever more insistently raised claim to plenary papal power which not even the authority of the Bible can bindingly curb, as Sixtus VI believed. In an anonymous lampoon entitled *Julius exclusus,* Erasmus alludes to his benefactor, the martial Julius II, and skewers a typical representative of this papacy with his pointed pen, exposing him to mockery and public contempt. Even Luther repeatedly rejected this malicious pamphlet for its causticity

and destructive effect. Yet just a short time later, he became convinced that the representatives of this overbearing papacy had to be seen as agents of the Antichrist within the Church, and combatted as such. Without wishing to excuse Luther's radical antipapal polemics which soon became unbearably rude, one will have to concede that it was enormously difficult and perhaps impossible for him to acknowledge the popes of his time as successors of St. Peter and representatives of a universal pastoral office. We should even admit that we also find it difficult to see the popes of the Middle Ages and the Renaissance as representatives of the Petrine office and ministry that we think of when we speak of the primacy and the plenary power of the papacy. If anywhere, it is in the papacy of the period that we have the principal cause of a central malfunctioning which necessarily affected the entire life of the Church. This is the meaning of Pope Adrian VI's confession of guilt before the Diet of Nuremberg in 1523, which John-Paul II recently repeated in his fashion. Once a central malfunctioning has set in, however, serious and even very good plans for reform, of which even during this period there was no lack, remain ineffectual because the damaged structures no longer admit the required reforms. Thus the papacy had to resist all reform councils because the conciliarism that prompted them struck the popes as a danger greater than the most dangerous and deplorable state of affairs. This meant that the structure of power and domination that was profoundly in need of reform but also threatened was now made stronger and that consequently the very reforms that had been intended were not carried out. This also explains why the powerful and morally irreproachable popes such as Julius II and Leo X actually did more harm to the Church than the degenerate ones like Alexander VI.

What was true of popes, the College of Cardinals, and the Curia applied proportionately to the bishops and their aristocratic cathedral chapters, as could be documented instructively by the example of the cardinal archbishop of Mainz Albrecht of Brandenburg. In spite of his rumored love for a baker's girl, he was no incarnation of moral degeneracy but a prince of the Church who, after a passing indecisiveness, courageously resisted the Reformation and remained loyal to the old Church. But he was also wholly a child of his time who saw no problem in uniting in his person no less than three episcopal sees and the electorship, and who had no scruples about paying off his pressing debts in Rome by that trade in indulgences that was to usher in the Reformation. Whtat excuses him in a human sense is at the same time what is truly scandalous here: the unperceptive matter-of-factness with which he, like so many of his peers, did what was visibly wrong.

Where Luther was born, in Kursachsen, one of the smaller German territorial states which was developing well under the government of Frederick the Wise (1486–1515), conditions were incomparably better. We have already mentioned the incorruptibility of the elector who was modest and intelligent enough to reject the imperial dignity that was offered him after Maximilian's death, an act that earned him not only the appreciation of the princes but of the entire German people. The epithet "the Wise" had originally been conferred on him for his knowledge of courtly etiquette. But he soon earned it also for his intelligent restraint in government and his developed sense of justice. If one adds his great kind heart and his modesty, Frederick emerges as one of the most appealing personalities among the princes of the period. An individualist in his life style, he did not hesitate to go counter to public opinion and sanctioned custom when his feelings dictated such a course. Since considerations of rank forbade him to marry the woman he loved, he contented himself with an extramarital relationship with the appealing Anna Weller and became a model father to the two sons, Bastel and Fritz, who sprang from this union. Otherwise, he lived his life as a member of the family of his brother and co-regent, Duke John, who was the father of many children. His leisure time was devoted to two honorable but dissimilar hobbies: he loved cabinetmaking and attained mastery in this craft. And being a man of considerable piety, he was a passionate collector of relics which, partly with Luther's help, he bought up everywhere. In the castle church at Wittenberg which he built himself, he then installed and exhibited them to the credulous as objects that would bring about the remission of sins.

The elector, who had humanistic interests, had, in 1502, founded a university in god-forsaken Wittenberg because he had wanted to annoy his cousin, Duke George of Saxony; and that institution was to become very important for Luther's development. But the intelligent protection which his prince afforded him in all his troubles was to prove even more important for the future reformer. A kind of mystery shrouds the relationship between the elector and the young monk and professor. For Luther never came to know his prince personally, presumably because the elector believed that it was only on this condition that he could protect him effectively. Even Wittenberg was not free of signs of profound tension. But in contrast to conditions at the imperial court or the Curia, there was no trace of mendacious ambivalence. One has the impression that Frederick saw

no conflict between his dangerous commitment in Luther's behalf and complete loyalty to the emperor and the old Church.

On the eve of the Reformation, profound dissension marks the entire spiritual and intellectual situation of Christianity. Though there are occasional compromises and syncretic forms, the theology of the universities and of the studies carried on in the religious orders is dominated by the confrontation of the more or less irreconcilable approaches of the *via antiqua* and the Occamistic *via moderna.* The old opposition between conciliarist and papalist theology heightened the tension. The new approaches of the "Platonic Academy" or of what was otherwise the quite encouraging reforms of a theology that went back to the Bible and the Church Fathers merely created confusion. There were signs of a danger that communication between the various styles of thought and systems might cease. Although the parties largely continued to use the same concepts, mutual understanding was becoming ever more difficult. In the Reuchlin controversy and as a result of the malicious pamphlet the *Letters of Obscure Men,* the proverbial disputatiousness of theologians led to a dangerous polarization. The advocates of the "good old doctrine" wrongly felt that they had been compromised and reacted with the old tricks of the still powerful. The representatives of the "new" indulged in an ever bolder, and also self-important, criticism. The "devout" turned away and sought satisfaction in the mystically tinged circles of *Theologia Teutsch* ("German Theology") or *Devotio Moderna* ("Modern Devotion").

Pre-reformist and late-medieval popular piety in its wide-ranging forms is even more confusing. Although there was certainly no lack of primitive superstition, dangerous superficiality, and crude exploitation of the sacred, it would be falsifying reality were one to deny the profundity and genuineness that could be found in the personal sphere in the striving for inwardness and spirituality, and in the sphere of communal piety in sermons and church music, but principally in religious art. Yet when we examine the inner connections more closely, two insights suggest themselves immediately: the overall impression confirms what was said above about the inner conflict as a consequence of a pivotal malfunctioning of life. In his portrayal of Christ's resurrection, the painter Matthias Grünewald bodies forth what we mean here: against a background of darkest night, Christ rises from the grave in a blinding aura of light. Threatening darkness and the supernaturally blazing light clash irreconcilably. The light does not illuminate the darkness and the darkness does not conquer the light. But the glaring light makes the darkness even darker, as the darkness makes the light more garish. The entire situation also suggests that the old Church was incapable of assimilating the abundance of positive approaches; as a result, it was principally in connection with the Reformation that they became effective and productive.

A complete analysis of the historical situation would have to deal with the development of a new human image and a new life-feeling, the simmering unrest that first seized peasants, visionaries, and apocalyptics and then spread to the entire social structure and transformed it. Whenever Luther's biography calls for such a more thoroughgoing treatment, we will return to these matters. For the moment and in conclusion, it will suffice to note that the Reformation had become historically inevitable (J. Lortz). In terms of the image of a profound organic malfunction of the life of the Church, this means that the church of the popes, which naturally did not stop being a church, went to great length to cure the symptoms of an illness that kept it from credibly and effectively fulfilling its mission in Christendom. Unfortunately even Luther did not succeed in immediately bringing the necessary cure. True, the intensity of his concern provides the thrust toward that depth in which an effective cure had to begin. But the unavoidable defense and the equally unavoidable onesidedness of the attack unfortunately led to a life-threatening shock that caused the unity of Christ's Church temporarily to disintegrate although this had not been Luther's intent. Is was a condition that was not rectified until the Church succeeded in a common effort to institute a comprehensive reform in whose course the concerns of the Reformation were brought to fruition.

## 2. LUTHER'S BIRTH, HIS YOUTH AND SCHOOLING, HIS ALLEGED "FATHER COMPLEX"

After the preceding reflections on the historical background, we now report as simply as possible on Luther's life, beginning with his birth, his parents, and his schooling.

Martin Luther was not a native of Eisleben although the accidents of his life brought it about that he died between two and three o'clock in the morning of February 18, 1546, in the very same town in which, according to Melanchthon, he was born into this sad world shortly before midnight on November 10, 1483. The date of birth is less certain than the date of death, however, for neither Luther nor his mother were completely sure about the former, a circumstance which neither then nor now is at all unusual, as country priests know only too well. The only thing that counts and that is remembered is the speediest possible baptism. And so the small child was given the name of the saint of the day, Martin of Tours, when he was baptized a day after his birth in the Brückenviertel church of Sts. Peter and Paul, by the parish priest Bartholomäus Bennebecher. We know nothing about any godparents and there are no records that might tell us something about whatever relations and connections the parents might have had in the town. It does seem, however, that there had been an earlier male child who had died. We only know that it was shortly before Martin's birth that the parents had come from the region around Eisenach and that by early summer of the following year, the family moved to Mansfeld, a fact which can only be explained by the father's profession. The house in which the child was born still stands. Judging by the impression it makes, the family can hardly have belonged to the poorest of the poor. We know nothing precise about the age or marriage of the parents. There are two conflicting versions concerning the mother's Christian and maiden names. According to one, the mother, whose Christian name sometimes appears as Margaretha, sometimes as Hannah, was a Ziegler and thus the daughter of one of the wealthiest peasant families in the village of Möhra, the place of birth of both parents which lay some three hours' walk south of Eisenach. According to the second version, which I take to be the more reliable one, the mother was a Lindemann and came from a respected burgher family in Eisenach. The traditional reservation about this name is easily explained by a terribly slanderous story which, though not invented by Johannes Cochläus, was nonetheless successfully peddled by him. According to it, Margaretha Lindemann had worked as a "bath maid" in a public bath in Eisenach prior to her hasty marriage to Hans Luder. In that place of employment, she allegedly had dealing with the devil in human shape and thus received her Martin as an incubus. To eliminate any basis for this disgraceful calumny, all mention of the mother's hometown was painstakingly avoided later.

There is no doubt, however, that Hans Luder, Martin's father—a name that may be derived from Lothar—came from an old landowning family in Möhra that has continued to inhabit its village of origin and its hereditary position as small landowners into the twentieth century. Since the High Middle Ages, they had been free landowners who only paid a small ground rent and whose only master was the elector. They were well-to-do and debt free without being actually wealthy. The precondition for the preservation of their property was a law of inheritance that made it possible to avoid all division of property. It was always only the youngest son who inherited, a circumstance that naturally had unpleasant consequences for the older siblings if marriage into another landowning family proved impossible. This had happened to Martin's father, "Big Hans," as he was called, who, being the eldest of four sons, had no right to the inheritance and therefore saw himself obliged to take up the mining of copper schist which was carried on in neighboring Kupfersuhl.

Although Big Hans was thus no farmer but a miner, Luther maintained throughout his life that he was a farmer's son and of peasant stock. What is special about this is certainly not that Luther felt himself a peasant and referred to his peasant origin with pride (M. Brecht). It is rather that, beginning with his school days, Luther increasingly considered himself to be a person who had been molded by an urban culture, and he invokes his peasant origin to underline the progress from peasant son to professor and adversary of the pope. Yet he would have obtained the same effect had he emphasized with equal vigor his origin as the son of a "poor miner." We will see in a moment that, oddly enough, Luther did not do this, or did it only infrequently, and not with the same insistence. For compared with that of a farmer, his father's profession was difficult, interesting, and quite modern. In other words, due to his father's profession, little Martin grows up in a nearly modern ambiance yet makes nothing of that fact.

In both a technical and an economic sense, the profession of miner made demands on the father that were not easily met. The copper schist, which in those days was either strip-mined in the Mansfeld area or mined at a shallow depth, was smelted on charcoal and worked into crude copper. Such foundries were either hereditary property or rented from the counts of the region. Luther's father was such a lessee. Quite apart from the technical effort, the running of a foundry not only required luck in the finding and sale of the ore but some knowledge of economics and considerable capital to pay the wages, construct the mines, and keep the furnaces going. Since the smelters did not own the necessary capital, the trading companies advanced it. They also bought the rude copper which they worked into silver or copper before reselling it. The profitability of such small enterprises was therefore contingent on a number of factors, and it happened often enough that those smelters who worked for their own account did not earn enough and were therefore unable to repay their debts in time. They then incurred burdensome obligations with the trading companies or even returned to the lower status of simple miners.

After extremely difficult beginnings, Big Hans did not escape any of the worries and risks that attended such an enterprise. It seems that he had some initial success, for he soon made his appearance as one of the "Four" who represented the community vis-à-vis the council in Mansfeld. But he had to work hard and count every penny. In 1505, there were still four sons and an equal number of daughters to provide for. By 1510, he seems to have made it. Three daughters and Martin's younger brother Jacob, who had taken up his father's profession, married into mining families. The plans his father had for Martin can also be understood from this perspective: smelters always found themselves embroiled in some legal dispute and constantly needed cash, and this is the reason it was expected that little Martin would come to the aid of the firm in the quickest possible way through the study of law and a wealthy marriage.

But "man proposes and God disposes," and unfortunately He does not always dispose as man proposed. This applies to Big Hans not only with reference to his son but also to his business. A document from the time shortly before the father's death gives us precise information about the business failures and modest successes of the "Luder smelting works." According to it, Big Hans and his Mansfeld partner Hans Lüttich already owed thousands of gulden to their company at a very early date. During the first years of the century, money was earned and the debts paid off. Big Hans even leased several additional foundries. This is the time during which the Erfurt student Martin is set down as "wealthy" in the registrar's records. And in 1507 the angry father showed up with twenty horsemen as his son was celebrating his first mass and donated twenty gulden to the monastery. But then years of failure and dearth followed during which the debt-ridden businessman had no more than fifty gulden to live on. It was not until 1529 that the debts could once again be paid off and some money put aside. In any event, when father Hans died in 1530, he left his heirs an estate of 1,250 gulden which was not a large fortune but twice what the farm in Möhra would have brought. Big Hans was thus not as successful as the biographers have occasionally asserted but neither was he a failure, not professionally and not as husband and father.

It is obvious that the extremely difficult years during which the father, beset by constant financial worries, tried to build a life for himself and his family through hard work did not fail to have some effect on Martin's childhood. Whenever Luther speaks of that childhood and his parental home, he remembers poverty, thrift, and severity. He does not forget that his overburdened mother had to gather the necessary firewood in the forest and carry it home on her back. And he remembered all his life that his study cost his father "much sweat and hard work."

As in families the world over, it was the severe, angry father, a man who always lived under stress, that set the atmosphere in the home. The Luders generally had a reputation for disputatiousness and belligerence. This is as true of the father's brother ("Little Hans") as of the younger son Jacob, who initially could not make his way in Mansfeld and whose name appears over a period of years in the town records as that of a brawler. But one must be careful not to infer too much about the character of the father or of Luther himself from this observation. Yet stress, severity, and anger were not without their significance for the education of the child. It is fairly obvious, generally speaking, that parents in the Middle Ages failed to entertain modern notions of education. They made hardly any concessions to the distinctive character of their children but treated all alike. For them, one child was like any other, and in addition to food, clothing, and indispensable care, children needed severity and an occasional thrashing if they were going to amount to something. Like countless other parents of the time, they were quick to reach for the rod and not excessively circumspect in its use. The stories the older and rather loquacious Luther tells about these matters in his *Table Talk* are sufficiently known. Being late and much emended recollections, they require careful interpretation and should not be read like the diary entries of a child or the records of a youth welfare office. There is, in particular, the story according to which the irate mother thrashed the poor boy for having stolen a nut until she drew blood. Luther goes on to comment—and this has stimulated interpreters of all persuasions—that it was this severe upbringing that drove him into the monastery, an explanation that is anything but reliable, however plausible it may sound. In another report about the "stolen nut," Luther says of his father that he "whipped me so that I ran away and felt ugly toward him." But Luther also mentions that after this severe punishment his father did everything he could "to win me back." This suggests that Big Hans was no inhuman tyrant but simply an excitable father with principles who apparently could not always restrain himself. Like all sons who remember a strict father, Luther then goes on to say that the beatings did him no harm.

It seems prudent to me not to criticize the vigorous upbringing too harshly, and especially not to measure it by the yardstick of an "antiauthoritarian education," a concept the good parents simply could have no knowledge of. Most importantly it is necessary to guard against the attempt to use the methods and means of modern psychology, psychiatry, or psychotherapy to discover Luther's disturbed personality in these reports. For the strict upbringing caused neither a psychological trauma in what was admittedly a sensitive child, nor did Luther suffer from a "father complex" for which his father—or an Oedipus complex for which his mother—would have been responsible.

To the extent that the sources permit any judgment whatever, everything was much simpler, more genuine, and real. It is undeniable that there was tension and conflict between father and son, and this may have begun in childhood. It also seems that the overworked mother was somewhat melancholy, as is true of many mothers in a similar situation. But a song his mother sang and which Luther mentions repeatedly—"No one really cares for you or me but that is our own fault"—really doesn't indicate more than that the mother loved songs which, like most folk songs, were a little sad, and that the son possibly inherited his mother's musical talent. According to the *Table Talk*, the father also sang and joked over an occasional tankard of wine or when he had had a tankard too many. But such documentation can be misleading when it is interpreted as proof of the father's alcoholism. We can be perfectly confident that Luther could distinguish between harmless inebriation and actual alcoholism, and he does in fact make this distinction when he compares a real drunkard among his relations with his carousing father.

In addition to the murky reports in the *Table Talk* which are difficult to interpret, there is other documentation and especially facts that cast a somewhat kinder light on the grim picture of the thrashing parents. There are, first, the two houses in Eisleben and Mansfeld in which Luther spent his childhood. If one allows the impression these two buildings make to sink in a little, one will concede that Luther was one of those fortunate beings who never lacked a "home." This home saw more than work, punishment, and upbraiding, it was also a place where people sang, celebrated, and even played. Since the road leading from the house in Mansfeld to school occasionally turned into mud and filth, the child was carried to school when this became necessary. We are thus entitled to feel that little Martin was given a very human and Christian education albeit not an individualized one. That the devil, poltergeists, fairies, witches, and mermaids played an important role, as they did in medieval popular belief, is no reason to feel alarm. For besides the threats and anxieties, there was a powerful God, more powerful than such beings, and there were the angels and the saints, and ultimate victory over the stupid devil, an occasion that was celebrated at Easter, in the *risus pascalis* ("Easter laugh"), to the sound of drums and trumpets. This world of the spirit which made such a deep impression during childhood even stood up under the learned and often polemical criticism of the reformer, as is impressively proved by Luther's unbroken love for the Mother of God, the Guardian Angels, and the beloved saints. Because the father, a man who had never seen the inside of a school, was concerned about this, little Martin was given a sound education. It is probably that the father began sending the little fellow to the Mansfeld town school on the feast of St. Gregory, 1488, which he attended for eight years until he had learned everything it had to offer.

School is another subject that has proven fruitful for psychologists even today. For the medieval school, whose teaching methods and curriculum ultimately went back to Charlemagne, was a grind, a place that strikes us as difficult and objectionable and in which the instructors were even handier with the rod than Big Hans. Luther's *Table Talk* leaves us with a terrible impression of his incompetent teachers and their almost devilishly refined punishments. There are two things I find disturbing about these reports: There is, first, the obvious literary tendency to use the hellish background of the schools under the papacy in order to let the "Christian school" of the Reformation emerge all the more gloriously. But there is also the fact that from his severely criticized school and the "rod masters" whom he vilifies time and again Luther learned a great deal more than— an allegedly ideal course offering notwithstanding—our high school students seem able to master. It must be admitted, of course, that the modern school offers a wealth of subjects that is incomparably greater than the pathetic three called *Trivium* in medieval schools. It must also be admitted that the meager rudiments of grammar, logic, and rhetoric according to hopelessly antiquated books— the grammar of Aelius Donatus dates from late antiquity, the "Alexander" (a rhymed syntax and metrics) from the twelfth century—were quite literally beaten into the students. And it is also true that cramming and beating instilled fear in them and that psychologically sensitive children like our Martin passed through "hell"

and "purgatory" at the same time. But all admissions of this sort do not lead to a fair judgment. Nor is there any point in the observation that the elimination of caning and the introduction of a very subtle pedagogy has clearly failed to remove fears and prevent neuroses but has significantly increased them instead. What is called for is a thoroughly critical examination which has its point of departure in the fact that the fear little Martin felt of school and family must be see as the norm and that we must resist the temptation to represent Luther's childhood and school days in the light of later reports or to see them from the perspective of our modern sensitivity and view them as a "martyrdom." An abundance of important facts supports such a decision: when all is said and done, there can be no doubt that Luther learned a great deal in that reviled school, such as Latin, for example, and most assuredly not the dog Latin of Scholasticism nor just the crude combination of Latin and German which, as the *Table Talk* and the sermons show, he mastered with great perfection. The Latin he learned served as the foundation of all knowledge and was a thoroughly alive, creatively used language. True, he does complain that he got to read "no histories" in school. But he knew his special favorites—Terence, Aesop's fables, and the moral maxims of the Pseudo-Cato —thoroughly. In this context, it is illuminating and will probably delight many schoolchildren that Martin neither could nor had to learn arithmetic in school. But neither school nor father should be blamed for this. For in contrast to the father who could not read but calculated exceedingly well, little Martin totally lacked that talent, as his later "tax statements" impressively show. And finally, there is certainly no lack of fond and happy memories of the Eisenach school years and the teachers he knew there.

All in all, we would raise the following objections to the primitive or "scientifically" stylized legend of Luther's martyrdom at home and in school:

Having completed the first stage of schooling, Luther left his parents' home in Mansfeld when he was fourteen years old and thus at an age when most of the famous children of the Middle Ages had long since finished their *trivium*. Philip Melanchthon was just twelve when he went to Heidelberg University. From that perspective, our Martin rather strikes one as a "late bloomer" who had trouble leaving the family nest. We therefore owe it to Big Hans to note that he, a man otherwise so intent on success, did nothing to harm his son by pushing him on to maximum efforts. Nor is there any basis for the belief that the angry father drove the son out of the house or that the son fled from a home and a school in which caning was such common practice. This striking freedom continued to prevail during the rest of his school years. In Magdeburg also, no one drove the boy although here the paternal direction of Martin's future becomes visible in a few instances. But this planning, which was clearly influenced by the decision of another smelter, was not at all rigid. Thus Luther moves on to Eisenach a year later, a town in which he had many relatives and made many good friends with whom he kept in touch over the years. That he had to earn his living or part of it in both towns by singing for alms in the streets is completely in keeping with medieval custom and was not particularly onerous for the boy. Like a sponge, Martin absorbed all the impressions the "big city" of Magdeburg with its population of twenty-five thousand had to offer. Here, he encountered the Brethren of the Common Life, heard music, and experienced the liturgy at the cathedral as a choir boy. He was deeply impressed by the example of Prince William of Anhalt, a poor Franciscan who begged in the streets for bread for Christ's poor. An even stronger shaping force seems to have been the impressions in Eisenach, in the home of his relative Konrad Hutter, the sacristan of the church of St. Nikolas, or in the home of the mayor, Heinrich Schalbe, at Kunz Cotta's or in the merry circle around the Franciscan friar Johannes Braun. It seems that it was among Braun's friends that Martin first consciously experienced the veneration for St. Anne that was soon to give a decisive turn to his life. In Eisenach, he was also impressed by the happy marriage of the Schalbes and came into contact with remarkable women such as the mayor's wife and her daughter Ursula Cotta who were so utterly different from his overworked mother back home.

The development of young Martin, which took an apparently seamless course without deep external or internal crises and whose result for that very reason is very suggestive, becomes apparent here. Already in Eisenach, the distinctive quality of the young scholar's entire background was clearly "no longer peasantlike but urban, that of a burgher" (M. Brecht). If it is equally true that throughout his life Luther invoked his peasant origins and simply ignored what strikes one as the modern ambiance of a smelter's family in which he spent his entire childhood, we can infer something of importance here which gives us a clue to his entire development. For if his father's professional world and the plans for the son that came out of that world were alien and always remained so, the decision he made a few years later to become a monk does not represent a break in his development either but was germinally present in it though not in the form of a conscious motivation. But for that very reason,

the distance he felt toward his father's plans and the development this gave rise to must never at any moment be interpreted as a conscious or unconscious "protest" against the father. Nor does such a development presuppose the rejection of the father by the son caused or touched off by Big Hans' strictness. It becomes clear once again that the problem that arose between father and son was nothing of minor importance and certainly entailed very serious psychological hardship for both yet, for all that, it is an everyday problem which countless fathers and sons have had to deal with and resolve ever since, not least in our time.

## 3. STUDY IN ERFURT: FROM BACHELOR OF ARTS TO MASTER OF ARTS

With the summer term of 1501, the beginning of his studies at Erfurt University, an important new phase began for Martin. Much could be written about this town with its twenty thousand inhabitants and prestigious university which had been founded as the fifth German university after Prague, Vienna, Heidelberg, and Cologne. But more important than any number of scholarly details is the observation that none of the ideas and expectations young men today connect with their move from school to university can be applied to Luther's time. For while it is true that the eighteen-year-old escaped the caning of the schoolmasters by this step, he did not exchange the compulsion of school for the academic freedom which even the merest beginners at our universities invoke these days. Rather, medieval universities were institutions that in their teaching tended to tighten rather than to loosen the close ties that bound students to the school. This is something the young man who registered as "Martinus ludher ex Mansfeld" discovered when the dean of humanities asked which college he had chosen. For it was by compelling the student to live in one that the university effectively supervised the life style of its charges. In Erfurt, the refusal of a college to accept a student was tantmount to exclusion from the university.

We do not know with complete certainty which college Luther chose. According to a number of sources, he decided in favor of the smaller, well-reputed St. George's, which was close to the Augustinian friary and which the students jokingly called the "Beer-Bag." According to other sources, it was the famous Amplonian college near St. Michael's Church, popularly known as

"Heaven's Gate," in which Luther took up residence. But whether "Beer-Bag" or "Heaven's Gate," the residential rules and education were the same. From "wake-up" call at four in the morning to "lights out" at eight in the evening, the daily schedule was minutely ordered. The students slept in large dormitories and studied in halls set aside for the purpose. Two meals were served at ten in the morning and at five in the afternoon, with meat being served four times a week. The food was substantial and adequate. Exercises began at six in the morning and were followed by lectures that were resumed after the morning meal and continued until five o'clock. During the study period, the students were not allowed to leave the building and the closing time of the gates was strictly enforced. Although beer was served in the college, gambling, excessive drinking, and relations with the opposite sex were banned. The students had to speak Latin with each other, wore a uniform, and were expected to participate in daily mass and the canonical hours. In sum, it was a schedule and an order that could not deny its monastic model. Anyone who, like the author, has spent twelve semesters as a boarder in an old-fashioned tridentine seminary is in a position to judge the rigor of such an order with a measure of fairness and without exaggeration. Those without similar experience will not believe how much freedom such a strict schedule actually offers to the development of young and zestful men.

Instruction and study at the humanities faculty were similarly regimented. Basically, the subjects were the same as in school except that there was some difference in the material. The most important was logic which was taught according to the thirteenth century manual of Petrus Hispanus and the commentary on Aristotle of Porphyrius. The curriculum also included the most important writings of Aristotle who was also the primary source of natural philosophy. The lectures were supplemented by exercises in logic and physics. In the disputations, the students had to defend theses their teachers had formulated. As early as the end of September 1502, Luther was admitted to the bachelor's examination which he passed elegantly rather than brilliantly or, to put it differently, with average grades. He now had to wear the dress of the baccalaureus and, although still a student, he also had to assume certain teaching duties in grammar, rhetoric, and logic.

Only a small number of students aspired to the master's degree which was the conclusion of the study of philosophy. In this second part of his philosophical studies, Luther first but unsuccessfully studied Euclidean geometry and arithmetic as well as music and Aristotle's metaphysical and ethical writings. In January 1505, he concluded his philosophical study with the master's examination. This time, he passed brilliantly, that is, as the second in his class. As a sign of his new dignity, he was given the master's reddish brown beret and ring. His inaugural lecture was followed by the customary ceremonies consisting of a feast and a torchlight parade. Luther, who loved such festivities, incurred considerable expense, and the proud father, who henceforth stopped addressing his son with the familiar second person singular, never balked at paying for it all.

This is the place to consider briefly the significance the study of philosophy had in Luther's later development. In this matter, as in the question regarding his schooling, we cannot take the generally negative judgment of his later statements quite literally. And this not because it is a psychological fact that, in retrospect, most great men speak contemptuously of their student days. What is involved instead is a circumstance that is difficult to judge, that is, the fact that even teachings and ideas that we later passionately reject as false and combat may yet have played a decisive role in determining the contents and form of our newly won convictions. This is true first of all of the way of thinking and the learning and teaching methods. Throughout his life, Erfurt exerted an influence on Luther's analysis of texts, the organization of his ideas, the formulation of his theses, conclusions, and proofs, his type of controversy, and his delivery. His passionate fight against Scholasticism notwithstanding, Luther always clung to the form and method of the Scholastic disputation, that is, he considered it suitable to ground, give greater depth to, and defend the truth that he drew from the Bible and the theology of the Fathers. The way of thinking that goes along with disputation cannot be radically separated from the underlying logic, the laws of thought, and the concept of truth that characterize the Scholastic philosophy he had learned in Erfurt. This means that even as Luther developed into an "antiphilosopher," he always remained the "philosopher" in a certain sense, and "philosopher" was also his nickname at college. Ultimately, it is this "academic" schooling and style of thinking whose absence he repeatedly rather arrogantly criticized in his controversy with the Swiss reformer Zwingli who, being an autodidact, had not had such an education.

The question becomes even more difficult when we ask specifically what influence the Erfurt teachers and their teaching had on Luther, for in the Middle Ages "academic freedom" either did not exist at all or was severely restricted. The professors were obliged by oath to adhere in their lectures to the orientation the university subscribed to. If we can believe Luther's later statements, it was the "sect" of the English Franciscan William of Occam, which was also called the *via moderna*, that ruled in Erfurt. But these are crude slogans which do not wholly correspond to reality. For it seems that it was a nominalist orientation that was not wholly Occam's but was also shaped by Gregory of Rimini—*Doctor authenticus* and general of the Order of Augustinian Hermits († 1358)—and Johann Rucherat von Wesel who was not precisely a man of universal renown. Although toward the end of his life the latter also had problems because of his teaching, it was the pride of the Erfurt ecclesiastics never to have been suspected of heresy.

This can be shown rather impresively by the two professors, Jodokus Trutfetter von Eisenach and Bartholomäus Arnoldi von Usingen, who were not only teachers but friends of Luther. Both advocated a doctrine that implied a separation of reason and faith. Everything in this world is subject to the judgment of critical reason alone. In theology also, reason retains a clearly critical function. But this does not lead to conflict because in what has been revealed, only faith can advance us, and this means the obedience of faith that the Bible and church dogma are entitled to demand even when they contradict reason. The approach of the Erfurt nominalists thus contains a kind of "scriptural principle" and makes possible a peaceful coexistence of philosophy and theology which, in spite of its dangers, did not exclude an honest commitment of scholars to the Church. This tie is confirmed by the later academic careers and lives of Luther's two teachers: Trutfetter and Usingen took the degree of doctor of philosophy. Both were or became monks, and Usingen even entered the Erfurt Augustinian friary due to Luther's influence.

Because there are inconsistencies, it is not easy to say how significantly the nominalism of Erfurt influenced Luther's intellectual and spiritual development. But we can sense more or less which elements may have had a positive, and which a negative, impact. Nominalist logic, though not epistemology, clearly proved stimulating, and nominalist theology with its emphasis on faith and Scripture and its rejection of reason in this sphere could not fail to make an impression on him. But from the very beginning, Luther also rejected the hollow abstraction of nominalist thinking as he did the theology of the schools that resulted from it and that was alien to the Bible. He did not care for bloodless abstractions and insisted on the priority of "substance" over "grammar" throughout his life.

To the extent that it was already stirring in Erfurt at the time, humanism also affected Luther. As early as the second half of the fifteenth century, a considerable number of electives were offered in addition to the obligatory courses. They dealt with classical Latin authors such als Cicero, Vergil, Ovid, and Terence. Nor did the Erfurt colleges remain closed to the influence of humanism. The rectors were humanists, like Matern Pistoris and Johannes Knaes, and there were humanist workgroups whose activities brought a loosening of the otherwise strictly regimented studies and which apparently also had a social side. It is probably in this way that Luther became acquainted with a fellow student, the humanist Johann Jäger von Dornheim, who under the pseudonym Crotus Rubeanus, later wrote the famous *Letters of Obscure Men,* an amusing and malicious satire of college life. It testifies to Luther's intellectual flexibility that the worn path of a prescribed academic order did not keep him from making use of the elective humanistic offerings. The influence humanism had on him is noticeable—he even took his copy of Vergil and Plautus into the monastery with him—but we should not exaggerate it.

Having passed his master's examination brilliantly, Luther had to give lectures and hold exercises in the faculty of humanities. But he also could and was supposed to begin study at one of the higher faculties. When we compare the situation of the talented young master to the academic career of his teachers and weigh the meaning his friendship with these leading university scholars had for him, it would appear that Luther's career in Erfurt was assured at this point, even without further studies. The sparse sources for this important phase contain no indication that Luther seriously considered such a possibility. Yet it forms part of the background of the decision he, a circumspect scholar who could certainly choose among a number of possible alternatives, had to make. How, and for which faculty, would he decide?

## 4. THE ATTEMPT TO STUDY LAW, STOTTERNHEIM, THE MONASTERY

The career the proud father took for granted was something the son was aware of and had never rejected, but it was certainly not a carefully considered and settled matter. There is the additional circumstance that this was the first time Luther had several months' time during which to reflect about problems which only became such when the situation was actually at hand. That Luther could not openly discuss these matters with his father certainly made his reflections no easier, nor did he really have any scope for a decision of his own. Apart from a teaching career, there was no way out: medicine was out of the question for practical reasons, not because quotas already existed at that time but because the faculty simply did not function properly yet. Theology was excluded by the firm intent to marry a wealthy woman, and thus the law remained as the only realistic alternative which, except for reservations Luther himself did not clearly understand, had everything on its side.

So he returned to the university where he had to begin giving his lectures as a master of arts on April 24 and where, seemingly as a matter of course, he began his new studies on May 19, after the solemn faculty mass in honor of St. Ivos of Chartres, the patron of the Erfurt jurists. There would have been no problem if Luther had not broken off his newly started studies a few weeks later and made a decision no one was prepared for. What had happened? What reasons for Luther's behavior can be found?

Anyone with some knowledge of human nature and some familiarity with the reactions of talented young scholars will first ask whether there might not be reasons that are related to Luther's feelings about the law. Even students of his caliber feel at first that there is much that is interesting, yet drop the discipline after some initial familiarity because they recognize instinctively that it will never make them happy. Is it possible to show that, analogous to his lack of talent for mathematics, Luther had antipathy toward the law that surfaced only during the first few weeks when he was familiarizing himself with the statutes of the new faculty or was reading the *Corpus Juris* and the commentary of the great jurist Accursius which he had just purchased? This supposition receives some support from the fact that Luther later not only continued to express his distaste for the law, because he considered it uncertain and dependent on interpretation and subject to distortion, but that in the course of one comment of this sort he specifically mentions his youthful reading of Accursius.

There are other clues which may be interpreted as signs of an inner process which, in its entirety, will probably remain Luther's secret. There are sources, for example, that report a curious melancholy at this time which the sudden death from the plague of two fellow students who had passed their examinations with him explains only in part. But the thought of death and anxiety over one's salvation prompted many young men to

enter the monastery in those days. This complex acquired additional motivating force when two professors of jurisprudence who had been stricken by the plague stated before their death that they wished they had been monks, an experience Luther had during these months.

This is what the scant sources tell us about Luther's state of mind when, on June 20, right in the middle of the semester, he abruptly left Erfurt to visit his parents in Mansfeld. He never indicated the reason for this journey. His father may have called him home to discuss his marriage, and the possibility that he was simply tired of the law cannot be excluded. All that is certain is that the monastery was not discussed by either father or son. Luther merely reports that he made the long journey to Mansfeld on foot which took three days at least. This is also how he had traveled home during the Easter vacation of the preceding year. On that occasion, his sword had become entangled between his legs and had torn a vein in one of them, causing a life-threatening wound because the loss of blood had been severe. With his swollen leg in a tourniquet that soon came loose, he had had to lie down and wait for a physician. Facing death, he had implored the mother of God for help but had made no vow. Although his recovery at home did not proceed without complications, he soon dismissed the danger from his mind and, while still abed and recuperating, learned to play the lute without benefit of a teacher. On the return journey from Mansfeld to Erfurt on July 2, 1505, Luther reacted in a significantly different way in an almost identical situation. A few hours' walk from Erfurt, near the village of Stotternheim, a violent thunderstorm overtook him. Lightning struck close to him and hurled him to the ground. In mortal fear, he called on St. Anne for help and added the vow: "Help, St. Anne! I will become a monk."

This vow had a marked effect on Luther's relatives and friends and also on wider circles of the Erfurt public although reactions differed. Later, it was through Luther himself and the indignant reply of his enemies that it became the slogan in the fight for and against monasticism. To this day, it is quoted again and again by biographers, historians, and theologians, and not infrequently it is misunderstood. But those scholars who deserve to be taken seriously are unanimous in their belief that Luther's vow, however sudden, represents the result of an inner development which the sources at least hint at. We therefore agree with H. Boehmer who asserts that spiritually Luther was already on his way to the monastery when the stroke of lightning near Stotternheim hurled him down.

But this comes nowhere close to answering all the questions that suggest themselves in this connection. What is the meaning of a vow that backs up a call for help? How binding is a promise made in such a serious predicament? An answer to this question is difficult or even impossible, for such vows have become alien to us, and not just to enlightened Protestants. Medieval man thought and felt differently about the matter. Without pharmacies, operating rooms, and health insurance, all the help they had in their countless trials and tribulations was God and the saints who plead our cause before Him. They were not ashamed to promise God spiritual works—such as prayers, alms, and pilgrimages, the building of churches, chapels, and altars, indeed even their lives—and refused as a matter of principle to make a "deal" with the Almighty out of it. For this reason, they also did not try to welsh on their obligation by claiming before God or their confessor that they had acted from the compulsion of their situation and that their vow was therefore not truly voluntary, or only imperfectly so. There were borderline cases, no doubt, which made a modification or revocation of the vow a necessity. It may also be taken for granted that there was abuse in this sphere and that there existed the primitive and religiously very dangerous tendency to put something over on God or the divine, as it were. But this must not be generalized. Normally, people at that time fulfilled their vows to God although this does not mean that they may not later have reflected on the seriousness of the obligation they had assumed and experienced its fulfillment as an oppressive burden. This was also Luther's reaction, as we will see.

But Luther's friends, the monastic officials, and especially his relatives also had their views regarding the Stotternheim vow, and everyone sought to influence him to do what they thought best.

As always in such cases, there were friends who understood and supported his decision. But others felt the world had collapsed and went to great length to get him to change his mind. It can be neither asserted nor denied with absolute certainty that there was also a weeping young girl among these latter since no halfway dependable source mentions anything of the sort. But in the case of men like Luther, sources are occasionally destroyed or "dressed up," so that the absence of any such report means nothing either. Literati, filmmakers, and psychologists should therefore feel free to invent whatever they please, provided they impute no sexual problems to Luther, for it may be taken for certain that Martin knew perfectly well what he was giving up and that he did not pretend that the love of women was something ugly that must be shunned.

Most people, though not nearly all, were convinced that a supernatural power had intervened in Luther's life: his angry and powerless father thought it must be the devil and the work of witches. Johann Nathin, Luther's teacher in the monastery, on the other hand, compared the Stotternheim episode to the conversion of St. Paul before the gates of Damascus.

It says something for Luther's realism that he never used that comparison, although at a later time he never hesitated to identify with Paul. Luther reacted as both a Christian and a human being. He did not simply rush from Stotternheim into the monastery but took two weeks to consider the consequences of his decision, to say his final good-byes, and to burn his bridges behind him. If, in retrospect, he mentions "remorse" during these weeks, it is a recollection which, like many others relating to his monastic life, portrays reality inaccurately. What is true about the recollection is that he felt the heavy burden the fulfillment of his vow meant for him. These final weeks were overcast by the melancholy seriousness people feel when they make final decisions, renounce obligations, pay debts, sell their belongings, and say their fairewells. In spite of the lacerating tension of these final days, Luther acted normally, calmly, and resolutely—in exactly the way he had lived up to this moment. Thirty-four years later, he will remember that memorable day: on the eve of the feast of St. Alexius, the evening of July 15 (not July 16 as biographers erroneously date it), Luther called his friends and acquaintances together for a last meal before they escort him to the monastery on the following day. When one reads the text with some knowledge of both Luther and life, one feels one can visualize the scene: he is sitting among friends in a comfortable Erfurt inn with a sad innkeeper's daughter. The reader imagines he can hear the conversations, as it were, and, after a night of eating and drinking, senses the chill of the early morning hours as the friends escort him to the monastery gate. The historical reality is harsher and more restrained but no less impressive for that. Given the situation, there is no chance that there was a final meal in some inn. And in a college, the friends certainly would not have been able to prolong their celebration until dawn. Nor does the source make any such assertion. Like all other nights, this night was spent in the dormitory, alone, as the college rules required, and Luther then fulfilled his fateful vow in the early hours of July 16. His friends cried when they embraced Martin a final time at the gate of the "Black Cloister," as it was popularly known. But Martin persevered and, his later bitter criticism of monasticism notwithstanding, went through with a decision which, as an act of total surrender to God, he never disavowed. Thus he states in his *Table Talk* of July 16, 1539, that God has understood and accepted his Stotternheim vow and his invocation of St. Anne "hebraically": "Anne" means "through grace" (Anne or Hannah is related to the Hebrew word *ḥēn* meaning "grace" or "favor"), "not according to the law" (in the sense of a merely legally enforced fulfillment of the promise). All in all, even the entrance into the monastery manifested divine grace and a divine promise. This is the reason there is no absence of light in this difficult hour, and that light will continue to shine, especially in the "Black Cloister."

# II

## 1. THE ERFURT CLOISTER: FROM NOVICE TO FRIAR AND PRIEST

As the gate fell shut and his dejected friends were left behind, another gate opened onto a kind of life that was certainly not altogether new to Luther but which only reveals itself for what it truly is to the person who commits himself to it without reservation.

It is part of the experience of all religious orders that the decision to embark on such a life requires thorough scrutiny, both by the applicant and by the order and the superiors. Luther began his life as a religious with the so-called postulancy which lasted for about two months.

The porter announced the postulant, who almost certainly was not visiting the monastery for the first time, to the prior, the Lothringian Winand von Diedenhofen. The prior took the postulant into the monastery church and from there, after a brief prayer, into the guest house, the oldest building of the Erfurt cloister and originally a burgher's house. Here, Luther lived during the next few weeks and familiarized himself with monastic life. In addition to conversation, the general confession he made to the prior was an important element in his examination by the superiors. Advising the parents, whose consent did not constitute an indispensable precondition for admission according to church law, was part of a clarification the prior considered important. Luther therefore wrote them from the monastery. Big Hans raged with anger and disappointment. He renounced his son and went back to addressing him with the familiar, and in this case reproachful, *du*, as he had before the master's examination. The death of two sons and the rumor that Martin also had died, as well as the mediation of relatives gradually induced the father to bow to the inevitable.

In Luther's case, the process of clarification involved the acquisition of a more detailed knowledge of the order, its history, rules, customs, constitution, and, more especially, its spirit. It was a matter of reaffirming a decision that had already been made when he chose the Black Cloister. Why, considering the abundance of religious orders, in Erfurt, did Luther choose the Order of Hermits of St. Augustine? The Erfurt Augustinians, as they were popularly called, were "observant" or "reformed" and thus known for their discipline. They were much stricter than the Augustinian Canons at the Augusttor or the Benedictines on the Petersberg. But since they were much less strict than the Carthusians, whose monastery lay in the southern part of the town, the severity of the discipline can have been neither the sole nor the decisive motive for Luther's choice.

If we search for other possible motives and look back at Luther's university studies at Erfurt, everything suggests that it was the "Augustinianism" of the Augustinians that decided him. Luther's later statement that even as a novice he had never considered becoming a priest, let alone a doctor of theology, does not really militate against this assumption. For while the novice knew that not he but his superiors would decide the use the order would make of him, and the course of studies that would be relevant to such employment, he also knew that they took the special aptitude and education of the monks into account when they made their decision, knew that the Erfurt cloister had its own "university"—the so-called *studium generale*—where not a few of the former masters of the faculty of arts taught, and that his previous training precluded his becoming a simple lay brother even if such had been his preference. Moreover, the fact that Johann Lang, Luther's friend and fellow master of arts, joined the order at about the same time he did speaks for the special relationship that existed between the faculty of arts and the Erfurt cloister.

It is against this background that it becomes fairly clear why Luther decided against the Dominicans or Franciscans. For while he considered the Dominicans to be very learned, he also felt they were arrogant and conceited. Besides, they represented the *via antiqua* which Luther's schooling made it impossible for him to follow. The Franciscans, on the other hand, were superstitious and stupid in his opinion, although this naturally did not apply to the great theologians of the order such as Bonaventure and Scotus but to its excessively popular preaching and ministry. Generally speaking, Luther did not care for the two orders because, along with many of his contemporaries, he believed that their eternal bickering and disputes were responsible for the wretched situation in which theology found itself.

What Luther discovered about the order as he reflected on his first impressions in the monastery guest house and during his subsequent novitiate can be only sketched here. It had been through the consolidation of several Italian congregations of hermits that the Augustinian Hermits had come into existence during the thirteenth century. All these groups shared a preference for the solitary life, excessively severe penitence, and the absence of a clear constitution. This led to difficulties with the established mendicant orders since the hermits, who also soon began wandering and begging and some of whom had, from the very beginning, tended the most repulsive cases of illness and disease in the towns, were confused with the Franciscans because of the similarity of their garb. In 1256, Pope Alexander IV succeeded in welding the various congregations into the order of Hermits of St. Augustine. But the Augustinians soon stopped being hermits, for at an early date the universities of Europe, the schools, and the cities became their principal spheres of activity. The exceptional liveliness of the new order can be explained neither by the adoption of the ancient Rule of St. Augustine and supplementary constitutions nor the recognition in 1503 of the Augustinians as a mendicant order of friars, although the privileges this entailed were certainly not insignificant. The reasons are more profound and clearly connected with the love of the order for "the great father Augustine" and a relation between the piety and theology this gave rise to and the Augustinianism of the thirteenth century. During the course of the fourteenth century, this great order did not escape the general decadence that overtook all monastic orders, but during the following century the reform of an increasingly strong observance movement sought to stem this trend. The presence and conflict of conventuals and observants in a single order naturally led to tensions and power struggles. The houses in which observance was practiced were run by vicars whose position was so powerful that even the prior general who resided in Rome could not simply remove them. It can not have failed to impress Luther that the initiative for reform did not necessarily came from Rome. Andreas Proles was the vicar of the Saxon Reformed Congregation. Originally, this association had five houses. When, in 1503, Proles turned the Saxon Reformed Congregation over to Johann von Staupitz, it numbered twenty-seven houses all over Germany.

Johann von Staupitz and Luther are closely connected, and we should indicate at least the most important dates of his life: Born in 1468 in Motterwitz near Liesnig, he came from an old aristocratic Meissen family. After studies in Cologne and Leipzig, he became an Augustinian, probably in Munich. He began the study of theology in Tübingen in 1497, where he was also prior and obtained the doctorate in theology in 1500. Frederick the Wise, who knew him since his youth, sought his advice in 1502 when he founded Wittenberg University where Staupitz became Bible professor.

A few comments on the history of the Erfurt monastery are in order. Established in 1266, it became the largest monastery in both the Saxon Province of conventuals and in the Reformed Congregation. In the early fourteenth century, Erfurt became the seat of the order's own course of general studies (*studium generale*). Because the Augustinians furnished the city with a professor of theology in order to save tax money, a tie between the order and the university was established. Famous teachers, such as Heinrich Friemar the elder, Jordan von Sachsen, Johann Zachariae (who had allegedly defeated Hus in a debate at Constance and lay buried before the altar), or Johann Bauer von Dorsten and his disciple Johann von Paltz, had been superintendents of studies.

The early gothic choir of the cloister church, whose multi-colored windows depicted scenes from the life of Christ, St. Martin, and St. Augustine, dates from this period. Like all other monasteries, the one in Erfurt had a cloister, a chapter house, a dormitory with narrow, unheated cells, a refectory with kitchen, a heated room in which one could warm onself in winter, a reception area and consulting rooms, stables, barns, and even its own brewery.

Just as piety and thirst do not exclude each other, so personal poverty and monastic wealth do not necessarily conflict. Even more, just as the hard manual and agricultural work of the monks had once led to the creation of large fortunes, so did the begging by truly poor mendicants at a later time. Such ownership required a legal fiction, for actually mendicant orders were forbidden the possession of any common property. This explains how the Erfurt cloister could actually own a great deal of capital and land. In addition, there was the regular income in the form of alms that flowed in from the various districts in which begging was carried on and which extended as far as the environs of Jena and Weimar. And finally, there were the mass stipends which constituted a not insignificant source of income for the friar-priests when they fulfilled their obligations by celebrating their private masses. The existence of three brotherhoods—of

St. Catharine, of St. Augustine, and of St. Anne—in connection with the Erfurt cloister is of significance from this perspective.

In the Erfurt cloister, Luther thus saw and experienced all those things for which he later so bitterly reproached monks and Church. Here, it is important to understand that this was undoubtedly a source of the most dangerous abuses but that the reform-minded Erfurt Augustinians initially avoided them or kept them within tolerable limits.

It is also in this context that one should judge the comment that the constitutions of the Augustinian Hermits did not regulate the life of the friars in accordance with the vow of poverty, or did so insufficiently. This is the reason why, during times of decay, there were Augustinians who, like the monks and canons of the older orders, owned property and money, a circumstance which could not but contribute to the decay of the entire communal life of the friars. In the Erfurt observant cloister, such massive degenerative symptoms were absent, of course, but we know from observations Luther made that the friars did own small amounts of money that allowed them to defray certain everyday expenses. Yet when one scrutinizes these statements—such as Luther's recurring complaint about his old, worn cowl which his own means did not suffice to replace—one finds that they do not really testify against, but to, the concrete and real poverty of the Augustinians of the period.

We have now reached the point where we can report his life as novice and friar in the Erfurt cloister primarily from Luther's own perspective. This does not mean, of course, that we can rely completely or even principally on Luther's late statements. The only method we can adopt is to take these retrospects into account but also to make use of reliable sources to correct those misrepresentations that occur for a variety of reasons when someone looks back on his life.

For the sake of greater clarity, I begin with a list of the most important dates: if the postulancy lasted for only a few weeks or two months at most, then Luther's novitiate began sometime during the fall of 1505. Since we know the length of the probationary period, it is at the earliest in the late summer of 1506 that Luther can have been admitted to profession and thus to the order. There followed the minor and the major orders whose dates we do now know with absolute certainty: the subdeaconate on September 19 or December 19, 1506; the deaconate on February 27, 1507; and priesthood on April 3 of the same year. Ordination in all cases was by the suffragan Johann Bonemilch who resided in Erfurt and was the titular bishop of Laasphe. From these sparse, reasonably certain dates, a number of important conclusions can be inferred:

It was the Erfurt superiors, not Staupitz the vicar general, who destined the highly talented Brother Martin—a man called by heaven itself, it seemed—for the career which reached its first culmination in the taking of holy orders. In view of the education of the ordinand, the superiors considered a scholarly preparation unnecessary, that is, they felt that a purely "technical" preparation according to Gabriel Biel's exposition of the mass was sufficient. The study of theology began directly after ordination. This seems to suggest that from the very beginning, the superiors never destined Luther for pastoral duties but for an academic career. With a view to his further development, they hastened the course of things to such an extent that they had to make use of their power of dispensation since on April 3, 1507, Luther had not yet reached the age of twenty-five which was canonically prescribed for ordination.

This overview and our conclusions suggest that we need not consider further the question of Luther's theological career and can concentrate all the more intently on his spiritual preparation for the religious life and priesthood, a matter that was of eminent significance for his development as a reformer. Following the daily schedule to which Luther had to submit since the beginning of his novitiate at the latest, we begin with external and physical matters. The choir office orders the life of the Augustinian as it does the schedule of all monks. Late at night, between one and two in the morning, the bell rouses the sleeping friars for Matins. At dawn, the actual morning prayer of the friars, Lauds, are sung. Subsequently, the community proceeds in carefully ordered rank to the chapter in the chapter house. Prime follows at six after which the community celebrates mass. Terce at nine is the beginning of the so-called Little Hours with Sext following at noon and None and Vespers at around three in the afternoon. After dusk, the day ends with Compline.

The first impression a layman has as he considers this schedule is that the friars never left the church. But this impression is misleading, as we shall see in a moment.

We begin with the simple matter of sleep which appears to have been much too brief. If we remember that even the medieval monks lived according to solar time and in principle without artificial illumination, we quickly realize that about eight hours sleep during the night in wintertime and about six during the summer plus one hour of rest in the early afternoon before None add up to a number that certainly did not affect health adversely. The friars slept in a white wool tunic in their unheated cells which was bearable, considering that they were hardened. Nor was their physical hygiene dictated by the ascesis of the desert Fathers. They washed daily, using water they themselves blessed upon rising. They shaved head and beard at regular intervals and even bathed on certain days of the year. Their linen underpants and white socks were washed, regularly, of course.

Meals followed a similar pattern. Except for periods of fasting, the friars had their noon meal shortly after twelve, the evening meal around six. Like all Christians, the Augustinians abstained from meat on Fridays and on the vigils of great saints. During the periods of fasting—from All Saints' Day till Christmas and from the Sunday before Ash Wednesday to Holy Saturday—Wednesdays and Saturdays were days of abstinence. In addition, the evening meal was reduced to the consumption of some beer and wine and side dishes such as gingerbread or fruit and salad. The prior could order an appropriate diet for the sick or those young friars who required it. Compared with the nutrition of peasants and burghers of the period, or compared with modern diets designed to reduce weight, food at Erfurt was more than adequate and fasting not excessive.

It is not easy to describe the Augustinian dress. At first glance, it seems as if they had put, one on top of the other, all the pieces of clothing once worn by the various hermit groups. Above the previously mentioned linen underpants, they wore a white shirt, a short and a long white wool tunic, a black leather belt, the scapular which consisted of two crossed strips of cloth and the long white *cappa* with collar. Above all this, they wore the characteristic black cowl with narrow or wide sleeves (wide for choir dress), leather belt, and black hood, an appearance that presumably explains the name "Black Cloister." The white undergarments were visible only along the hem of the cowl and the neck. The white garment was and still is worn indoors, in regions where a confusion with Dominicans could not occur. On journeys, the Augustinians also wore a black coat and a hat. In winter time, the fur of domestic animals and felt slippers were permitted. If one has a little imagination, one asks oneself involuntarily how with all these clothes—in bed a pillow and two wool blankets were also used—the allegedly "God-pleasing" hardship of shivering during the winter could have been possible, or what one should make of Luther's recurring recollection that he almost froze to death in his cowl during services.

As we move from externals to what lies below the surface, we briefly mention the monastic "rubrics" which modern man finds either ridiculous or hateful and certainly unbearable. In liturgical texts, *rubrum* refers to the rules in either red (Latin *ruber*) ink or print that lay down what prayers are to be chosen and specify all the ceremonies down to the lighting and extinguishing of candles. Like the liturgy, the entire life of the monk—from rising in the morning until bedtime, from his conduct during choir office and the numerous and different reverences, from behavior at table, during study, and on journeys to the sign language during the *silentium* and extending to the bell signals and the order of dress—is governed in the most minute detail by precise rules whose violation is punished by a variety of sanctions. Learning all of these rules took up a significant part of the novice's time. The danger to dependent personalities from such an excessive ordering of all aspects of life is obvious. But it is equally obvious that in a world of matter and spirit the inner requires the outer, and this applies not just to intersubjective relationships but also to man's life with God. Not without a certain onesidedness, Luther criticized these rules for being mere externalities, lies, and moral constraint. But beyond such polemical attacks on monastic life, he always insisted on the importance of external forms if the inner and the spiritual is to be visualized and made incarnate, especially in the realm of the sacramental.

Similar considerations apply to the choir office in which the inner and spiritual act of the praise and adoration of God is embodied in the *opus Dei* of the praying community: the "work of God" consisting in psalms, hymns, lessons, antiphons, responses and versicles, and prayers. The choir office is the original form of monastic prayer, and at a very early date it became the model for all prayer in church. It may even be said that the history of the choir office or of the breviary provides us with a clear indication of the greatness and wretchedness of the pilgrim Church. We should add that all of the criticism Luther later expressed had already been expressed before him, that the rebukes were certainly not unfounded and, at the very least, did in fact point to serious problems, but that a onesidedly negative criticism simply did justice neither to the nature of the choir office nor to the Erfurt practice of it. For a critical examination of this entire set of questions, three key terms which we encounter time and again in the history of the choir office and its reforms suggest themselves:

The term *quantum* has to do with the length and extent of the breviary. The times when the monks of Cluny took pride in extending the time of their prayers to eight hours, moaning under the "leaden mass" of all the psalms yet feeling pride in "officially" praying in behalf of the Church as a whole were long past. Under the leadership of St. Bernard of Clairvaux whom Luther venerated throughout his life, the Cistercians had already reduced their office to the duration of the Cluniac Prime because they wanted more time for physical work, a change from which they derived considerable spiritual benefit. As part of this development and actually going beyond it, the Augustinians, who as mendicant friars were not really monks in the sense of the old monastic orders, used the Roman breviary, like the Franciscans, rather than the considerably longer monastic one. According to this breviary, the nightly Matins, including the short introductory Marian Office and the concluding Lauds, lasted a little more than one hour. Even though Lauds was directly followed by chapter, the friars had time until Prime at six which they could spend in contemplative prayer, the reading of the Bible, study, or the celebration of private masses. The intervals between the Little Hours, which lasted hardly more than fifteen minutes, were even longer. Things were arranged in such fashion that the public choir office ended and climaxed in the personal, meditative prayer of the individual friar. But the choir office undoubtedly also had the considerable advantage that, if only quantitatively, it consisted largely of psalms and Bible readings which, due to the choral singing and the nature of the reading, especially impressed themselves on the memory. If Luther, like countless medieval monks before him, later knew the Psalter and extensive passages of the Bible by heart, this was due less to personal study than to the much maligned choir office.

Of course, the choir office also had its dangers and problems. This can be demonstrated easily by the silent prayers that were said in preparation for the choir office. For here, the Lord's Prayer or the recitation of the creed became simply a way of measuring the duration of a silence that should actually have served the meditative preparation for the choir office. In the case of the lay brother, this danger becomes even more pronounced. As members of the order without monastic profession, they were not really obliged to participate in the choir office but in an office of their own which consisted of countless Lord's Prayers recited silently during the choir office of the monks. The reason for this type of office (to which, in spite of all reservations, we do not wish to deny the quality of prayer), that is, the lack of linguistic schooling, certainly did not hold for the lay brothers only. A quantitatively determined quota of prayers always brings with it the danger that those who pray will not understand what they pray, or will understand it

only in part. Luther's criticism of the medieval choir service, especially at the cathedral chapters, is undoubtedly not without justification. But such criticisms are not fundamental and do not, or cannot be shown to, apply to the choir office at Erfurt.

The choir office or the Hours must then be considered from the point of view of the *officium,* that is, from the point of view of the service that every monk must perform. The one who prayed or sang what did not correspond to the set order, who ignored the set times, or omitted parts of the breviary became guilty of a venial sin. But he who failed to pray the Hours altogether was considered a schismatic because he had refused the service that was owed to God. Anyone who has ever taken seriously the obligation to participate in choir office or the breviary knows what this means. It is not the obligation as such that is problematic. For the person who means to lead a spiritual life, be it as monk or as priest, simply cannot do so without regular and intensive prayer. But this obligation does become problematic when it is given a petty and anxious or a legalistic interpretation. Catholic assertions that, while still a novice, Luther neglected the choir office for weeks because he felt an inner resistance and was disobedient are polemical legends to which any shred of credibility must be denied. For a novice who must participate in the choir office under the supervision of his master, such an infraction is simply unthinkable. At the very earliest, it was after his ordination that problems developed for Luther, for it was customary to dispense certain friars wholly or in part from the common choir service when they were engaged in intensive study or teaching. In such cases, the friars were obliged to pray the breviary privately, away from the choir. This may have resulted in difficulties which are often reported and with which every person praying the breviary is familiar. But here also, one will have to guard against taking the recollections of the *Table Talk* as if they were Gospel. The story of one of Luther's colleagues, for example, who allegedly prayed the Hours "twice over a period of years" strikes me as incongruous and untrustworthy. Historically more credible is the story of an Erfurt theologian who paid someone to pray his Hours for him, a way of doing things that the conscientious Luther allegedly rejected. But even Luther's supposed choice, to make up for the hours he had missed on lecture—free weekends and while fasting, is questionable, at least in its detail: in 1520, it was not just weeks but three entire months that he was behind in his obligations. From a higher perspective, it is the cliché underlying these recollections that argues against their reliability. One will have to ask whether the picture of an individual whom monasticism has turned into someone who is excessively scrupulous and who gradually frees himself from this nightmare by reading the Bible really corresponds to what happened. If it could be shown that this is not the case, those delightfully scary stories are all part of a "Luther legend" and either the product of the editors of the *Table Talk* or Luther's own doing. In looking back on his life, he may have succumbed to the temptation to use the stylistic means of hagiography to embellish his past "for the greater honor of the pure Gospel."

The final key term to be used in a critical evaluation of the choir office is the phrase *opus Dei* ("work of God"). It is true, of course, that the breviary and, more particularly, the solemn choir office involved a good deal of training and effort. To the extent that Gregorian chant or what was taken for it had not been drummed into them in school, the novices had a great deal to learn. There were, in addition, the previously mentioned red rubrics that were much more difficult to memorize than the rules of conduct which finally became routine. Part of this drudgery is learning how to read and pronounce correctly, to learn how to comprehend and vocalize the biblical and other Latin texts in a dignified manner. Involuntarily, I am reminded of my own students. I fear what would happen were I to call on them to recite a *lectio brevis* ("short lesson"), let alone the magnificent *Exultet* of the Easter liturgy, and this in spite of a foolproof system for indicating accents. As a country priest, I also know that this difficulty persists, if in a somewhat different form, even since the vernacular was introduced. We should therefore view the justifiably praised principle of "comprehensibility" with a measure of scepticism. It simply does not solve all problems overnight, and even creates new ones.

Apart from the rubrics, Brother Martin did not have the slightest technical difficulties. There are, of course, other matters that might be mentioned and which underline that aspect of the choir office that is mere drudgery. It is only natural that the office should become no more than a routine performance when simple monks succumb to the temptation to place the "quantity" of completed psalms into the scale before God or when they anticipate their eternal reward for the trouble of the psalmody in this life and insist on being honored above all others *pro psalmis et lacrymis* ("for psalms and tears"). The service also becomes drudgery when it tortures and tyrannizes the conscience as a falsely understood obligation or, conversely, when it degenerates into a kind of ascetic high-performance sport.

I will not dispute that such degeneration occurred in history, or that it might recur at any time for as long as men succumb to the temptation to look for nothing but their own advantage in whatever they do. What I do dispute—and this in part by invoking the "reforming" Luther—is the secret imputation that the choir office is such drudgery by its very nature. Should that be true, I wonder who, in Erfurt, might have encouraged and seduced the novice or friar to engage in such an effort. It cannot have been the wise old novice master nor the fatherly prior who most likely coined the comment about the hotheads among the young friars who always wanted to knock down twelve pins even though a mere nine were standing in the lane.

In summary, the following comments seem appropriate to the choir office: Luther had difficulties with the highly structured and regimented common prayer. He preferred the personal, free-flowing *oratio mentalis* ("mental prayer"). The constant constraint which interfered with or even suppressed his unusual spontaneity was even more disturbing to him in reciting the office privately than publicly. It is certain that difficulties or crises arose here and that they became all the more acute the more he tried to resolve them by a massive employment of the will and under the dictate of his scrupulosity. But we should guard against exaggerations. For close to crisis though Luther's distress may have been, it was anything but unique and certainly not abnormal. Such vexations are described in the manuals of the spiritual life and neither then nor now are confessors helpless when confronted with them. In the course of time, Luther found solutions for his problems, and they were not that he simply stopped praying. We will avoid exaggeration most effectively if we compare the praying friar and the praying reformer, for such a comparison readily shows that prayer as the "work of faith," the structure of the community's liturgy, the length of public or private prayer, the kneeling and crossing oneself, the binding order of prayer in church and family, or the biblical substance of prayer were none of them things that disturbed the reformer at all. But the comparison also has an eminently positive result for it shows that the vilified choir office with its psalms, hymns and sequences left a resounding echo in the songs and liturgical texts of the reformer. Liturgical instruction in the Erfurt novitiate must have been outstanding if we can judge it by its later fruit such as the formula for ordination that Luther created. Anyone with some experience in the life of prayer knows that what the praying Luther allegedly lacked so completely, the "certainty of the heart" and the "confident Amen," may never be taken as matters of course.

# ILLUSTRATION SEQUENCE I

## BIRTH—YOUTH—STUDIES—AUGUSTINIAN FRIAR
1483–1506

1 Model of the printing press of Johann Gutenberg from Mainz. Gutenberg's invention of printing with movable metal type, which he had come to master around 1450, significantly contributed to the rapid spread of Martin Luther's writings.—Mainz, Gutenberg Museum.

2 Hans Luther († 1530), Martin Luther's father. Painting by Lucas Cranach the Elder (around 1527).—Wartburg Collection.

3 Margarete Luther († 1531), Martin Luther's mother. Painting by Lucas Cranach the Elder (around 1527).—Wartburg Collection.

4 The illustration shows the copper schist mining and the type of foundry operated by Luther's father. Detail of the epitaph of the Stossnach family (around 1536) from the "old cemetery" in Eisleben.—Eisleben, municipal museum in house where Martin Luther was born (*1483).

5 House of the Luther family in Mansfeld where the family moved from Eisleben in 1484.

6 References to the Wartburg as the seat of the Landgraves of Thüringia occur as early as 1080. Around 1200, the castle was enlarged by Landgrave Hermann I and restored in the nineteenth century. From 1498–1501, Luther attended school in Eisenach and lived disguised as "Junker Jörg" in the Wartburg from 1521–22 where he translated the New Testament into German.

7 The burning of the Dominican Girolamo Savonarola (1452–1498) as a heretic on the Piazza della Signoria in Florence (detail) was, like the burning of Jan Hus at the Council of Constance in 1415, a symptom of the pre-Reformation unrest already present in the Church when Luther was a schoolboy. Painting by Fra Bartolomeo (1472–1517), Florence, Museo di San Marco.

ANNO · 1530 · AM · 29 · TAG · IVNY · IST · HANS · LVTH
D · MARTINVS ·                    · VATER · INN · GOT
VERSCHIE                               DENN · ⚔

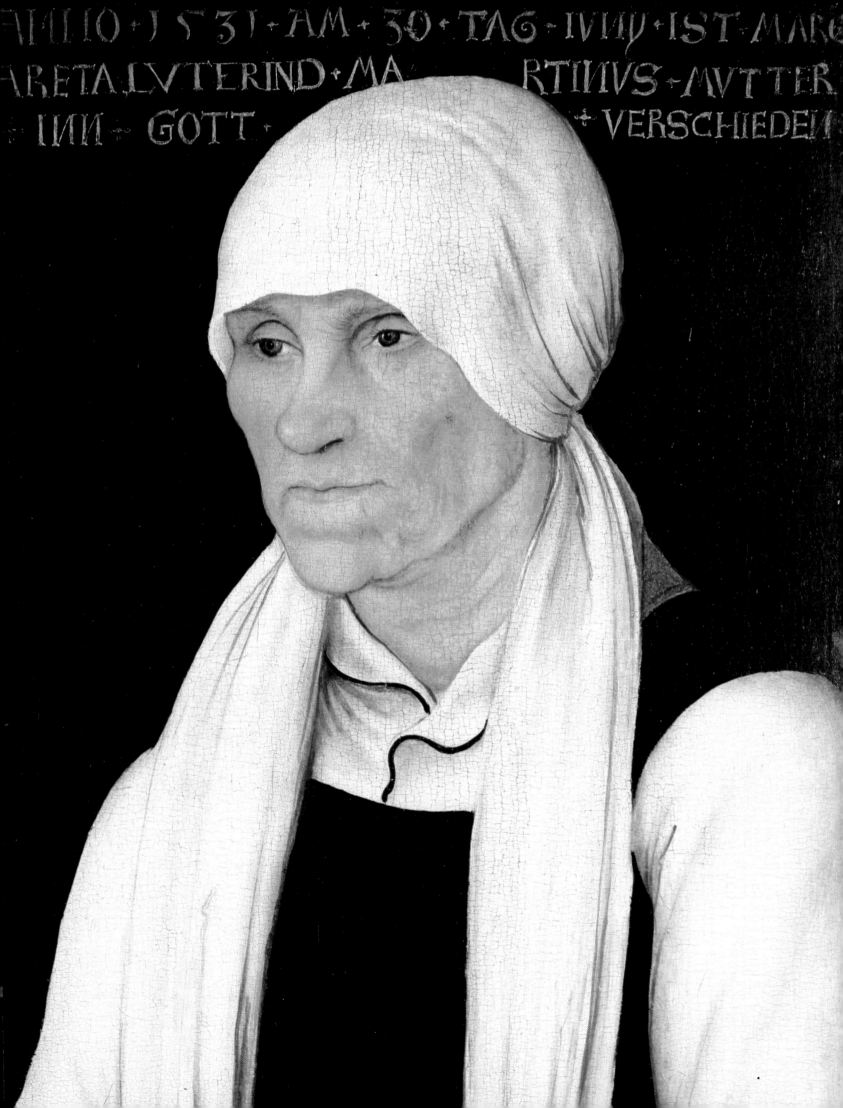
IM ILIO · 1531 · AM · 30 · TAG · IVNIJ · IST · MARG
ARETA · LVTERIND · MA        RTIINVS · MVTTER
· INN · GOTT ·                         + · VERSCHIEDEN

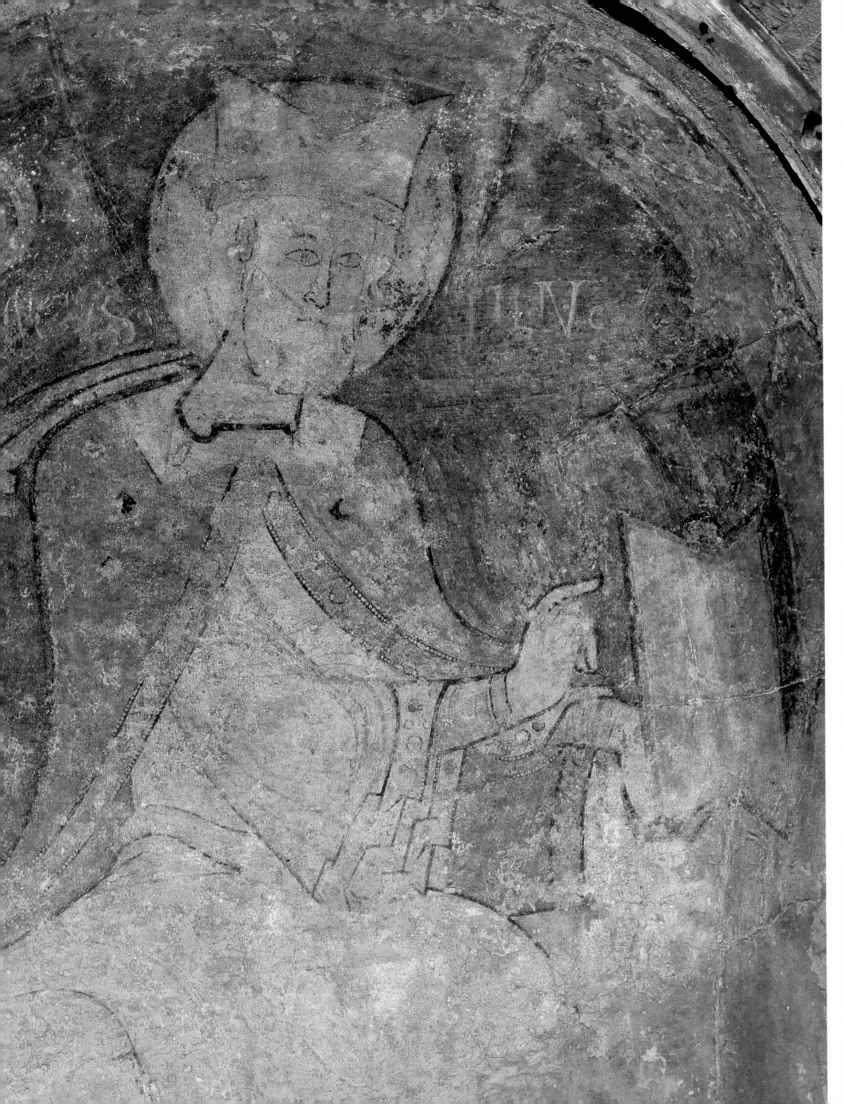

8 View into the church of St. George in Eisenach where Luther sang in the choir as a schoolboy. The present structure dates back largely to the 17th century.

9 View of the cathedral (14th cent.) and the church of St. Severus (13th–15th centuries) in Erfurt. Luther began studying in the faculty of arts of Erfurt University in 1501. He was ordained in the cathedral in 1507.

10 S. Augustine (354–430) was the author of what is probably the oldest rule for monks in the West. It also governed life in the Erfurt Augustinian monastery which Luther entered in 1505. — Fresco (12th cent.) in Saint Sernin, Toulouse.

11 Pietà (around 1360) in Erfurt cathedral. Luther, who felt a particular reverence for Mary throughout his life, probably knew this statue.

12 St. Anne carrying her daughter Mary with the child Jesus on her arm. Statue (around 1330) on the "Triangle Portal" of Erfurt cathedral. Luther knew this statue of St. Anne whose help he implored when he almost died in a thunderstorm near the village of Stotternheim on July 5, 1505, and vowed to become a monk.

13 Cloister in the Augustinian monastery in Erfurt which Luther entered as a novice on July 16, 1505.

14 Slab covering the grave of Johann Zachariae, one of the principal accusers of Jan Hus at the Council of Constance, in front of the high altar of the Augustinian church in Erfurt (13th cent.). During his profession and reception into the order in the early summer of 1506, Luther prostrated himself on this slab.

Of considerably less significance for the spiritual life of the friars was the chapter of faults which, during Luther's time in the monastery, took place only once a week. This performance which is a bit of a show and is insupportable for the modern sensibility took place regularly on Fridays, shortly before dawn, and followed the daily chapter. The chapter of faults dealt with the thousands of possible infractions of house and monastery rules mentioned previously. Being infractions of the obedience that had been vowed, they were not without spiritual significance. Normally, the friars accused themselves. But infractions could also be "proclaimed" by their fellows. Instances of venial guilt were preponderant, and in these cases everything was forgiven when the guilty monk beat his chest. More consequential violations were punished by imposing the recitation of psalms or three days of fasting. Serious or very serious cases, such as rebellion, flight from the monastery, stubborn persistence in mortal sin, and so forth, all too often eluded the chapter of faults and could be forgiven only by sacramental penance.

If Luther later criticized the practice of the chapter of faults because here something that was no sin was punished as one, and the individual's conscience was therefore being tyrannized, his attacks overshoot the mark. The whole practice may sometimes have been childlike or even childish and was certainly not suitable for educating the monks toward the "freedom of God's children," but does this mean that one should deny all pedagogic and spiritual significance to this old and venerable institution? There is no question that the monks made a clear distinction between guilt to be acknowledged in chapter and sin to be confessed privately. The sources also leave no doubt that Luther was not driven into any sort of guilt complex, however seriously Brother Martin may have taken his monastic obligations.

With sin, we come to sacramental confession, and with confession to all those real or putative torments Luther suffered in this connection if the customary accounts are to be credited. And due to the idea untold people have of confession, these accounts are taken as fact. Without prejudice, we will first attempt to clarify what place confession occupied in the life of the monks, and what confessional practice was like.

From its beginning, monasticism had an instinctive discernment of sin in its many forms and its mysterious power over the heart of man. The constitution of the Augustinians made it the friars' duty to seriously examine their conscience every day, and to confess once a week. The regular confessor was normally the prior, and it was he alone who could forgive mortal sins such as serious sexual transgressions or theft. Venial sins could be confessed to any friar-priest. To the extent that confession served spiritual guidance, the friars turned to specific father confessors such as the novice master or other experienced fathers. In addition to weekly confession, there was the general confession which comprised the entire life or certain extended periods of it. It was obligatory only at the time of admission to the monastery. At other times, it was used with circumspection and care was taken to avoid repetitions unless there was a clear need. As in the case of all Christians, confession consisted of as complete and contrite an avowal of sins as possible by the penitent, and the absolution and imposition of an appropriate penance by the confessor. In addition to guides for the examination of conscience, there were manuals like the *Summa Angelica* by Angelo de Clavasio which Luther knew and did not esteem highly. But what concrete knowledge of Luther's practice and of his father confessors do we actually have?

According to his later recollections, Luther made much more frequent use of confession than the rule prescribed so that the sources initially convey an impression of morbid scrupulosity. For Luther not only confessed thoroughly but claims to have done so for hours. He clearly doubted the validity of his confessions and questioned the efficacy of absolution for that reason. Not content with a general confession to the prior, he says that there were two additional ones: one in Erfurt to the *praeceptor,* by which term he may have referred to the novice master; the second one later, in Rome, where the powers of the father confessors were especially extensive and certain. There are comments that testify to Luther's anxiety concerning the completeness of his confessions: he claims to have run back to the priest when, having just finished, another sin occurred to him. Later, as a priest, he reports that, having already confessed in preparation for mass, he signalled to the father confessor at the altar and confessed a second time while it was in process. According to his recollections, monks cannot get enough of confession: "We wear out the father confessors," he writes.

If we had to credit these and similar statements, we would have to judge that Luther was a pathological case whom even the art of modern psychotherapy could never have cured completely.

But the comments that have come down to us are not persuasive and can be questioned under a variety of aspects. They are not the diary entries of a tormented and self-tormenting monk but the *Table Talk* of a reformer who is wholly sure of himself and who, addressing his friends, colleagues and disciples, points to the tortures of a dark, long since mastered past. In statements in which Luther does not cite his personal but the common experiences in accusation of the malpractice of monastic confession, this becomes especially evident. But since even in his recollections, Luther does not denigrate the past as a matter of principle and since he makes quite positive statements about his former father confessors in this context, we find a good many irreconcilabilities and even contradictions in the reports.

We have already mentioned Prior Winand in this connection. While we do not know much about him, he would appear to have been an intelligent and experienced superior who fulfilled his task of spiritual guidance with much circumspection, insight and understanding, and whose fatherly authority was always respected by Luther. More positive and more detailed are Luther's recollections of another father confessor, his novice master, Johann von Greffenstein. Luther always speaks of him with great respect and describes him as an old and utterly kind, devout and learned monk who, "even under the cowl, was without doubt a true Christian." From him, Luther learned that the confessor occasionally encounters cases which all the wisdom in the world cannot wholly explain either morally and theologically or legally, and which one must therefore content oneself to recommend to the grace of God. But I doubt that this fully accounts for Luther's later advice to Philip of Hesse. What can be asserted quite confidently is that Luther learned much that he used in his own practice as father confessor, and that the wise novice master certainly did not drive his difficult charge into some sort of neurosis because he imposed excessive demands on him. This is equally true of Johann von Staupitz who, as extraordinary father confessor, decisively influenced Luther's development.

If we judge the Erfurt practice of confession by looking at Luther's father confessors, it becomes impossible to sustain the thesis that seeks to account for Luther's crises over confession by postulating a growing rebellion against the fundamentally wrong system of Catholic confession as practiced in the monastery. But a thesis which is usually put forward by Catholics and according to which Luther really was the pathological case that is mirrored in the retrospects can be refuted even more easily. For is it likely that his confessors who were also his superiors would have admitted a neurotic, a person of notorious scrupulosity, to the novitiate, profession, and ordination, and later to the teaching of theology and leading functions in the order? It is very important to develop a clear picture about all these mistaken judgments

that so clearly stem from confessional prejudice. For only then do we get closer to reality which is much more complicated that historians and especially theologians will admit even today.

But what more deeply relevant questions can be raised here, once it has been shown that Luther was no psychopath and the sacrament of penance no fundamentally un-Christian horror? Are Luther's difficulties with confession, like his difficulties with the choir office and the chapter of faults no more than minor complications, the result of a few improper exaggerations and differences in personal style? That even as a reformer Luther clung to regular and frequent private confession throughout his life, indeed that he considered it a source of strength and consolation without which he could not have resisted the temptation of the devil, would seem to point in this direction. But such an indication does not take us very far. It is only the question why something that tormented and frightened him in the monastery should later have strengthened and consoled him that will open up new perspectives and backgrounds. For it is in the light of this question—which only arises, of course, when one takes note of two fundamentally different ways of understanding the sacrament of penance—that Luther's relevant texts gradually begin to speak.

There is a whole number of texts in which Luther keeps repeating that he remained uncertain of the absolution granted him after confession, or that he doubted that God had truly forgiven his sins. While this poses no problem for suspicious Catholic readers provided they feel certain that Luther's uncertainty can only be due to an incomplete and therefore invalid confession, critical Protestant readers are readily reassured when told that it was the absence of the certainty of salvation and the evil Catholic "performance principle" that made Luther unsure. There is no need to prove that, in the absence of proof, the "Catholic" explanation is untenable; it is also repulsively self-righteous. But that should not prevent us from recognizing that the apparently critical "Protestant" explanation explains nothing whatever. For every honest Catholic seminarian or youth ever who confessed his sins with the seriousness and conscientiousness of the Erfurt friars can invoke his own experience and assert before God and the world that he normally, though not invariably, experienced absolution as a relief and a blessing. Why does Luther tell us that he often failed to have this experience while a friar? For he does not say that he never felt it in his heart. This must have a plausible reason which must have found some echo in Luther's recollections unless they are to be dismissed as pure invention, which they are not.

There are in fact statements that explain Luther's doubts about forgiveness that are plausible, do not require a far-fetched interpretation, and take his situation into account. I am referring to the not so very rare passages in which he mentions that he did not always succeed in mobilizing the required contrition. In back of this lies a large problem that has to do with the theology of penance but that plagued Luther not as a theological but as a practical problem. We are dealing here with the concrete question whether in confession "attrition" is a sufficient disposition for the forgiveness of sins or whether a contrite heart is indispensable. Anyone who reflects a little about this because he feels the burden in his own heart will soon understand something he didn't understand before. For if someone feels attrition, it is because he fears purgatory and hell and does not wish to lose the promised bliss of heaven. He thus thinks first of himself and only secondarily of God because he fears and needs Him. But the person who feels contrition feels deep in his heart how much his sins conflict with the love of God, the love He feels for us and the love we owe to Him. Everyone who has ever been touched by that true and great love is familiar with the shame that is connected with attrition. And he or she knows with an equally intimate knowledge the difficulty or even impossibility of a repentence in which we wholly disregard ourselves out of love for God or where we finally love ourselves for God's sake alone.

This suggests Luther's dilemma which inevitably developed into the crisis whose spiritual and theological solution determined his whole life and work. At this moment we are concerned only with the first tentative steps on a long path. Still, it must be said even at this point that this path proves how great the heart of the young friar was and that it is a path we take because we are led, not because we choose it on our own.

Back to Luther and the questions that beset him at the time. With the instinct of someone who is being guided, he rejected attrition as a solution and did not look for reassuring counsel in the conventional piety of the day. Instead, he stayed with the demanded contrition which was unattainable to him, and thus involved himself in a maze of irresolvable questions. We do not know precisely how well he already knew the Occamist thesis according to which man's "natural powers" enable him to love God above all else. It is certain, however, that the young friars were instructed to "awaken" the unattainable contrition and that the order's own absolution formula in use at Erfurt made it the indispensable precondition for the effective remission of sins. Luther undoubtedly did all he could to "awaken" the unattainable

contrition; the result was that he got himself deeper and deeper into the maze. The harder he tried, the more clearly he realized that the will has no power over the love of the heart. The less he felt the remorse of such love in his heart, the more uncertain became the remission of his sins. It was a perfect circle. How did Luther escape from it?

From this perspective, a number of otherwise incomprehensible statements make sense. For what does it mean that Luther doubts his own purity and believes all remaining impurity to be ineradicable? This comment cannot be explained by reference to sinful sexual stirrings, for Luther credibly assures us that he did not experience temptations of that sort. In Erfurt, he saw no women and he already knew at an early time that the sinfulness of occasional nocturnal emissions did not lie in the process itself but in the individual's free consent. But the moment we interpret impurity as the impure desires of a love directed toward the self, the remark becomes perfectly clear.

On this basis, Luther's difficulty in distinguishing between venial and grievous sins can be explained with equal ease. Both involve the incapacity to love God with the love that is owed Him, both separate from God. There is the additional fact that gross sins such a whoring, murder, and theft become insignificant from this perspective when compared with the spiritual sins of a perverse heart which, because of its perverse love and precisely because of its virtues, sins against God.

These considerations also suggest why all the excellent advice of eminent father confessors could not help Luther and why even Johann von Staupitz could not resolve the matter. For in his situation, what good could the advice to put all hope in God's mercy do him? Or what use was the reprimand: "God ist not angry with you, you are angry with God"? Even Staupitz did not understand this complicated penitent who wanted to confess to him the "real knot," but which he, Staupitz, dismissed as "peccadillos." Considering that Staupitz later freed Luther from the anxiety caused by the doctrine of grace, his clear failure to understand this earlier distress is a matter of considerable moment. For judging by what we know of the vicar general's theology and spirituality as shaped by Thomas Aquinas and Augustine, Staupitz was in no position to advance a reasonably plausible solution to Luther's problem of "pure love." It will be shown in what follows that Luther could find no effective help within the framework of the *via antiqua* or the mysticism he knew. The young monk therefore found himself alone with his problem. But we must remember that at that time Luther saw neither the full depth nor scope of the problem and that theoretical helplessness does not necessarily exclude various kinds of practical remedies. The problem Luther had to deal with from this moment on did not lead to an unbearable permanent burden, let alone a rapidly accelerating crisis which he then solved by a single stroke as hell was staring him in the face. If such a primitive comparison is admissible, Luther experienced something like a toothache. The pain set in suddenly or faded, a condition that did not preclude times of euphoria. The pain returns as long as man has teeth, and as long as he reaches out in hope and faith to perfect his pathetic love.

It is obvious that the problem we have sketched had a central bearing on the few remaining points still to be discussed. This applies especially to Luther's attitude toward life in the monastery for which he prepared for an entire year during his novitiate and to which, acting as a free agent, he committed himself by a vow in the fall of 1506.

Whenever Catholic and Protestant authors have dealt with Luther's time in the monastery, admission to the novitiate and profession before the prior play a special role. One has the impression that, depending on the point of view of the author, the analysis which is usually performed in this connection of the prayers of the profession ceremony itself emphasizes either grace or the works to be performed under obedience. These matters having so often been presented in considerable detail, there is no need to repeat. An even more important reason for not repeating them is that Luther's attitude toward a monk's life cannot be explained in this way. For the decisive rejection of monasticism that was taking shape in Luther's mind because he saw it as drudgery does not negate works as the expression of a surrender of the self that is sustained by grace. It will be shown that his rejection of a corrupted monasticism notwithstanding, Luther never disputed the meaning and justification of a binding monastic vow. Luther's fundamental question reemerges here, for he is concerned with a vow that commits us to a loving, and therefore free, surrender to God and neighbor. Once again, the problem lies in the connection of freely given love and a wholly serious lifelong obligation. When, through his profession, he commited himself to a life in poverty, chastity, and obedience according to the rules and constitutions of the order, he had at best a sketchy sense of the problem. Yet his fundamental question enhances the seriousness and integrity of the decision Luther's profession involved. He took it very seriously indeed, just as seriously as the symbolic investiture with what were now consecrated monastic garments (the garments worn during the novitiate were not consecrated). The comparison with the baptismal dress which makes monastic profession appear a kind of second baptism apparently did not disturb him at all. Nor did it have to, since a perfectly orthodox understanding of it was possible.

We can be certain that Luther made this definitive decision in the faith and that he never regretted it. His later recollections with their massive criticism of the busy-work of the Erfurt Augustinians strike one as ideologically exaggerated and simply do not correspond to reality. There is absolutely no basis for the charge of arbitrarily chosen, conspicuous works (*opera electitia et speciosa*) of rigorous asceticism in the areas of fasting, penitential exercises, and inhuman obedience by which monks allegedly distinguished themselves from ordinary Christians and gave themselves airs as a privileged class. Quite the opposite is the case. In its reasonable strictness, the "roughness" of the life of the Augustinian friars rather makes a blessedly normal impression. Everything is oriented toward the service which the friars have to perform in the ministry, at the university, or in schools. From prayer and intensive study in preparation for teaching and preaching to a poor but certainly not exaggeratedly poor life it is difficult to discover any "work" that Luther did not also do as a reformer. After his profession and during the years thereafter, he behaves as if he would never leave the monastery. For this, there are reliable proofs that date from a later time and which we will discuss below. At this point, we merely mention the record of an indulgence for the Erfurt convent which is dated 1508 and lists the names of the friars living there at the time. Prior Winand is followed by the names of the teachers at the Erfurt *studium generale* where, behind Johann Nathin as the director of monastic studies, Luther is mentioned as lecturer in philosophy. As early as 1508, Luther thus was in sixth place among the dignitaries of his convent.

In conclusion, Luther's training for the priesthood, his first mass, and his devotion to the mass must be dealt with at this point.

As suggested above, Luther's preparation for ordination was primarily practical and did not include the study of theology, a procedure that was not at all unusual at the time. Since the celebration of mass represents the most important priestly function, preparation centered on this task. Luther used the standard work of the Tübingen theologian and nominalist Gabriel Biel, the *Canon Missae,* which first appeared in 1499 and which, in eighty-nine lessons, deals clearly and in detail with the entire liturgy of the mass and related theological questions concerning the powers of consecration and the presence of Christ in the sacrament. Biel had succeeded in bringing all theological, spiritual, and practical questions into relation with each other. Rather ironically, Luther praises the competence of Biel's work in his *Table Talk,* saying that his authority in matters relating to the mass exceeded that of Holy Scripture. But reminiscing about his studies, he recalls that his heart had bled while he read it. Here, we once again encounter Luther's fundamental problem which became significantly more acute as he considered the solemn celebration of the mass and the reception of the physically present Christ who was also understood to preside over the final judgment.

What made him dubious about the remission of sins in confession made him all the more skeptical about the worthiness of which an upright Christian had to be morally certain before he received the Eucharist. Luther already had difficulties with the daily communal mass at which the friars were to communicate at least sixteen times a year. In both intensity and scope, these difficulties increased considerably after Luther had been ordained and had to take on the task of holding private celebrations of endowed masses at the monastery. In addition to the mere participation in the Eucharist, it now was necessary to celebrate mass correctly.

According to his reminiscences Luther's first mass on May 2, 1507, turned into an occasion where all these difficulties combined and almost precipitated a crisis-like collapse. The invitation he sent to his friend Johannes Braun in Eisenach already reveals a certain excitement on the part of the young celebrant who, having been called to the dignity of the priestly office, feels all the more a miserable sinner and is also afraid of being unable to celebrate without error. The presence of his strict and as yet unreconciled father, who made his appearance with twenty horsemen and contributed the almost princely gift of twenty gulden to defray the expenses of the banquet, presumably increased Luther's nervousness. A crisis allegedly erupted during the canon of the mass when, in the course of the introductory invocation, "Therefore, most merciful father ..." (others mention other passages), he claims to have succumbed to the overwhelming majesty of God whom he must address, directly and without a mediator in order to offer Him, the living and eternal God, the gifts of the altar. According to his reminiscences, Luther wanted to rush away from the altar and would supposedly have done so had the assisting priest, the prior of the novice master, not restrained him. Although it is difficult to interpret the various versions of the report, the historicity of the reminiscence is not in dispute. While the Catholic version

takes this incident as impressive proof that Luther was too confused to understand even so clear a text, its Protestant counterpart emphasizes that in the liturgy of the mass Christ is not only mediator but also judge.

Although I have no desire to question the historical core of the recollection, I consider this retrospect, like so many others, to be seriously flawed and the conflicting interpretations more than questionable. Nor does the incident become more credible when one remembers that such stories about first masses were told more than once during the Middle Ages, by the humanist Mutian among others. If Mutian delayed his first mass for years, he presumably had motives that had no connection with Luther's difficulties. It would seem that when we see it properly and reduce it to its presumably true core, Luther's reaction was a quasi-normal difficulty which many conscientious neophytes experienced during their first mass, and continue to experience today, a fact which finds nearly official confirmation in the liturgical office of the *presbyter assistens.* To this day, I remember the intensely elating and simultaneously oppressive experience I had when I celebrated my first mass, feelings which my assisting priest and father confessor could confirm were he alive today. When I remember how, about ten years after my ordination, a police official, who was not known to suffer from religious delusions, confided to me that he had felt great anxiety for me at my first mass — he claimed that the terrible seriousness in my face indicated to him that I would soon become an apostate — I am again struck by the terror that seized me back then. Without wishing to put myself in Luther's place, I may add in all modesty that at that time I had almost completed a paper on "pure love," though without having the slightest suspicion that Luther had been beset by the identical problem.

From this perspective, Luthers's fear during his first mass and his later masses is clearly motivated. It must be defined as serious moral distress but has nothing whatever to do with a pathologically onesided temperament. The horror story of a Luther still "confessing" during mass should be relegated to the same realm of "Protestant legend" as the "Catholic story" which Cochläus reports according to which the young monk once collapsed with the cry, "It is not I," when the biblical story about the cure of the deaf-mute was read during mass.

More credible in this connection are those reminiscences that testify to Luther's high regard for the office of priest during the celebration of the mass and which also mention his occasional euphoria when he had succeeded in celebrating mass in the way expected of him. It may also be that he succeeded in combining his devotion to mass with the veneration of the saints. But it is not here that we should look for the core which brought Luther in the course of a rather long development to view the mass as a real horror. What is meant here is the mass as "sacrifice," applied to the needs of the living and the dead, in short the mass that was being exploited for one's own advantage and misused as magic, the so-called "corner masses" of countless mass priests and monks who lived off the business they did with the Most Holy. But years were to pass until this kind of mass became a problem and an insupportable scandal for Luther. Compared to his fellow friars and later fellow reformers, Luther here appears as an archconservative who only laboriously detached himself from the traditional form of the mass, the silently prayed Canon, the Latin text, and the priest's vestments, and who continued to adhere to the old view in his understanding of the physical presence under the forms of bread and wine and in his idea of the administering and reception of the Eucharist. If one refrains from polemical formulas and relates the later criticism to false forms of the theology and practice of the mass, it becomes anything but easy to distinguish between Luther's lifelong high regard for the Eucharist and the purified Catholic mass. For the moment, in any event, Luther's critique remained within the framework of Catholic ideas. He criticized the frivolous practice of the Romans; he began to see the countless ceremonies and rubrics surrounding the mass as threatening superficiality; he fought against distraction during the prescribed prayers, especially during the consecration. He soon had trouble with devotion to the eucharistic Host outside of mass.

The *Table Talk* in which he remembers a Corpus Christi procession in Wittenberg shows clearly that occasionally, such recollections are not only objectively correct but contain observations of actual historical occurrences. Luther recalls, for example, that the monks from Zerbst also participated in the procession. Because these monks had come a considerable distance to join the procession, it was interrupted to feed the hungry in the city hall. What sets off Luther's angry astonishment is the observation that during the meal, the "Lord" God in his monstrance was simply stored in a small room and that God accepted such treatment without retaliation. One will agree with Luther that such ill usage of the Eucharist can seem a problem. But this problem cannot be eliminated by doing away with processions or by the effort to limit the number of wafers to be consecrated as precisely as possible to the number of communicants. The corresponding practices of Protestant ministers and sacristans when they remove the remains of Communion would also have been punished as sacrilege by Luther the reformer.

We therefore conclude our reflections on this important point by observing that the neophyte's problems with the mass were nothing out of the ordinary though it is true that they were the cause of weighty concerns. We must recognize the fact that tensions and conflicts have always been found, and continue to be found, in the calling and life of a priest, and that the priesthood contains far greater risks than other walks of life. It should be added, however, that neither these difficulties nor the anxiety-creating question concerning the love of God intensified to the point where they became a fundamental crisis that would unambiguously account for Luther's subsequent development.

## 2. FROM STUDENT OF THEOLOGY IN ERFURT TO PROFESSOR IN WITTENBERG

Although Luther's future seemed settled, it appears that there were monks and superiors in the Erfurt monastery who tried to hamper the dramatic rise of a friar who was allegedly being compared to St. Paul. Father Martin was assigned to the cleaning of latrines and begging in the countryside, for example, a story that has a marked flavor of monastic legend about it. But even if Luther should really have come into contact with cleaning rags and beggar's sack, this cannot have gone on for long, for we know that directly after celebrating his first mass and as early as the summer semester of 1507, he immediately began the study of theology. In the interest of saving space, I will confine myself to indicating the technical details of the curriculum. In Erfurt, Luther would first have had to attend lectures, especially on Peter Lombard, for a period of five years, and would also have had to go through the prescribed disputations. But he earned his doctorate in five and one-half years because the statutes provided for shorter courses for monks, courses which could be shortened even further when necessary or when a student enjoyed special favor. It is striking how little the conditions of academic life have changed since Luther's day. It is still a matter of considerable moment for theologians from religious orders to which groups within an order they belong. The rivalries between the various houses and, especially, between the various universities persist, and much depends on whose protegé a young scholar becomes.

Luther benefited first from the interest Johann Nathin, professor of theology and head of the *studium generale,* took in him as long as he made his own the views of his teacher on policies to be pursued by the order. Since Nathin belonged to the circle of Erfurt nominalists, Luther had probably come to know him during his philosophical studies. As a teacher of theology, Nathin did not make a deep impression on him although his marginal comments on Peter Lombard's *Sentences* and on Augustine betray the influence of the Occamist tradition which prevailed in Erfurt. Luther still believed that man's will is free and that, at least indirectly, he can by his good works earn the merit that God then rewards through His grace. It is not His absolute power and arbitrariness but His compassion that is emphasized. To the extent that man does what he can, God will not withhold grace. More important are the beginnings of a critique

of Aristotle and of an Aristotelian theology. Luther recognized ever more clearly that we must orient our thinking by the Bible and that the "rancid rules" of logic do not suffice to measure God in His revelation. Nominalism and his preference for a biblical theology made access to scholastics such as Thomas Aquinas and Scotus more difficult during this time.

It should be added that in keeping with the custom of the period Luther had also been a lecturer in philosophy in the Erfurt *studium* since the summer semester of 1508.

His studies were considerably speeded up when, in the fall of the same year, the vicar general, Johann von Staupitz, called him to Wittenberg as lecturer in philosophy because his predecessor Wolfgang Ostermayr had been given a leave. Since it was up to the Augustinians to fill this professorship at the recently founded university, Luther spent a rather joyless year lecturing on Aristotle's *Nichomachean Ethics.* But that he could now pursue his theological studies under the direction of Staupitz who was the dean of the theological faculty at the time was a considerable benefit. For obvious reasons, Staupitz now hastened his student along. On March 9, 1509, Luther qualified for the *baccalaureus biblicus* which was followed in the fall of the same year by the examination for the *baccalaureus sententiarius.* Even before the newly graduated baccalaureus could give the public inaugural lecture which was customary after this examination, he was transferred back to Erfurt, perhaps because he was urgently needed, perhaps because his superiors did not wish to see him working in another monastery and at another university. Because of his accelerated studies in Wittenberg, Luther at first had problems in Erfurt. Only with difficulty did he secure permission to give the compulsory lectures on the *Sentences* of Peter Lombard. In their hurry, the Erfurt people forgot to demand that he take the oath incumbent on those members of the Erfurt faculty who were admitted to the biblical baccalaureate and which required that they refrain from obtaining the theological doctorate at any other university. Luther gave his lectures on Peter Lombard in Erfurt and, having dealt with book two of the *Sentences,* obtained the degree of *sententiarius formatus.* He presumably did not complete his lectures before his journey to Rome which would mean that this was not done until after his return in the spring of 1511. This is probably the reason the copy of the text Luther used contained no comments relating to the fourth book and that we unfortunately do now know for that reason what position the young sententiarius took on the problem of God's justice which is treated in *dist.* 46.

But since Luther's order politics which had been the same as those of Father Nathin changed after his return from Rome as he now adopted the views of Vicar General Staupitz, considerable tension developed between Luther and the extremely sensitive Nathin. To resolve the complicated situation, Staupitz ordered Luther's transfer to Wittenberg, and in September 1511 he and Johann Lang returned there to stay. The Erfurt people did not immediately understand what this loss meant, and when they finally did, it was too late. For the chapter of the Reformed Congregation had taken the following decision in May 1512: Lang was to take over the teaching position in philosophy that Luther had occupied a short time earlier as a substitute and which, along with the Bible professorship, was part of the teaching obligations the Augustinians had assumed at the new university. Luther was made sub-prior of the small Wittenberg friary in which, after his promotion, he was to assume the direction of the *studium generale.* The Erfurt people reacted with a lasting bad humor which Luther would come to feel. Behind all this, one senses the machinations of Staupitz who gave up his professorship in 1512 and therefore needed a successor because his obligations in the order began to take up more and more of his time.

In view of this background, it makes no sense to allege that after his arrival in Wittenberg, Luther's situation was wholly indeterminate. For it is precisely the famous scene under the pear tree in the cloister yard that proves that as regards the plans of the order everything about Luther's future had in fact been settled, and this in spite of the fact that after the promotion of 1511, Staupitz could have chosen among any of candidates within the order. But the vicar general and his councilors had decided that, in sending Luther on for the doctorate in theology and in commissioning him to preach to the community, he should finally be given the position to which his talents predestined him. That Luther, having thus had his future laid out for him, immediately listed fifteen reasons why this should not be done and claimed that, for reasons of health, he was simply unable to bear up under the stress of the tasks assigned to him can easily be explained by the humility of the friar or the literary cliché of the late reminiscences and must not be interpreted as proof of Luther's indecisiveness, let alone rejection of the plans that had been made for him. The same applies to Luther's letters on this subject in which he states that he is not interested in obtaining the doctorate in theology and that he had resisted the plans of the vicar general to the point of disobedience and reemphasizes his incapacity and his unworthiness for such a task.

The statement is completely inproblematical if we put ourselves in Luther's place and consider the historical difference between his call and a modern negotiation for a professorship where the candidate naturally believes himself to be the best qualified among all candidates and presents himself accordingly.

This does not exclude the possibility that for Luther, though not for Staupitz, there were a number of personal and specific reasons which deserved to be considered even if he was basically prepared to accept. The mere choice between Erfurt and Wittenberg, between the large friary and one that was smaller and still in the initial stages of its development, between the famous university and one that had just been founded, was not obvious. As a small town with the characteristics of a village, situated on the periphery of civilization, with narrow streets that threatened to disappear in the mud and its quarrelsome citizens, Wittenberg can hardly have seemed attractive to Luther. The same applies to the brethren he left behind and those whom he found at Wittenberg. True, there was no lack of old friends such as Wenzelaus Link who had just earned his doctorate in theology and was the prior of the small monastery. And there was, more importantly, the vital friendship with Staupitz. But this friendship was really just developing at the time and the falling out with Nathin did not involve a radical break in his relations with the old monastery in which his teacher and friend Usingen would not become a monk until 1512.

The same holds true for the colleagues in the Wittenberg theological faculty: the Thomist Petrus Lupinus, the Scotist Nikolaus von Amsdorf, a nephew of Staupitz, or the equivocal Andreas Bodenstein who called himself Karlstadt after his place of birth and was trying to work out a theologically not altogether clear compromise between Thomism and Scotism. There really was no such thing as a "Wittenberg theology" at the time, for while there were new approaches like the coexistence of various schools among the theologians and the humanists, and a nominalism without Occam, things had something provisional and makeshift about them. The new university was enmeshed in the crises of its founding years.

Quite apart from Luther's inner difficulties, there were also personal reasons. The Wittenberg teaching post with its numerous compulsory lectures and disputations and the simultaneous course of studies and new examinations in 1509, the unusual hardship of the journey to Rome, the new theological lectures, and the quarrel over matters affecting the order had all taken their toll. If one remembers in addition that Luther never in his life changed positions with flying colors, it becomes perfectly understandable why, in his new situation, Luther should have preferred obedience to impulsive decisions of his own. The greater the temporal distance from the event and the more insight into the significance of his change in course grows, the more urgent becomes the need to make the entire later development with its unforeseeable consequences a matter of the obedience of faith, not the result of personal decision.

From the perspective of the historian, it was probably perfectly simple and ordinary reasons that caused the delay in the promotion and the assumption of his teaching. Among them was the simple fact, for example, that neither Staupitz nor the monastery had the money to pay for Luther's promotion fees because such a large number of Augustinian theologians had obtained higher degrees in 1511, which is why Staupitz had to persuade the elector to assume this burden. With the assurance that the biblical professorship Staupitz had given up would be taken over by Luther for life, Frederick the Wise finally paid. On October 12, 1512, Staupitz received the required fifty gulden from the court treasury in Leipzig.

Another reason may have been that, in view of the shortness of his training and the interruption of his studies by the journey to Rome, it really proved impossible to promote Luther more quickly lest the impression be created that the entire process had been inadequate because excessively compressed, an impression that would have been harmful to both Luther and Wittenberg. The fact that the general of the order did not appoint Luther as theological lecturer until October 6, 1513, may be due to countless insignificant reasons and was of little consequence in this context.

In October 1512, Luther finally received the doctorate, the preparatory acts of candidacy, permission by the chancellor, and the oath of obedience to the Church having been attended to. On the afternoon of October 18, the three-hour long preliminary celebration began where the baccalaureates disputed with each other and the new doctor disputed with the masters. The promoter —in Luther's case it was Karlstadt—was scheduled to end the celebration with a witty speech but one may doubt that he succeeded. On the morning of October 19, there followed the awarding of the doctorate. The ceremony took place in the castle church and consisted of another speech by the new doctor, the swearing of the oath, instruction in the duties of a master, and the presentation of the doctor's insignia: a shut and an open Bible, the doctor's cap and gold ring. After the kiss of peace and the blessing, the new doctor then pronounced an encomium on theology. The celebration ended with a

disputation between two doctors about an open theological question which was decided by the new doctor. A large banquet for the faculty with music by the elector's celebrated orchestra ended the eventful day. With admission to the senate of the theological faculty on October 21 and a final defense, Luther had now become a full-fledged professor.

As might have been expected, this was not the end of the matter. Luther had not forgotten, of course, to invite his teacher Nathin and his other Erfurt superiors to the ceremony. But the latter not only did not accept his invitation but embarked on an ugly campaign against him which was not to end until 1515. Calling attention to the customary oath of the University of Erfurt which forbade the individual to acquire a doctor's degree at any other university, they accused Luther of having violated it. But because in their hurry they had forgotten to have Luther swear it in time, their criticism was unfounded. Even today, the important question concerning the date and nature of Luther's first Wittenberg lecture cannot be answered with absolute certainty. We do know, however, that in the winter semester 1513/14 he lectured on the Psalms and that these lectures, the so-called *Dictata super Psalterium*, continued on into the winter term 1514/15, and perhaps even to the following summer semester. But it is quite possible that another set of lectures preceded this one, and that his subject may have been the Epistle to Titus or Judges or perhaps Genesis, especially the story of Abraham which Luther treated throughout his life in sermons and lectures. It is certain that he lectured on the epistles of Paul—Romans (1515/16) and Galatians (1516/17)—and the Epistle to the Hebrews (1517/18) in the following years. In the winter semester 1518/19, he turned back to the Psalms. He gave two-hour lectures, at six in the morning during the summer, at seven during the winter. Beginning in 1516, he lectured at one in the afternoon.

This unusually crowded schedule was supplemented by a number of disputations and countless sermons which he gave in the monastery or the town church. Apart from further marginal comments and the quickly swelling correspondence, there were publications on the Seven Penitential Psalms or sermons on the Ten Commandments and the Lord's Prayer.

If Luther really did hesitate to accept the task that had been chosen for him, then our esteem for Staupitz grows, for on the basis of objective criteria this man ignored all the subjective doubts of his disciple and was confirmed in his judgment. As professor of Bible, Luther proved himself. Using the Bible as his guide and working his way through all the distortions of Scholastic theology, he found his way back to the beginnings of a biblical theology in which the story of Abraham or of Christ happens anew for every reader, as it were. This is the reason why neither the ecclesiastical condemnation of certain exaggerated pronouncements nor a systematizing inclusion in a supposedly "reformist doctrine" which cannot be derived from Luther's work allows us to quickly dismiss it. Luther also proved himself as a preacher. For the theology that concerned him not only demanded that he proclaim it, it is ultimately identical with such proclamation. That is why the most profound direction of his teaching cannot be understood without his preaching.

## 3. LUTHER AS FRIAR AND SUPERIOR OF HIS ORDER

Luther's retrospective recollections of monasticism suffer from an internal contradiction. On the one hand, he always emphasizes his undivided and over-eager engagement in behalf of monasticism, and the statements along these lines can always be understood both as self-accusation and as self-defense. But on the other hand, the reminiscences of negative experiences constitute an ever more violent accusation of monasticism, the motive being the radical criticism of an institution he had recognized as unfit and meretricious. From the point of view of the backward-looking Luther, the contradiction can be more or less explained and therefore removed. But when we ask how Luther actually experienced the religious life and how he should be judged as a religious, this contradiction persists and significantly reduces the value of the retrospective statements. The contradiction in the retrospects provides us with only one positive pointer to an answer, for it justifies the observation that Luther's original experience of monasticism differed from his later judgment of it. This means that we should answer the question concerning Luther's monasticism without bothering about the *Table Talk* or other retrospects. Fortunately, there is no lack of objective sources and facts or of biographical statements that are not suspect and by which Luther himself answers the question we are raising here.

As we search for relevant sources and facts, we remember first the unbroken and successful monastic career. As early as 1508, Luther is part of the monastic élite of the Erfurt friary. This is shown not only by his position as lecturer but by his previously mentioned journey to Rome. When we examine all known details of this journey, we discover no compelling grounds for the customary account according to which Luther was merely the junior partner in this enterprise. We do not know who his companion was and therefore cannot assert that he was older and more experienced than Father Martin. But we do know that at the age of twenty-seven Luther was old enough for such an undertaking that he was one of the men Johann Nathin trusted, and that both had already negotiated this matter in Halle. What was involved here? Without examining the difficult details and the earlier history of the problem at length, we can summarize as follows: among the Augustinian Hermits, reform had led to the creation of legally autonomous reformed congregations which did not coincide geographically with the original and never relinquished constitution of the various provinces of the order under the direction of the general in Rome. The legal autonomy of the reformed congregation appeared to guarantee the stricter observance which could be disturbed neither by the provincials nor the general. The co-existence of, or conflict between, two autonomous groups of communities within a single order, however, became a serious danger to its unity as time went on. This was the reason that General Aegidius of Viterbo, a man who sympathized with the reform, attempted to re-establish, at least in Germany, the threatened unity of the order without compromising the reform. Johann von Staupitz was persuaded to give his support to a plan which was to re-establish the unity of the two branches of the order by conferring the offices of vicar general and prior provincial on a single person, or to initiate such a development. Since this plan was not without danger for the reformed communities, a countermovement within the reformed congregation quickly sprang up. The soul of the resistance which naturally also turned against Staupitz were the so-called "renitent cloisters" among which, during the final phase, the Erfurt cloister and Nathin were prominent. From the perspective of monasticism, it is therefore illuminating that Luther sided with the demands of the strict reformed party and thus against the mediating attempt of the vicar general to create a union.

It was in this matter that Luther and another monk whose identity is unknown to us traveled to Rome in November 1510. It was the object of the delegation to ask the general of the order in Rome for permission for an appeal by the renitent cloisters to the Papal See which would prevent the plan for union.

As a devout pilgrim in Rome, Luther experienced and saw a great deal, though he did not have the opportunity to see the procurator general who gave a negative response to the request of the delegation. It seems that Luther felt Rome to be more important for the salvation of his soul than an affair in which he could not accomplish much against the general of his order and his own vicar general. And since Luther, though eager for reform, was no zealot by nature, he decided against Nathin's project after his return and supported the mediating policy of the vicar general. Although this change in position earned him the enmity of his old teacher, the sources provide no basis for the assumption that in his adoption of Staupitz's position, Luther allowed himself to be guided by irrelevant considerations of personal profit. Without wishing to attribute a greater importance to this matter than it deserves, one may say that Luther's place was among the followers of the vicar general rather than among Nathin's adherents. For is it not much better to serve both reform and unity if there is any chance of doing so? The theme itself is highly significant. But it would appear that neither for Staupitz, who soon gave up his union plan for practical reasons, nor for Luther did it play a role that would entitle us to draw far-reaching conclusions.

More important in our context than the journey to Rome is the fact that the congregation chapter meeting in Cologne in 1512 appointed Luther sub-prior of the Wittenberg cloister and that the same chapter in Gotha chose him, on May 1, 1515, to be the vicar provincial of the ten Augustinian houses in Meissen and Thuringia for a period of three years. If as sub-prior he was the second ranking superior of the Wittenberg cloister, he now had the spiritual and canonical responsibility for ten important communities such as Dresden, Erfurt, Neustadt, Orla, Gotha, Langensalza, Eisleben, Nordhausen, and Magdeburg whenever the vicar general was absent, which was often. As vicar provincial, Luther had to fulfill the entire range of obligations of a superior, if we can judge by the correspondence that has come down to us. They extended from participation in financial dealings to the canonically prescribed visits to monasteries under his jurisdiction between April and June 1516, and included the support and guidance of a prior in difficulties, the demotion of that official and the election of a suitable successor, the counseling of the new Erfurt prior Johann Lang in delicate questions of monastic order such as the complicated issue of flight from one monastery and the joining of another, the counseling of other superiors, and the rendering of spiritual help to difficult and troubled monks. It would be an attractive task to set forth the picture of Luther as vicar provincial,

using his own letters and biographical documents as a basis. I confine myself to roughly sketching the upshot of such a portrayal. In the mirror of this three-year correspondence, Luther emerges as a model friar and superior of the monasteries and friars under his jurisdiction. He is thoroughly familiar with the rules, the constitutions, and the general law of the order. As superior, he distinguishes himself by his psychological knowledge, his judgment, and his friendliness, but equally by the courage to make authoritative decisions. All in all, he is wholly and without reservation a friar, a Christian, and yet already the Luther we know, even though still wearing the cowl as if it were part of his body.

Of greatest importance in this connection are letters such as the one dated April 5, 1516, which he sent to his former fellow monk Georg Spenlein who had been transferred to Memmingen. For they show impressively that for Luther the admonition to lead a true monastic life seamlessly connects with those approaches which he will identify as the core of his reformist breakthrough in the great retrospect of 1545. Fragments of letters to the Premonstratensian provost Georg Mascow in Leitzkau near Zerbst tend in the same direction. The second of these has, because of its concluding statement, become a source of misinterpretation time and again, though the context makes the meaning clear. For at the end of the letter, Luther asks the addressee for his prayer to their common Lord, and emphasizes: "For I confess to you that every day, my life approaches hell more closely because I am becoming worse and more miserable every day." Luther signs the letter "the banished son of Adam, Martin Luther Augustinian"—banished from heaven, a precise designation of the theological position of someone suffering from the consequences of original sin. Anyone who interprets this confession of a daily "deterioration" as a criticism of the useless drudgery of monasticism and an expression of growing predestinarian fears takes neither the connection to the first fragment nor the situation and the theological background, that is, the concurrent lecture on the Epistle to the Romans, into account. For the first fragment consoles the provost, who is depressed over the decline of monasticism, with the seemingly paradoxical advice that he avoid at all cost the use of a kind of pious violence in an effort to improve things, for that would involve him in a quarrel with the majority for the minority's sake. According to the parable about the wheat and the chaff, he would do better to put up with the latter for the sake of the former and to let both grow till harvest day. The situation of the second fragment is determined by the experience of the plague, which indiscriminately destroys humans and cattle and which, by the sighs of mortal creatures, recalls to consciousness our sins and our misery even though it should really be understood as a sign of grace rather than of wrath. Given the background of the Epistle to the Romans, the experience of a progressive deterioration can readily be explained as the expression of the *peccator fieri*. For only if we "become sinners" by recognizing as "sin" our incapacity for a loving fulfillment of the law, do we receive in faith the "justice of Christ" and can then live through that justice.

The oppressive burden of work that Luther had to bear as professor and vicar provincial, especially in 1516, is additional reason for understanding the sigh of "the banished son of Adam." The degree to which Luther's as yet wholly monastic piety already contains the reformist beginnings could finally be shown by his correspondence with the Augustinian Georg Leiffer whom he already knew in Erfurt and who had consoled him during his early sufferings in the monastery. Leiffer, who lectured in the Erfurt *studium generale,* was an old man at this time and seems to have found himself in the dark night of faith and the cross. As Luther consoles him by pointing to the destiny he shares with Christ, the outlines of the reformist theology of the cross emerge. Luther also suggests that the troubled father consult with another old friend, his former teacher Bartholomäus von Usingen who had entered the Erfurt Augustinian cloister at Luther's promptings in 1512. Leiffer, he writes, could find no better "paraclete and consoler" than the man who lives up to his name "Christopherus and Stauropherus" ("Christ-bearer" and "Cross-

bearer")—the words from a letter to Usingen— "by always carrying in the body the death of Jesus" (2 Cor. 4:10). It therefore would appear that Usingen received "Christopherus" as his new name at profession unless the name is being used metaphorically and alludes to the friend's inner situation. During the decisive years 1517/18, even Luther called himself for a time "Martinus Eleutherius" which may be understood either as a grecizing periphrasis of the family name—"Luder"—"Lauter"—or as the allegorical designation of someone who, being "free," sets about become a "liberator."

Whatever the case may be concerning Usingen's name, it is certain that Luther participated in his friend's profession in his own way. When, in recent times, Usingen's grave in the old Würzburg Augustinian cloister was opened, a medal bearing the inscription "Erfurt 1512" was found. If one may be permitted to hypothesize that Luther gave this simple gift to his friend to commemorate the day of his profession, we can conclude as follows: the old "Christopherus" who wore Christ's cross on his body until the day he died in the monastery and who violently disapproved of Luther's later decision yet continued to wear this reminder of his old friend around his neck until the end.

Whatever may be made of this somewhat sentimental suggestion, the accuracy of this concluding observation is beyond all doubt: in spite of his later negative decision, Luther also understood his monasticism without reservation and qualification as the imitation of Christ which is the reason that his life as friar was no delusion even though he and his friends later viewed and portrayed it as such.

## 4. FROM FRIAR TO REFORMER

We are now finally in a position to answer the question as to what one should make of Luther's spiritual assaults and struggles in the monastery. What was their nature, and what significance do they have in Luther's development as a reformer? If we review the results of our reflections up to this point, we can answer the first question as follows: as novice, cleric, and friar-priest, and in Wittenberg as professor and vicar provincial of his order, Luther had a number of difficulties and problems which resulted from the monastic mode of life and his personality. It cannot be denied that these difficulties were exacerbated by the achievement principle which Luther initially followed, and that occasionally and for periods of time these problems congealed into real crises. Yet when one judges these phenomena objectively and fairly, one will discover that Luther's crises—we are momentarily leaving the problem of "pure love" out of account—did not transcend the limits of the normal, that they were not caused by the monastic life style as such and that they could have been resolved inside the monastery.

It is only Luther's special problem that requires clarification. It has already been shown that the problem had its origin in Luther's practice of confession. It seems that absolution in Erfurt required "contrition" as the precondition for the effective remission of sins. In contrast to his fellow friars to whom the practice of confession caused no problems in this respect, this becomes an oppressively excessive demand for Luther. He cannot rouse the required contrition, certainly not by his own power, nor even through grace or the virtue of the love that is "infused" in our heart through justifying grace. The reason for the failure is Luther's conviction that he must feel and experience contrition as a determining power in his heart, as the expression of a surrender that is owed God, that cannot be replaced by a compromise and especially not by the imperfect "gallows repentence" (attrition) which repents of sins merely because it wants its heavenly reward and is fearful of punishment in hell or purgatory. The ultimately unsuccessful though arduous attempt to "rouse" such contrition became the source of further insights and led to a problematic that extended beyond confession and the celebration of the mass.

Before developing this matter further and giving an answer to the second question, I will temporarily conclude consideration of this point by defining Luther's special problem from a more formal perspective.

To the extent that the fundamental question clearly became a problem for Luther alone, and to the extent that his otherwise excellent confessors and spiritual guides could not help the troubled friar in his distress, the question shows that Luther's case is unusual after all and ultimately comes to take on considerable significance. Concretely, this means that for the friars at the Erfurt Augustinian monastery, Luther was not merely a singular but an alien problem that neither arose nor could readily be dealt with within the framework of the contemporary piety, spirituality, and theology of monasticism.

But while recognizing the distinctive character of the case, one will have to guard against exaggerations. For although the Catholicism of the period saw the problem of "pure love" as something strange, it was not wholly unknown nor, more importantly, a demonstrably un-Catholic problem. Instead, it is rooted in Holy Scripture, emerges in certain Fathers and saints, occasionally preoccupies mysticism and mystics, and disquiets theologians and especially the teaching of the church. Generally speaking, one may call the problem a kind of borderline case whose riskiness makes one shrink back from it but which keeps returning and arises especially where the totality and the distinctive quality of a life in faith and as an imitation of Christ is concerned. But this also means that there is nothing about monasticism that would as a matter of principle have made impossible a Catholic solution of this problem even though it is true that Luther found no help in Erfurt.

This provides us with an important premise as we answer the second question, that is, what Luther's monastic battles meant for his development as a reformer. For if, in the majority of cases, Luther's difficulties can be defined as normal crises even though they occasionally became quite acute, and if his special problem had no monastic cause, we may begin our answer with a negative observation of considerable import, for now it may be taken as established that monasticism was not the cause of Luther's failure and that therefore Catholic monasticism must not be viewed as the dark background from which Luther detached and freed himself in a painful process, or that he developed in a "reformist" direction as a result of this negative influence. This also applies to the special problem that demonstrably affected both his spiritual and his theological development profoundly. In view of the causes of this development, we may say that although it was decisive for the elaboration of all those approaches that later come to constitute the "reformist" element, it did not make Luther's leaving the monastery a theological necessity.

# ILLUSTRATION SEQUENCE II

# PRIEST—JOURNEY TO ROME— PROFESSOR AT WITTENBERG— INDULGENCE CONTROVERSY 1507–1518

15  Luther as friar. Colored woodcut by Cranach the Elder. Luther is wearing the cap of a doctor of theology which he became in 1512.—Bretten, Melanchthon Museum.

16  The *auditorium coelicum* above the eastern cloister of Erfurt cathedral where Luther gave his inaugural lecture as *sententiarius* in 1510 after he had completed his study of theology, some of which was directed by the vicar general of the order, Johann von Staupitz, in Wittenberg.

17  As vicar general of the German Augustinians, Johann von Staupitz (*around 1465/70, †1524) decisively furthered Luther's scholarly career. He saw to it that Luther was called from Erfurt to the recently founded university at Wittenberg where Luther became his successor as professor of biblical studies in 1512. To avoid having to take steps against Luther the reformer, Staupitz later resigned from his positions in the order, joined the Benedictine order, and died as the head of the Benedictine abbey in Salzburg.—Painting (16th cent.) in St. Peter's Abbey in Salzburg.

18  Together with an unknown brother from his order, Martin Luther walked across the Alps to Rome in November 1510 because negotiations concerning the position of the Reformed Congregation within the Order of the Augustinian Hermits—the Erfurt monastery among them— were to be conducted there.— The Alps near the San Bernardino Pass.

19  In Rome, Luther stayed in the monastery of the Augustinian Hermits, next door to Santa Maria del Popolo.

20  The basilica of Santa Maria Maggiore, one of the seven principal churches in Rome, was visited by every pilgrim in Rome, including Luther. With its 5th-century mosaics, its gilded, coffered ceiling, and mighty rows of columns, it is one of the most impressive of Roman churches. Luther never remarked upon the sights of Rome.

21  View from the tower of the castle church in Wittenberg of the façade of the town church (cf. no. 53). After his return from Rome, Luther was sub-prior of the Augustinian cloister, preacher, and professor of biblical studies here.

22  Christ as universal judge. Stone relief (14th cent.). Once located on the northern outside wall of the parish church of St. Mary in Wittenberg, it is today in the sacristy of that church. Because of its terrible severity, Luther could not bear to look at this image and hurried past it shielding his eyes with his hand, as he recalls in his *Table Talk*.

IOHANNES TETZELIUS LIPSIENSIS
MISNICUS, MONACHUS ORDINIS SANCTI DOMINICI
FRANCOFURTI AD ODERAM PRÆCO, FORNICARIUS ET
NUNDINATOR, BULLARUM PAPALIUM
INDULGENTIARUM Anno 1517.
Denatus d. 7 August. Anno 1519.

23   The apostle Paul. Painting by Masaccio (1426), part of an altar painting in several sections for the church of Santa Maria del Carmine in Pisa.—Pisa, Museo Nazionale di San Matteo.—In his lectures, Luther repeatedly discussed Paul and his epistles. We have reliable knowledge of lectures on the Epistle to the Romans (1515/16) and the Epistle to the Galatians (1516/17).

24   Tower of the castle and the castle church at Wittenberg which also became the university church in 1503. In this church, which was renovated in 1885/92 in neo-gothic style, Luther's solemn promotion took place on October 19, 1512. It is uncertain whether he affixed his ninety-five theses which were intended as a call to a disputation to the portal that served as the university "bulletin board." Luther still lies buried in this church (cf. no. 89).

25   Johann Tetzel, O.P. (ca. 1465–1519) was a preacher of indulgences on behalf of Pope Leo X, who needed money for the construction of St. Peter's in Rome, and Cardinal Albrecht of Mainz, who could not repay his "pious debts." The banking house of Fugger had lent this prince of the Church a large amount of money which was to be repaid in this fashion. The traffic in indulgences was the occasion for Luther's theses in 1517.—The woodcut shows Tetzel preaching with a chest of money and a letter of indulgence; above is the bull of indulgences and Pope Leo X, whose bull on the rebuilding of St. Peter's gave rise to the indulgence dispute.—Constance, Rosgartenmuseum.

26   Pope Leo X (Giovanni de' Medici) discusses further construction of St. Peter's in Rome with Michelangelo. To finance this, the wretched trade in indulgences was instituted. Painting (1506) by Jacopo da Empoli.—Florence, Casa Buonarotti.

27   Martin Luther in conversation with Cardinal Cajetan (Thomas de Vio) during the Diet of Augsburg in 1518. Pope Leo X had ordered the cardinal to settle matters by persuading Luther to recant. Luther fled from the town without awaiting the end of the interrogations. He could not know that the cardinal had received new instructions according to which he was to show leniency in his dealings with Luther because the pope needed the good will of Frederick the Wise, Luther's prince, in dealing with the question of the succession of the ill Emperor Maximilian. In 1519, the pope sent a new mediator, Karl von Miltitz, who bestowed the Golden Rose of Virtue on Frederick. Only when this attempt to suppress the spreading reformist movement failed and Maximilian's succession was clarified did the pope issue the bull threatening the excommunication of Luther (around 1520) which was followed, in 1521, by the bull of excommunication.—Colored woodcut from the *Histories of Ludwig Rabus* (1557). Wittenberg, Lutherhalle.

28   Triumph of St. Thomas Aquinas. Thomas Aquinas, 1225–1274, scholastic theologian and Doctor of the Church. He wrote commentaries on all the books of the Bible and made Aristotle's philosophy accessible to theology. It is his particular accomplishment that he perfected the introductory work of early scholasticism and presented all of theology in the *Summa Theologica* and other works.—Painting (14th cent.) by F. Traini (?). Pisa, Santa Catarina.

29   Devils are leading a pope and a bishop into the jaws of hell. This relief in wood which was created in Franconia in the early sixteenth century clearly shows the disappointment and the anger people of the period felt toward the Church of Rome and its head. It is such feelings that led to Martin Luther's Reformation.—Collection in Coburg Castle.

This thesis will initially surprise and confuse the reader. For if not this development, then what did make Luther the "reformer" whom we admire or criticize? But what appears so certain to us that we consider all further questions superfluous can quite easily and persuasively be shown to be less so. For if it was really this development that caused Luther to become a "reformer," why then did he not simply leave the monastery after he had developed his fundamental approach? Why does he, alone and deserted, continue on in the Black Cloister in Wittenberg until 1523 although the large majority of his fellow friars had long since decided in favor of the freedom of the gospel. Were they more "reformist" than the "reformer?" And what, finally, was the "reformist" element and the cause of the Reformation as we know it if Luther could develop its essential foundations as a friar and without encountering resistance when we consider that he publicly defended them before his order at the Heidelberg chapter in 1518, even after initial criticisms had set in?

This brings us back to the concrete question concerning the effect Luther's special problem had on his further development and what it meant for the elaboration of his theology. Because I am concerned with exploring this matter in some depth, I must momentarily add a further measure of confusion and suggest that in the almost unanimous belief of Luther scholars, the problem of "pure love" is not considered a typical reformist approach, a comment I make here in all its provisionality so that, in the course of further discussion, it may gradually penetrate consciousness.

Above, we briefly addressed this question in its original context, in connection with the contrition that must be awakened during confession. Now we must show how, in the course of theological reflection, the original question necessarily takes on greater amplitude. Anyone who, like Luther, attempts constantly and through the use of all of his or her powers and yet in vain to "mobilize" the requisite act of contrition will soon be confronted by the disturbing question whether the will has any power over the love of the heart at all or, more fundamentally still, whether the will to love is already love. We are taken a little further when we critically examine the reassuring information that we have the virtue of "infused love" through the sacramentally mediated justifying grace and that we abide "in this love" as long as we obey the commands and prohibitions of the law in what we do. The individual who, like Luther, judges such love to be insufficient because it allows the heart to be very far from God, and who thinks through the same question in terms of the Pauline theology of the law, is swept into a veritable vortex of extremely difficult theological problems: if only love can fulfill the law, what about the works of the law? Are they simply useless or even harmful because a mere facade of fulfillment of the law? But if works are necessary as an expression of a loving surrender to God, how does one become *voluntarius ad legem,* that is, how does one find one's way to that spontaneous and gladdening "willingness" of a love that engenders its works as a tree its fruit? It is such considerations that underlie Luther's understanding of the law: as long as the law commands works while promising reward and threatening punishment, it is like the pedagogue in Paul or in medieval schools who beats into the boys what they would not accept otherwise. But then the very constraint of the law thwarts what it demands from us, for do not carrot and stick arouse precisely that "covetousness" which the law—"you shall not covet"—forbids under threat of punishment? And doesn't the law in this way frustrate the very thing that alone can be its fulfillment, the all-comprehending love of God and man? Luther insists on the harsh demand that only love fulfills the new law although or because as the law of our heart and the law of life of the "new man," the all-determining love supplants the constraining law of Moses (and this is something the later Antinomians do not understand because they are too anxious and too simple in their haste to exchange the constraint of the law for the freedom of the gospel). God has a strict and inalienable right to this love, or we owe Him that love that frees us from all dominion and all constraint of the law.

Love thus has a central, supreme meaning for Luther: If only love is the fulfillment of the law, it alone is that "righteousness" which man cannot manufacture through works but which, in its entirety, must be God's gift so that we might live through and finally in it before and with God. But if God's love for us and our love for God and neighbor liberates us from all terror and all law, then love is identical with the "freedom of a Christian" which Luther demanded time and again, a freedom that liberates us from servitude to sonship and through love then makes us freely take upon ourselves the "form of a servant" in the discipleship of free obedience to our "self-emptying" Lord.

But if the love that fulfills the law and frees us is identical with our righteousness before God, Luther can understand the nature of injustice and sin only in this context. It is strange how the question about love affects our understanding of sin and sins. Illuminating one problem by another initially creates confusion. Without surrendering its place in the practice of confession and the care of souls—for Luther always knew that the "nocturnal emission" of the same experience of "daydreaming" boys is no sin without the assent of the will—the unquestionable distinction between "venial" and "mortal" sin becomes hazy at first. For if sin is ultimately the refusal of or incapacity for the total surrender to God in love, then venial sin also separates us from God, for it represents a guilty lessening of such love. There also occurs a shift in accent and a change in the evaluation of sin: the serious sins of those who stray from the path toward the "left" appear as much less serious than the "secret sins" of the Pharisees who stray toward the "right" and fall. For no one disputes the sinfulness of murder, adultery and theft whereas it is only with difficulty that the objective fulfillment of the law that is guided by a pathological love is recognized as sin. In Luther's perspective—and it is theologically indisputable—sin is the greater the more splendid and sacred the good or the virtue man violates in his pathological self-love. Man's sin is greatest when, in view of all his virtues and achievements and in the enjoyment of his own virtuousness, he comes to feel that, through his fulfillment of the law, he has attained that perfection of love to which God owes the reward of heaven. The person who lives and acts from this conviction desecrates the "highest good," for he misuses the omnipotent God Himself in using Him as a means to his own blessedness. It is against this background that Luther's frequently misunderstood and easily misunderstandable, rather pointed phrases must be seen which, to the annoyance of the devout, inform us that it is precisely the "good works" of the Christians that should be feared as "mortal sins."

This context allows us to show what Luther means when he keeps calling on us to "sin bravely," when he opens our eyes to the mystery of "abiding sin," or represents the justification of man through God as the "becoming a sinner" which then leads to the seemingly so problematical definition of righteousness as being "simultaneously a sinner and justified." For in these somewhat confusing phrases, it is precisely not sins that cry to the heavens nor the "secret plague" of a perfection in "love" that has been achieved on one's own that is at stake. All that is involved here is the sin that can only be recognized through faith and that consists in the fact that even under and in the grace of God, we are still in no position to offer God the love we owe Him. But it must be seen that with the recognition and confession of this failure as "sin," man's situation has already fundamentally changed as far as Luther is concerned, for as we accept God's judgment that we are sinners and do so contrary to all appearance and contrary also to our self-estimate, the creative power of His word declares us to be just and there begins the real justification and, along with it, the strengthening and recovery of our sick love which attains perfection in and through death.

If this is so, Luther accomplishes through his *simul justus et peccator* a revaluation of sin as *felix culpa* which the fifth-century monks in their devout eagerness for works no longer understood and which is why they simply erased the mysterious phrase about "blessed sin" from the parchments of the Easter liturgy. Then God transforms the "sin that dominates us" into the "sin we dominate" where our incapacity which we experience as sin brings us the community with Christ who has become sin for us and who through his cross as sacrament leads us, as "fellow crucified," to resurrection and the birth of the "new man."

It would now have to be shown that Luther read the secret of the question about love which was agitating him off the cross of Christ, and this is the reason his theology of love has his theology of the cross as its immediate precondition. We understand that in the cross of His son, God hides Himself and His work and also His love and grace under their opposite. Whoever begins to live out of the mystery of divine love necessarily experiences the freely given and flowing love of God as the crucifixion of his miserable human love which only seeks itself and even on the cross does not lose sight of it. But what is hidden under the concealing veil of the opposite is already present for faith and promotes salvation.

Concerning this approach which is so important for Luther's mature theology, we will merely introduce one additional idea that deserves attention here because in the history of Luther interpretation and beginning with Luther himself, it has caused the love that was so important for Luther's theological development to recede more and more behind faith and to fade almost entirely from consciousness. The reason for, and the initial stage of, this process is actually quite plausible and of considerable theological significance. For if, throughout life, the Christian does not attain that perfect love that is owed God on the one hand, and if Luther understands faith not only as the devout acceptance of divine revelation but primarily as the obedient and confiding surrender of man to God on the other, it seems plausible that Luther should associate perfect faith with an as yet imperfect love. Such a nexus seems to make sense because, according to Scripture, there is a connection. Thus Luther thinks he is justified in saying that through its devotion "cheerful faith" anticipates the spontaneous "joy" of love and thereby promotes its growth. From the perspective of his theology of the cross, there is profound meaning in the statement that the devotion of faith conceals the devotion of love and also takes its place until the love of God has attained perfection. It makes profound sense when in view of his still feeble and sick love, the Christian can at least be certain in his belief in its perfection.

But it can also be shown that even in Luther, this splendid beginning was not without dangers for our consciousness of love. The strongly emphasized formula "by faith alone" already makes this clear though Luther did not mean this to militate against either hope or a properly understood love but only against justification by works. But when in disputes with Catholic theologians, this pointed formula is used to attack their approach of a "faith" that is "formed through love" and only lives through love, an unintended direct threat to love finally arises in Luther. True, it does not occur to him to dispute the triad of divine virtues to which St. Paul so solemnly testified. Nor is the defense of faith a betrayal of love, and the rejection of "effective love" is far from being an attempt to do away with *agape* which is Paul's name for love. Yet Luther does go too far when he returns like for like and counters the attack on "Evangelical faith" with one on "Catholic *caritas*" and states: "we put faith in the place of love." This central phrase from the great commentary on the Epistle to the Galatians (1531) clearly goes too far, for here faith not merely "represents" love but "replaces" or "drives" it from the position which, according to Scripture and the tradition of the Christian religion including Luther, it deserves. The former "queen" is demoted to "servant girl" whose commerce henceforth is no longer with God but only with man. Driven from the king's "bridal chamber," she no longer lives from the devotion of her heart but torments herself under the constraint of the law in order to serve man through its works. This new ranking of love which demonstrably contradicts the unchanged fundament of Luther's theology unfortunately had historical effects. For already his contemporaries and even more those who came after him referred to Luther's polemical stratagem as "reformist" and were finally even proud to have sent "Catholic *caritas*" into the washhouse and the cowbarn.

The dream of Frederick the Wise at Schweinitz in 1517 on the outcome of the posting of the 95 Theses against indulgences. Luther recounts the dream in his Table Talk.

Schweinitz

Paul Leo X.

85

Although the reader would presumably be interested in discovering more about the central importance the love of God has in Luther's theology, I break off this exposition, important elements of which require further discussion at greater depth. For a biography of Luther unfortunately involves more than the significance the love of God has in his theology. But because Luther differed from almost all "star" theologians in being proud of the fact that the fundamental problems of his theology were grasped by mere teen-agers in Wittenberg and elsewhere, I am hopeful that the unprejudiced reader will have seen what is at stake. But because the perspective we have advanced here is new and unusual, it seems appropriate to summarize the results of our reflections in their bearing on the further course of our discussion.

Title page of On the Freedom of a Christian Man (November 1520), which, with its prefatory letter to Pope Leo X, represents the last attempt at reconciliation inspired by Karl von Miltitz. This is the last of the three great programmatic works of 1520.

If my thesis is correct, Luther's very own theology and the fundamental question that gives it its form and impetus can be claimed by neither the "Catholic" nor the "reformist" creed of the period although the command that God be loved is of course as binding in the papal church as it is in the churches of the Reformation. What is exciting about Luther is that he bursts the framework of the old church without therefore leaving it, and that he does not establish a "new church" whose "reformist configuration" would be a function of its rejection of Catholicism. From this perspective, the uncommon and pronounced ecumenical potential of Luther's fundamental concerns becomes apparent. He resembles Abraham with whom, as with Paul, he identified throughout his life. Being called on by God, he abandons everything but remains a stranger in the land that has been promised him although a stranger, of course, who in his faith in God's word already has all he needs to live, particularly the friendship and love of God who speaks to him in his heart. A person who goes along with Luther's questions and accompanies him on Abraham's path will quickly realize that in Luther also, he has found a "father in the faith."

If my approach is correct, it also contains perfectly concrete insights that correct present judgment about Luther and the Reformation. For henceforth we will neither be able to maintain that in its form as monasticism the Catholic faith had been overcome by Luther once and for all and been replaced by the Reformed. Nor is the opposite thesis tenable according to which the Catholicism Luther overcame within himself was not Catholic at all, or that he heretically rediscovered for himself important elements of the Catholic faith. This is not to say that these theses are radically false. Indeed, they were and are unavoidable preliminaries to a real encounter with Luther. But where we do encounter him and engage his problems, and where, on our common path, we are suddenly beset by the question whether we might not be able to grasp Luther's faith as the possibility of our own, a line of demarcation which we considered impassable heretofore is suddenly crossed. The insight that occurs at that moment has direct consequences which also affect our presentation. For if the implicit assumption concerning the fundamental irreconcilability of the two creeds does not correspond to Luther's development and his fundamental theological concerns, the question about the contents of the Reformed faith also falls by the wayside, as does the question concerning the time at which Luther recognized and experienced it in a liberating breakthrough.

This means that the further presentation of Luther's

biography becomes immeasurably simpler. For that most difficult problem in all of Luther research, that is, the necessity to determine the contents and time of the so-called "tower experience" with the greatest possible precision, a problem that countless controversies have rendered virtually irresolvable also loses all urgency.

Of course, there also arises this new question: How can the course of the Reformation, troublesome to this very day, be explained? Even when we ask different questions, we clearly cannot completely abstract from Luther's further theological development and his fundamental concerns. For as a theologian, Luther continues to intervene in the course of things and changes his positions in disputes. Conversely, the rapidly emerging critique of his Catholic adversaries and the resulting condemnation by the Church naturally directs itself at Luther's theological formulations and this gives rise to a host of new problems. But his position on the Peasant War and his very personal decision to leave the monastery and to marry must also be judged by his spiritual concerns. And even his role during the important phase where the Reformation became a church, a development for which he is no longer solely responsible, certainly has some relation to his theological conception and is not without consequences for his understanding of the Reformation.

Yet all of this, however problematic its detail, does not modify the significance of the insight presented above. For if we may and must make it our point of departure that Luther's theological concerns do not compellingly account for the direction of the Reformation, then it is historical reasons that significantly determine its tragic course.

Title page of Luther's first celebrated reforming work of 1520: To the Christian Nobility of the German Nation concerning the Reform of the Christian Estate.

# III

## 1. THE INDULGENCE CONTROVERSY AS OVERTURE TO THE CONTROVERSY WITH THE PAPAL CHURCH

It is true that indulgence is a fateful problem in the life of the Church that was not caused by the theologians. But since the failure of theology seems responsible for the exacerbation of the problem and since the battle was finally fought with theological weapons, it makes sense to recall with appropriate brevity how Luther clarified the theological position while teaching at Wittenberg and up to 1517.

Luther's position required clarification in two principal directions: vis-à-vis the scholastic theology of the period, especially the Erfurt theology which had had some influence on him. But it also required clarification vis-à-vis the reformist-theological approaches of humanism which, under Erasmus, was advancing to the status of a European power in the intellectual realm of the time.

In the first of these two instances, Luther clarified his position principally as part of his teaching activity in Wittenberg, as is true of most professors. More than in the lectures themselves, such clarification expresses itself in the promotion disputations of his first students. After the course of lectures on the Epistle to the Romans, one such climax unquestionably occurs on September 25, 1516, during the promotion of Bartholomäus Bernhardi from Feldkirch. It was in the course of a disputation on "Man's Capacity for Salvation without Grace." In keeping with the protest against the "swine theologians" and their thesis that man's natural powers sufficed to fulfill the command to love God, the disputation theses deny any capacity for salvation to man outside of grace. Without grace, man can neither fulfill the law nor do the good. Nor does man's free will suffice to turn toward grace and to prepare himself to receive it. We are thus dealing with a rejection of the famous nominalist thesis according to which God will not deny His grace to the person who does what he is capable of. The theses not only testify to the shaping influence of Paul but also evoke Augustine's authority to counter Scholasticism.

Disputations of this sort are especially suited to discover the position of respected colleagues. Although Nikolaus von Amsdorf would soon adopt Luther's position, Luther immediately sent the theses to Erfurt where his former teachers expressed annoyed surprise as they read this new material by a young professor who had outgrown their influence. Luther, who was anxious for a clarification, informed his famous teacher Johann Trutfetter in a letter a few months later that his rejection of Aristotle was becoming increasingly one of principle. But the reactions to the Bernardi disputation on the part of his Wittenberg colleagues Petrus Lupinus and Karlstadt were even sharper. Before an intensive study of Augustine induced Karlstadt to change his position radically, a rather violent dispute with Luther took place on the indulgence question. For when Karlstadt maintained that one would have to confess in the church of All Saints if one wished to obtain the indulgence granted there, and Luther promptly rejected this claim because he felt it hurt the Wittenberg ministry and the parish principle, the easily excited Karlstadt threatened to institute procedings against Luther for being a "heretic" and ignoring a papal privilege. But before he could make good on this threat, Karlstadt had converted to Augustine, the decisive impetus being his study of *De spiritu et litera* which he edited and commented upon. He now prepared himself to do battle in behalf of Augustine and Wittenberg theology. On April 26, 1517, when the relics were exhibited in the Wittenberg castle church, Karlstadt affixed 151 theses to the church portal. They were to be disputed for a period of several days by theologians chosen by the elector. The theses consisted essentially of quotations from Augustine and corresponded with Luther's views. Luther himself sent the theses which he called *paradoxa* on to Christoph Scheurl in Nuremberg who was to pass them on to Wenceslaus Link, who had in the meantime been transferred to that city, and other theologians.

The position that newly obtained in Wittenberg is unmistakably sounded when Luther writes to Johann Lang in Erfurt on May 18: "Our theology and Augustine are happily progressing and rule at our university through God's doing. Aristotle is declining and will soon disintegrate into a ruin. The traditional lectures on the *Sentences* disgust the students. No one can hope for listeners unless he lectures on the new theology, that is, on the Bible or Augustine or some other teacher with ecclesiastical authority."

A glance at the Wittenberg lecture schedule shows quite clearly that this statement to his friend was no mere boast. The fact that, in July 1517, Luther prepared some seven Augustinian theologians for their theological master's examination proves that the profound reform of studies had the approval of the heads of the order.

In view of this situation, it is tantamount to a programmatic statement when, on the occasion of Franz Günther's promotion to baccalaureus biblicus on September 4, 1517, Luther calls for a disputation *contra scholasticam Theologiam.* After an introductory endorsement of Augustine's judgment concerning man's incapacity for the good, the theses reject Gabriel Biel's doctrine concerning man's natural capacity for salvation, especially his capacity for the perfect love of God. There follows a group of theses against Aristotle, that is, against his understanding of righteousness—we do not become righteous through righteous acts, rather it is God's righteousness that enables us to act righteously—and against the importance for theology ascribed to him. A final group of theses deals with the significance grace has for obedience, free will, and the love of man. In conclusion, Luther states expressly that his comprehensive attack on Scholasticism contradicts neither the teaching of the Church nor that of its authentic teachers. The élite of Protestant Luther scholars who search for what is genuinely "reformist" maintain that neither theses nor lectures contain "the program of a new theology but [merely] a settling of accounts with the misguided Aristotelianism of traditional Scholasticism" (M. Brecht). This misjudgment is understandable since they fail to recognize the constructive significance this fundamental question has for Luther's theology. It can be conceded, of course, that Luther has not yet extended his questions to include the relationship between love and faith or other significant themes such as sacrament, office, and church.

The connection to the "theology of the cross," however, is fully recognized as one can tell from the dispatch of the theses to Lang where he again refers to them as *paradoxa.* Luther eagerly awaits the position of the Erfurt monastery. He is anxious to dispute his theses either before the public or in the monastery because he wants to get away from insignificant Wittenberg university. He has a strong desire to appear before the theological public and therefore even asks Scheurl to transmit his "paradoxes" to Johannes Eck, professor in Ingolstadt. But before Leipzig becomes a possibility, he wants at least to defend them before his order at the Heidelberg chapter of the Reformed Congregation, in April 1518.

On this occasion, a young Dominican, Martin Bucer, will listen to him enthusiastically and congratulate him on a theology that strikes him as "Erasmian" through and through. It is understandable why many contemporaries should have had this impression, for there is an abundance of common elements and key terms, from the common front against Scolasticism to the preference for paradoxical formulations and the program of a renewal of theology for which Scripture and the Church Fathers would be the source. The young Dominican could not know that as he clarified his position Luther achieved a result which he had obvious reasons to guard as a strict secret. For the correspondence with his closest friends— Georg Spalatin and Johann Lang—clearly shows that as early as 1516/17, his uncommon clearsightedness and intuition had shown him those aspects of the central question concerning Christ, grace, and justification in which he differed fundamentally from Erasmus and which precluded any alliance between him and humanism, although he carefully avoided premature engagement in a dispute that was all but inevitable. The ambiguity of the situation and Luther's truly unique powers of orientation become impressively clear when we consider that Justus Jonas, a passionate "fan" of Erasmus, joins Luther during these years and even though one of the most loyal disciples of his new master finds it extremely difficult to recognize that the two positions are irreconcilable. Not until 1525 will the still hesitant Luther publish his *De servo arbitrio* ans thereby engage in a dispute whose objective necessity he had already recognized and foreseen in 1516.

We have repeatedly emphasized that Luther felt great urgency to defend his "new theology" before the academic and ecclesiastical publics of contemporary theology. Quite differently from the way he had wished, he suddenly found himself in the limelight of history after presenting as a basis for a future disputation ninety-five theses on the meaning of indulgence to the competent bishops and his colleagues on the eve of All Saints' Day, 1517. That he affixed his theses to the portal of the Wittenberg castle church as Karlstadt had allegedly done before him has been disputed with good though not incontrovertible reason. There can be no doubt, however, that the image of a "hammer-wielding and zealous Luther" belongs to the realm of legend, however difficult it may be for devout churchgoers to surrender an idea they have come to cherish. For anyone who studies the clumsy structure of this document will recognize immediately and in spite of a few effective statements that Luther is not intentionally and skilfully using a manifesto to put fire to a temple he feels has been made into a robbers' den but that, as a theologian and spiritual guide, and under the heavy burden of a gigantic complex of problems, he formulates irrefutable questions which an intellectually childish and triumphantly self-assured Church had not recognized for centuries, or had either repressed or optimistically deflected.

This already tells us something decisive about the peculiarity and development of the indulgence problem which Luther initially confronted in the confessional when his penitents importuned him with the "indulgence letters" of the great plenary indulgence which were being sold in Jüterborg or Zerbst by Johann Tetzel. With a frightening matter-of-factness, Pope Leo X and Albrecht of Brandenburg, cardinal archbishop of Mainz (as well as of Magdeburg and Halberstadt), had proposed to draw on the "inexhaustible treasures of Christ and the Church" to finance the construction of St. Peter's Basilica in Rome and to pay off Albrecht's "pious debts," 43,000 gulden in dispensation fees (for the illegal accumulation of benefices) and in pallium tax, which had been financed by the banking house of Fugger.

Much more important than yet another disquisition on that hoary topic, the traffic in indulgences and all its details—be its object to arouse a pious indignation or to loyally defend the Church—is, from my point of view, the rarely raised and even more rarely correctly answered question: How had this growth of indulgences been possible at all in God's Church, and what did it mean for the faith and the life of that Church?

If one wishes to give a reasonably accurate answer, one has to go to some historical length. For, originally, indulgence was a problem of the ecclesiastical practice of penance which, similar to the veneration of the saints or the elaboration of the liturgy and the constitution of the Church, preceded all theological theory, for it is an expression of the life of the Church. Theology and theologians were not consulted until this pious practice encountered difficulties and required clarification or when its autonomous development availed itself of the help of theologians in order to promote its guiding concepts more effectively within the Church.

The first important beginnings of the later practice of indulgence must be looked for during that period when the old penance with its rigorous principle of *paenitentia una*, according to which the sinner is admitted only once to penance in the Church, was restructured and transformed into a practice that did justice to the needs of a missionary Church that was made up of Celts, Franks, and Anglo-Saxons. The solution, which was not found without some difficulty, consisted in having the priest absolve the sinner immediately upon confession of sin, the works of piety imposed as satisfaction only having to be performed after absolution. This involved the following important clarification as regards the remission of sins: eternal punishment in hell for mortal sins was remitted when absolution was granted, but the temporal punishments which aimed at the purification of love were expunged by satisfaction or purification in purgatory should the poor sinner die before being able to make satisfaction in this life. The fundamental change from the old sacrament of penance to private confession had the great advantage that the sinner could "confess" more often and no longer had to wait until he lay on his deathbed for readmission to the community of the Church and the remission of his sins. But like any transformation, this change had a problematical side: it was not really the modification of the understanding of satisfaction by the pagan-Germanic principle of restitution that was decisive in the development of indulgence but another simple problem connected with it. For the Irish-Scots who gave its new form to the practice of confession were such zealous penitents and imposed so large a quantity of satisfactions that the sum of pious works—from the performance of individual prayer and Draconian fasting and other self-imposed chastisements to life-long pilgrimages or the prohibition to carry arms—simply became too great and the demands made on the capacities of the individual penitent in both a physical and a temporal sense excessive. The problem that had to be solved therefore was a reduction in the quantity of works of piety of the new form of penitence was to remain practicable. The monastic fathers finally resolved the difficulty their devout zeal had created by recurring to a number of diverse ideas.

From penance as practiced during the persecutions of the early Church, they took the idea of "intercession" and "substitute penance" on the model of the "confessor" who, not having succumbed to torture, interceded after the persecution for a fallen brother and thus obtained his readmission to the Church. From the Germanic idea of restitution, they took the technique of combining longer, lighter penances and making them shorter and more severe. Through the introduction of substitute penance, the duration of these penances could then be significantly reduced. The result of all these reflections and calculations was set down in what were considered ecclesiastically binding Penitentials, according to whose instructions the priest administering penance was in a position, for example, to impose upon a penitent king a tariff of penances whereby the entire penance of one-hundred-and-twenty years could be performed in twelve days if twelve substitute penitents were used and the severity of the works of piety was increased correspondingly. Under Charlemagne, these Penitentials lost their quasi-legal status in ecclesiastical law but they continued to mold the idea Christians had of penance until well into the Middle Ages.

Against the background of these reflections on the history of penance, it becomes easy to identify and name all the characteristics of the system of medieval indulgence.

1) Indulgences derive from the pagan-Germanic principle of restitution, which is soon extended to deceased relatives because the old Germans thought and felt in terms of family and clan. They are equally based on the endeavor to work off the temporal punishment due to sins by the smallest possible effort. The orthodox and exemplary idea of "intercession" and "substitute penance" by the "confessor" or the "community" gave rise to the cruder notion of a "substitute penance" that was soon associated with the notion of an inexhaustible "treasure of the Church."

2) In connection with an intrinsically correct idea, the "temporal" punishment for sins that must be atoned for in time, the calculations of the penance tariff led to the childish and un-Christian quantification of the grace of indulgence. The partial remissions which dealt in millions of years seem much more dangerous than the total ones which, precisely because they were total remissions of all sins, soon made the numbers game impossible.

3) It is in keeping with the Germanic principle of restitution that it became perfectly natural to commute the original works of piety for financial obligations: money, gold, or other values.

This summarizes the most important though by no means all the errors of the practice of indulgence which, in the course of its historical development, was paradoxically elaborated with the help of theologians, and this brings us to the theory of the matter. In the early Middle Ages, remissions were at first very modest—a matter of forty or eighty days. On the occasion of the consecration of churches or chapels, they were granted by bishops to those who, as donors or in other ways, had made possible their construction. There was thus a morally sustainable relationship between penitential works and the remission of temporal punishments which was always distinguished from the remission of eternal punishment when sins were forgiven in sacramental penance. But as in the course of time indulgences increased significantly and the relationship between them and works of piety became unclear, difficulties arose for those who administered penance. Theology was consulted and judged correctly that when pious works were not performed, that deficiency would have to be made up for by the person who had granted excessive remission, namely the father confessor or the bishop. But because, in the meantime, armies of praying monks had awakened the consciousness and the need of a Christian community that had persisted in its Germanic modes of feeling and argument (hermits reported that the Cluniacs had literally prayed the black soul of grandfather Dagobert out of hell), because, in other words, not only the not so saintly crusaders and the throngs of not so pious pilgrims but also the enormous army of "poor souls" dying of thirst in purgatory were clamoring for remission, "substitute penance" soon proved inadequate. But in this unsuitable approach, the theologians with their razor-sharp distinctions discovered the possibility of an ever more perfect solution. For to move from "substitute penance" to the inexhaustible "treasure of Christ and his saints" which had been left to the pilgrim Church for its benefit did not prove a difficult expedition. Theology, ready to serve here as always, resolved the problem to the total satisfaction of all concerned: the "treasure of Christ," which was inexhaustible as a matter of principle, distributed with unerring certainty by the pope as the possessor of the highest power of the keys, was the theologians' seemingly ideal answer. Sustained by what was really the pagan interest of Christians to receive ever more extensive remissions ever more cheaply and reliably, well advised by a theology that was "ready to serve," and carefully administered by the pope and the dignitaries of the Church, indulgences now began to proliferate.

In connection with the cult of relics and pilgrimages, partial remissions not only reached dizzying record numbers of millions of years but escalated to total remission which only the pope, of course, could grant. Beginning in 1300, these total remissions had been tied to the jubilee year and pilgrimage to Rome but were soon also granted outside it. Remission for the "living," which Thomas Aquinas had confirmed as a possibility, expanded into remission for the "deceased" and the "poor souls in Purgatory." This gave rise to specific questions behind which we discern the first intimations of a timid criticism. Examples would be whether remission is granted through the power of a "judical decision" or merely in the sense of an "authorized intercession" on the part of the Church, or whether purchase of an indulgence for a deceased presupposed the purchaser's state of grace. Such questions were never authoritatively answered and thus became the arena of imaginative theologians and indulgence preachers with business acumen. Developing inhibitions and the criticism of men such as John Wycliff, Jan Hus, J. Ruchrat von Wesel, or Wessel Gansfort failed to stem this development. The income deriving from indulgences gradually rose to levels that inspired Emperor Maximilian with the dreams we mentioned earlier. It is true, of course, that some of these funds also benefited the "poor in Christ" because bridges, roads, and hospitals were built because they were used to commission works of art and art always serves everyone and therefore unhesitatingly accepts whatever awards are offered.

In one's criticism, one will have to guard against pious indignation and the zealous attempt to anticipate God's final judgment. It is the great advantage of Luther's theses on indulgence that they avoid such radical criticism. He knows indulgence too well "from the inside" and from the perspective of the medieval Christian. He knows that the lovingly assembled and exhibited collection of relics of his prince does not serve exclusively or even principally the making of money. He also knows that payments in the form of alms can assuredly express true penance, that the office of the keys must also administer penance judicially, and that we must represent each other before God, in prayer or by intercession, precisely as Christ interceded for us. But all this understanding does not calm Luther or make of him one of those apologists who contented themselves with defending the correctness of the practice of indulgence and simply advocated that it be cleansed of its worst abuses. Instead, he senses in and behind the contemporary traffic in indulgences what made it, directly or indirectly, a lethal danger to the faith and the life of the Church.

Without being a theoretical and formal heresy, the practice of indulgences in the Middle Ages weaves highly significant articles of the faith such as sin and forgiveness, penance and confession, grace and the power of the keys, the Church and its office, purgatory and hell into a highly compromising, ultimately pagan abuse that is motivated by the selfish desire for salvation and open to the possibility of being misunderstood and judged heretical.

Beyond this, indulgences reveal the failure of theology which is so ready to serve that it abets popular superstition and thus makes this blatantly misguided development possible in the first place. Popes and bishops succumbed to the temptation to live off the cheap sale of grace, to feel at the same time that they are the benefactors of the "poor" and the "poor souls," and to develop their positions of power in a way that necessarily undermined their real authority. Everyone profited from remissions in his own way, all used and cheated each other, all kept each other from availing themselves of the power of grace that would enable them to take the way of a penance which, through a return to God and service to one's neighbor, comprises all of life and can only be lived in the functioning community of the Church. The worst thing about this entire matter is that the ultimately deadly nexus was not caused by some monstrous heresy or failure but by the seemingly Christian but actually pagan, profoundly human desire to use the means of grace of the Church to obtain maximal results for oneself and one's own.

Given these facts, little is gained by the unquestionably correct assertion that the forgiveness of sins and of the eternal punishments those sins incur could only be achieved by a contrite and valid confession, and that despite all abuses, intercession for the "poor souls" retained its Christian meaning.

It is certainly to Luther's credit not to have used the pope's and the archbishop of Mainz's horrendous dealings with the Fuggers as the basis for a radical attack on the old Church. The letter to Albrecht of Brandenburg refrains from any polemical allusion to this matter, and where the theses mention the building of St. Peter's or the huckstering practice of indulgence sermons, his arguments do not lack respect for the pope, nor does his sharp criticism make him forgetful of his love for the Church. Justifiably, he recalls the nature of true penance as Christ demanded it, a penance that extends to life in its entirety and cannot be discharged by a few works. Ingeniously if not with total clarity, he points to the inner connection between purgatory and the necessary purification of love. Carefully and relevantly, he reminds his addressee of the limits of papal power in the granting of remission, especially remission for the dead. Cautiously, he brings up the problematical "treasure of the Church" which is being put to such cavalier use. Irrefutably, he underlines in a sequence of theses the absolute primacy of "good works of love" over all remissions. For the "works of love" not only serve the neighbor in his need but also make man "better" and "increase" love while indulgence at best frees us from "punishment."

But from another point of view, Luther's meritorious criticism had a decisive effect on him and the renewal he aspired to, and this precisely because it was well-founded. For the theses revealed the neuralgic points of the problematic of the medieval system of indulgences and thus compelled the sick Church of the period to take a position which, being involved in the indulgence traffic, it could not adopt unless it wished to run the risk of capitulation.

The correctness of this assertion can easily be demonstrated by the unfortunate course the discussion took. For although without Luther's knowledge and intent, the new medium of the printing press spread the theses throughout Germany with the speed of a forest fire, the reaction was initially unusually or characteristically restrained: a disputation may have been planned but none took place. While many colleagues secretly agreed with Luther, there was no lack of adversaries either. Even Karlstadt was not in favor of a radical criticism of indulgences, and the theological faculties needed time as they always do or reacted with summary opinions when they were obliged to do so, as was the case of the faculty in Mainz. The bishops Luther had addressed did not actually react with unfriendliness or nervousness but were initially stumped. Only the archbishop of Mainz had to take a position. The advisers in Aschaffenburg instituted the *processus inhibitorius*, the professors delivered themselves of "opinions," the archbishop "informed" Rome, and the pope became annoyed at all the German profundity and tried at first to act through the superior general of the Augustinian Hermits.

The first formal reactions come from Johann Tetzel and Johann Eck. Although the theses do not mention him by name, the indulgence commissioner felt the understandable need to defend himself, presumably he had to. He is as radical here as in his sermons: within three weeks, Luther will burn at the stake. But because Tetzel can take no official action against Luther, he tries at the academic level: on January 20, 1518, he starts a disputation in defense of indulgences at the University of Brandenburg in Frankfurt an der Oder. The theses had not been formulated by Tetzel but by the leading theologian at Frankfurt, Konrad Koch, called Wimpina. They propose to refute Luther's theses sentence by sentence. Unfortunately, they merely demonstrate an utter blindness to the problem Luther has raised. Luther had not quarrelled with sacramental penance and a defense of it was therefore no effective counter to his criticism of indulgences. In April or May, Tetzel reacted once more

to Luther's "Sermon on Indulgences and Grace" and, a little later, with a set of his own theses to Luther's theses in indulgences. To Luther's thesis of the primacy of works of love over all indulgences, the unfortunate Tetzel can answer only by referring to the scholastic *ordo caritatis*, according to which "ordered love of self" has primacy over "love of neighbor." Tetzel's new theses show what defense of the vulnerable indulgence traffic was being envisaged: with the highest power of the keys, the pope also has authority over indulgences and Church dogma. Since the pope cannot err and must not be questioned, let alone ridiculed, attacks on indulgences are attacks on the pope and the teachings of the Roman Church and therefore heresy. This is the first occasion this reproach is also levelled against the elector.

Tetzel's personally motivated and theologically primitive apologia was not taken seriously by Luther or the academics and bishops. This changed in the spring of 1518 when the Ingolstadt professor Johann Eck who had been considered a friend of Luther's up to this moment entered the discussion. Eck was a passionate "disputant" and about to discover an extensive sphere for that passion in his actually very laudable defense of a Church that was as vulnerable as it was reviled. *Obelisci* is the name of the signs scholars had been using since antiquity to identify those sentences in a corrupted text that were to be expunged. Playing the superior professor, Eck gave this title to a dissertation that he had originally intended for the bishop of Eichstätt and in which he dealt with the theses of the Augustinian from distant Wittenberg whom he treats as a Hussite and heretic, an insolent, ignorant know-nothing and even a contemnor of the pope.

This unfair and unexpected attack annoyed and disappointed Luther. It is said that he originally intended not to pursue the matter but then, pressed by his friends, he decided to send the arrogant and excited professor a proper response which he would entitle *Atserisci* (little stars), a term used by scholars to designate the valuable parts of a text. While Eck's attack was more polemical and he a figure of greater consequence, that attack had no more theological merit than Tetzel's. Although a definitive "declaration of war" had not yet been issued, the collision of two such fundamentally unlike intellects signalled the impending irreconcilable conflict that wholly failed to advance matters because Luther also let himself be goaded into deploying his own considerable polemical gift.

Here again, it was Karlstadt who saw to it that the next round would take place. Forgetting his earlier doubts about his colleague's excessively sharp critique of

# ILLUSTRATION SEQUENCE III

# THREAT OF EXCOMMUNICATION—
# DIET OF WORMS—
# "JUNKER JÖRG" AT THE WARTBURG
# 1519–1521

30  Burning of books on October 12, 1520, before the Elsterntor in Wittenberg. As the students toss books on canon law and works of scholastic theology into the fire, Luther, hardly noticed by the rest, commits the papal bull *Exsurge Domine* to the flames. The elector would not have permitted the demonstrative burning of a papal bull. Luther appears here with special clarity as an Augustinian Hermit.

31  Henry VIII of England who wrote the anti-Lutheran *Defense of the Seven Sacraments* for which he received the Golden Rose from the pope.—Painting by an unknown artist. London, National Portrait Gallery.

32  Charles V, German emperor from 1519, whom Luther faced at the Diet of Worms on April 17 and 18, 1521. The emperor who saw it as incumbent on himself to commit "all his realms, friends, his body and his blood, his life and his soul" to the preservation of the Catholic faith and the Catholic Church could only view Luther as a heretic whom, along with his followers, he saw it his duty to fight.—Painting by Barent van Orley (around 1521), Budapest.

33  Martin Luther, colored woodcut by Lucas Cranach the Elder (circa 1520).

34  Dr. Johann Eck (1486–1543), professor of theology at Ingolstadt University was Martin Luther's adversary in the Leipzig disputation during the summer of 1519. Detail of the bronze epitaph of J. Eck in the church of Unsere Liebe Frau in Ingolstadt.

35  The romanesque cathedral in Worms where Luther arrived on April 16, 1521, having been summoned by Emperor Charles V to present himself at the Diet.

36  Martin Luther before the emperor at the Diet of Worms. On April 17, 1521, Luther was called on to recant his writings in the bishop's residence. On April 18, he refused to recant before the emperor "because to do something against one's conscience is neither safe nor salutary. May God help me. Amen."—Colored woodcut (cf. nos. 27 and 30).

37  The imperial document by which Emperor Charles V outlawed Martin Luther who left Worms on April 26, 1521, under the escort of the imperial herald Caspar Sturm. The reading and diffusion of his writings had been placed under severe penalties. After hearing Luther, Charles V declared: "Henceforth, I will view him as a notorious heretic." Secret Vatican Archives.

1520

...eulentur libri

ich/Ich kan nicht anders.
Got helffe mir Amen.

Edict keyserlic/buytghegheuen by Raerle den viifften Ghecozen Keysere
des Roomschē rycke/Altijts des rijcs vermeerdere/Coninc Catholijck ꝛc
int zeer ōmaerde verzamen des helics Rijcke/te Woozms/int iaer ons hee
ren duust biijfhondert ende een en twintich.

¶ Ieghēs bzoeder Marti luther vā sente Augustyns oozdene/ōweckere
der oudē eñ ōwesene ketteriē/eñ heresiē/ eñ der nieuwer eē voozthzighere

¶ Ieghens alle de bouckē ōder Luthers name buytghegheuē/eñ die naer
maels buytghegheuē zullē werden/eñ der zeluer boucken van nū voozt an
Pzenters:coopers: eñ vercoopers.

¶ Ieghens Luthers mede zweerers/onthauders/of bedeckers eñ die hem
ionste draghen in wat manieren dat het zy.

¶ Ieghens opspzakelicke eñ famoise libellen of boucken   Oec ieghens
beilden of scilderien van dier manieren/ende harer butgheuers: pzenters
coopers: ende vercoopers van wat name of condicien zy zyn.

¶ Statuyt ende wet den pzenters/om te belettene eñ te ōbiedene tquaet
dwelke daghelics ghebuert by den mesbzuycke der louelicker conste van
pzentene.

   ¶De   Peynen.

¶ Uan Crȳme lese maieste.grotelic te mesdoene ieghens des Keysers ghe-
bodt/ende zwaerlic te ballene in zynder indignacie.

¶ Up confiscatie ende verbuerte van lisue ende van allen goede wat het
zy vaste of roerelic/waer af deen helft cōmen zal der Keyserlicker maiesteit
ende de andre den anbzynghere of wzoughere.   Bouen andre peynen
inde rechten begrepē. alzoot bzeeder blyct in dit ieghē wozdich edict.

Gottes wort
bleibt ewig.

# Biblia / das ist / die gantze Heilige Schrifft Deudsch.

## Mart. Luth.

## Wittemberg.

Begnadet mit Kürfurstlicher zu Sachsen freiheit.

Gedruckt durch Hans Lufft.

M. D. XXXIIII.

38   Georg Burkhardt from Spalt (1484–1545) known by his latinized name, Spalatin, was a friar like Luther. Called to Torgau in 1508 to educate one of the sons of the pretender to the throne of Electoral Saxony, he soon advanced to the post of confidential secretary to the elector Frederick the Wise. Spalatin, who was a very learned humanist, theologian and lawyer, played a decisive role in the elector's backing and protection of Luther after the Diet of Worms by, among other things, having him "kidnapped" and taken to the Wartburg.—Painting, 1537 (workshop of Lucas Cranach the Elder?), Karlsruhe, Kunsthalle.

39   Madonna with child and Sts. Catharine and Barbara. Center section of the so-called Dessauer Fürstenaltar which was donated by the elector Frederick the Wise and his brother Johann. Lucas Cranach the Elder whom Frederick the Wise called to Wittenberg in 1504 as court painter did this altar painting in 1510. It was originally intended for the castle church in Wittenberg which was also the church of Wittenberg University, founded in 1502. Luther probably knew this altar.—Dessau, Staatliche Galerie Schloss Georgium.

40   Elector Frederick the Wise (1463–1525) was Luther's prince and protector. On December 18, 1518, he refused, in a letter to the papal Curia, to surrender Luther to the authorities in Rome, and commented as follows: "If we were convinced that his teaching is impious and untenable, we would not defend him. It is our sole intent to fulfil the office of a Christian prince."—Detail of the bronze epitaph of the elector in the Wittenberg castle church by Peter Vischer the Younger (1527).

41   Martin Luther as "Junker Jörg." Returning from the Diet of Worms, Luther was "attacked" by Electoral-Saxon horsemen near Eisenach on May 9, 1521, and taken to the Wartburg where he lived in this disguise until the spring of 1522. In a letter to Spalatin, he wrote: "I had to wear a horseman's garb and let my hair and beard grow so that you would scarcely recognize me."—Painting (1521) by Lucas Cranach the Elder, Weimar, State Collection in the castle.

42   Luther's study at the Wartburg where, from 1521–1522, he translated the New Testament into German. The first publication of three thousand copies, an enormous number for the period, came out in September 1522.

43   Title page of the first edition of Luther's complete translation of the Bible with a woodcut by Lucas Cranach the Elder, published in Wittenberg in 1534. Bretten, Melanchthon Museum.

44   On the table of the Luther room at the Wartburg lies a copy of the second edition of Luther's complete translation of the Bible which was printed in Wittenberg in 1541 by Hans Lufft. The pages of the book contain corrections and marginalia by Luther and Melanchthon.

45   Erasmus of Rotterdam (1466–1536). Painting (1523) by Hans Holbein the Younger, Basle, Kunstmuseum.—Erasmus was the illegitimate child of a priest. Educated and trained as an Augustinian canon, he soon came to see it as his principal task to improve men morally by the Christian philosophy which he found in the New Testament and the Church Fathers. His fundamental maxim "back to the sources" has been of lasting significance. Erasmus' particular achievement was his editions of numerous writings of the Church Fathers and, even more important, the first edition of the Greek New Testament, in 1516.

indulgences and interested in publicity, he published Luther's theses against the *Obelisci* without the author's knowledge, an event that Eck could not ignore.

## 2. A CARDINAL'S HAT OR THE STAKE: LUTHER ON TRIAL

Before going on to Eck's successful attempt to lure Luther into the arena at Leipzig, we will report briefly how the quarrel continued and proceedings in Rome were instituted against Luther. Already at this point, it is clear that these actions may perhaps lead to a condemnation but certainly not to a clarifying decision.

After the interlude of the Heidelberg chapter before which Luther was allowed to defend the fundamental concerns, the *paradoxa* of his theology of the cross though not the indulgence question, he quickly prepared his extensive comment on the indulgence theses, the so-called *Resolutions,* for the printer. The document is preceded by a letter to Staupitz, whom he asks to transmit it to the pope, and a dedication to Leo X. In both letters, Luther is after the same thing: he defends his understanding of penance against the false interpretation by the Dominicans; he defends himself against the reproach that he has attacked the position of the pope, and acknowledges in his voice the voice of Christ, however the decision may turn out.

From Luther's perspective, this phrase is totally honest, without ambiguity or tactical cunning. For if the pope is the "voice of Christ," how can he decide against Christ? As yet, this question is not for Luther. But to us, it is already clear what Luther's answer will be, should he ever have to struggle with it. The terrible and unavoidable thing about the impending decision is that the fundamental assumption to which each side is committed has already settled the matter, yet the insistent fundamental problems that emerge here have been given no thought whatever. The indulgence problematic that so urgently requires resolution, yet is historically unresolvable, thus turns into the even more fateful question concerning the papacy.

While Luther has Staupitz pass his resolutions in to the pope, proceedings against him have been instituted in Rome, and it is irrelevant whether this occurred with or without Dominican help. Marius de Perusco, the papal finance official who was charged with the prosecution of the case requested that Luther be put on trial.

Leo X called on the court theologian Sylvester Prierias, a Dominican, to write a theological opinion, and charged the bishop Hieronymus Ghinucci with the preliminary judicial investigation. It took no more than three days to complete his opinion—an excessively speedy procedure that will cause some unhappiness later—and he submitted it to the court in early June. On August 7, the cardinal legate Thomas de Vio, better known as Cajetan, who was in Augsburg at the time, sent Luther the summons which called on him to defend himself in Rome within sixty days.

How Rome conceived of the proceedings becomes clear from Prierias' *Dialogue on the Power of the Pope against Luther's Theses,* which was handed to the accused along with the summons. Summarizing the argument that was designed either to make Luther recant or to burn him at the stake, we formulate as follows: the pope is the highest and infallible teacher of the Church in all questions of faith and morals. Indulgences are part of this. Anyone who attacks or questions indulgences therefore questions or disputes the power of the pope and is consequently a heretic. What was new here but plausible was the constant invocation of Thomas Aquinas as "teacher of the Church." The original problem had thus been significantly modified and further discussion newly defined: now it was only indirectly a question of indulgences. What was really and directly at stake was the position of the pope and the associated question concerning the Church. Luther can defend himself if he uses Scripture to attack this theological view of the papacy and the Church. In so doing, he unavoidably returns to the dangerous approaches of the "conciliarists." And his theological adversaries will do everything they can to drive him into this risky position.

Suddenly, events follow each other in rapid succession. After a papal brief of August 23 to the legate, the summons is withdrawn because the preliminary investigations are practically complete. The cardinal is to seize this friar who has been recognized as a notorious heretic and to keep him in custody until the end of the proceedings. Only if Luther should appear voluntarily before the cardinal and humbly ask to be forgiven for his boldness is Cajetan empowered to readmit the contrite sinner into the Church. Should he refuse, Cajetan is to excommunicate him and his adherents and to break all resistance with the punishments canonical law provides.

Concurrent attempts to induce the elector to withdraw his protection or to induce the heads of the order to surrender Luther do not produce the desired result.

Beginning in late August, politics, that is, Emperor Maximilian's plan to have himself elected king, changed the situation and placed Luther in a more favorable position. The legate needed the elector and, on September 11, Rome softened its instructions: Cajetan is now given the power to summon Luther and to accept his recantation or to condemn him. But he must not involve himself in a disputation.

Being a theologian of some standing and extremely conscientious, the legate read Luther's writings and composed a number of tracts on the questions they raised. Without changing the theological framework of the questions, he directed conversation to two points he considered central: he believed he had discovered the decisive difference concerning the doctrine of justification in Luther's thesis on the certainty of faith (and this has been the view of controversial theology to this day), and he followed Aquinas in viewing the doctrine of the "treasure of the Church" as the basis for the papal power of granting indulgences.

Ordered to Augsburg by Frederick the Wise, Luther finally makes his appearance on October 7. In spite of considerable efforts by both sides, the interrogation does not have a good result. As instructed, the cardinal insists on a "recantation" while Luther wishes to be heard and refuted. He cannot and will not understand that the submission demanded of him is not necessarily one in scholarly matters. Repeatedly and despite the cardinal's efforts, a discussion develops but no understanding is reached and the gap between the two points of view widens. Staupitz and the elector's advisers and other friends do not fail to support Luther. Because an attempt at a written apology does not fulfil the expectations of the cardinal, Luther appeals to the "pope who must be more adequately informed" and leaves town precipitately on the evening of October 20. Back in Wittenberg, he intends to appeal to the future council. But the question whether the pope himself might not be the Antichrist takes on an ever increasing urgency for him.

Before matters escalate, an important interlude occurs. Emperor Maximilian, the "last knight," dies in January 1519. Settling the imperial succession becomes the principal preoccupation of papal politics and Frederick the Wise the key figure in the process. The pope, concerned about the papal state and its destiny here on earth, momentarily forgets about "temporal punishments," his "power of indulgence," and the "notorious heretic" in distant Wittenberg. For a period of almost twenty months, the heresy trial is interrupted. During this time, the "poor souls" and the Church enjoy a respite and Luther can breathe a sigh of relief and work with superhuman energy to fulfill his tasks as preacher and professor. Although the renewal of the Church he strives for is not as yet hopeless, things are imperceptibly moving toward that "Reformation" that we know from history.

This interlude is filled by two contradictory events that cut across each other in time. The first is associated with Karl von Miltitz, the second with the passionate disputant Johann Eck.

The first action with its quality of chiaroscuro is part of the political deal papal diplomacy tried to strike with the Saxon elector. Karl von Miltitz (ca. 1490–1525), from the lesser Saxon nobility and acquainted with the elector through his father, chamberlain and secretary of His Holiness Leo X, hardly usable in Rome because of his poor Latin but intimately familiar with the language and customs of the Saxons, cunning, active, and not without some understanding of the situation in Germany and certainly not without ideas, suddenly seems the proper diplomat for Kursachsen. The garrulous and intrusive Junker in the service of the pope—Luther does not take him seriously and reacts with embarrassment to his sentimental "toasts" and "moist kisses"—does not enjoy a good reputation among historians. He is generally considered stupid, unreliable, and wilful, with a touch of the confidence man about him. His early death in what were still, in those days, the clear waters of the Main becomes a kind of symbol for a failed, ultimately absurd existence that was altogether too inconsequential for a historical mission. But even great men have fallen from barks into water and if one thinks a little about the situation and the task, one should really conclude that from the perspective of his masters, the chamberlain could appear perfectly suited to serve as nuncio with the Golden Rose of Virtue in distant Saxony, on a mission that was anything but transparent and undoubtedly made excessive demands on the secretive, allegedly arrogant cardinal legate Cajetan.

In discharging himself of his mission, Junker Karl did in fact prove skilful. He deposited the Golden Rose in the Fugger's safe before setting out on his good will journey to Nuremberg and Altenburg. At the various stops, the hospitably received nuncio drank his fill of wine and beer or even the stronger stuff he had had to do without in distant and refined Rome, and informed himself until far into the night of what the Germans were thinking. At the same time, he reveals to his astonished countrymen how people in the highest places in Rome actually feel about Luther. He tells his listeners about the annoyance of pope and Curia at the sloppy, much too quickly written and inflammatory Luther opinion of the auditor of the Sacred Palace, Prierias.

And it should be noted here that Junker Karl, as "diplomat," considers theology, especially that of the Dominicans and not excluding the great Cajetan, to be really rather superfluous. He tells his hosts that a "recantation" is required but that, from the Roman point of view, such a request for forgiveness does not mean that Luther has suffered a terrible blow theologically speaking, that such an act should be understood more along the lines of a reconciliation between father and son. Then the enthusiastic nuncio comes to the climax of his report. To prove the pope's fatherly sentiments, he alludes to the "state secret" that Leo X would be ready to bestow the cardinal's hat on Frederick the Wise's protegé to honor the elector and simultaneously to bring the *causa Lutheri* to the most favorable conclusion possible for the entire church.

The breathtaking stories of the garrulous chamberlain were certainly not credited in toto even at the time. Yet critical and experienced advisors in Kursachsen and the sober Nuremberg jurist Christoph Scheurl considered the reports substantially correct. As is customary in diplomacy, the elector used the compliant chamberlain, of course, inasmuch as his reports and offers were more than opportune, considering that in December he, the elector, had told Cajetan definitively that he would not surrender Luther since the Wittenberg professor had not been proved guilty of heresy, was open to correction, and always ready to dispute. But this does not mean that the elector believed Junker Karl had acted on his own or even against his instructions and made himself the mediator. What militates against such an assumption is primarily the fact that whereas the Curia may have seen things a little differently, the suspicious Cajetan undertook nothing against the incredible wilfulness of a young diplomat under his orders. The changed political situation due to Maximilian's death does not mean a great deal. For as far as the election of the king was concerned, the situation had been essentially the same since the end of August. And it would also be better for the not exactly untarnished reputation of papal diplomacy if we could assume that the Curia did not simply decide after the event to exploit the wilful actions of an intellectually limited chamberlain for its own ends. That this is what actually happened is beyond all doubt. For it was none other than Karl von Miltitz, not Cajetan, who was acting on the orders of the pope to win Frederick the Wise's assent to the plan regarding the imperial election. Acting in a clearly official manner, he was to advise the elector that one of his friends might be made a cardinal. In spite of his garrulity, Junker Karl thus had not told a fairy tale in Nuremberg some months earlier. He also

presented the Rose of Virtue and transmitted the valuable indulgence and penance privileges including the legitimation of Frederick's illegitimate children although not without bringing up the matter of a princely reward.

This does not mean that I wish to stifle the criticism that the ambitious Junker undoubtedly deserves if only because, as part of his plans, he made matters intolerably difficult for that poor sinner Tetzel. Yet it seems to me of the greatest historical, apologetic, and theological importance to at least experiment for once with the idea that Karl von Miltitz was not only serious but really did act on the pope's orders. For what makes it demonstrably impossible that a pope such as Leo X would initially have contented himself with the "childlike submission" of Luther, which is what the possibly childish Junker espoused? Is it not a fact that only this minimal solution still had a certain chance of success? The preliminary negotiations had made it clear that the indulgence problem, being a central problem of the Church, could not be resolved by disputations, and that the framework as Johann Eck and Prierias had changed it made a genuinely theological solution altogether impossible. What was more plausible from the papal perspective than to act in accordance with ecclesiastical discipline and at least to begin to move the problem toward a solution which doctrine made it impossible for either side to achieve then and there? In the light of this question, the image of the papal chamberlain changes: he no longer seems the pathetic and untrustworthy diplomat but, as a human being and a Christian, takes on the features of the nuncio of the Golden Rose who, now in childlike fashion, now childishly, attempts to bring about the seemingly impossible. And Leo X, who for twenty long months and for purely political motives did not concern himself with the truth, gains considerably if we assume that he would have dispensed temporarily with a theoretically precisely formulated "recantation" and thus tried to serve the discovery of truth as the situation demanded it by fatherly wisdom and kindness.

On the basis of the texts, it could be shown convincingly that this suggestion is no hypothesis but rests on a possibility that is both utopian and real. It may be called real because it shows the only road that could still have led to a solution. It must be called utopian because its realization quite simply made excessive demands on the strength of all participants. This could be shown by the example of Luther's letter of apology which he wrote early during the negotiations and addressed to the pope but which Junker Karl kept back because he did not feel confident that Leo X's "fatherly wisdom" would be able to deal with the arguments it contained. It could also be shown by the last document of the sequence which after Luther's condemnation, simply could no longer achieve any impact. This was the letter to Leo X, predated September 6, 1520, which Luther composed at the suggestion of the still hopeful chamberlain and intended to be a final and desperate attempt and which accompanied the treatise *The Freedom of a Christian Man* which he was to submit to the pope as a comprehensive justification of his concerns.

Although from the very beginning the chamberlain's plan had no chance of success, although he may also have been motivated by jealousy of Eck who, as the new nuncio, was responsible for the publication of the bull *Exsurge Domine*, although Luther himself had already called the pope "Antichrist," the papal image that emerges from Luther's letter is certainly not inaccurate nor, more importantly, insignificant. For it shows how the "Holy Father" and the sincerely pitied, "most miserable Leo" might never have become the "Antichrist" for Luther in the first place. Of course, only someone who thoroughly knows the authentic Bernard of Clairvaux and not his sugarsweet dummy can conceive of the possibility that in his relation to the "pious Leo," Luther might have been what St. Bernard was for "his Eugenius" at an earlier date. The devout Catholic who is used to measure Luther by the obedience of the "incomparable" St. Francis will reject my comparison as impious and absurd. One wonders whether our nuncio of the Rose of Virtue might have recognized a "potential Bernard" in the Wittenberg friar. Caution demands that I leave this question unanswered although his childish plan certainly points in that direction.

As regards Luther himself, it is a historical fact that because of his understandable rejection of the bizarre and unlikable Saxon Junker, but especially through his dangerous overestimation of theology and doctrine, he contributed significantly to the failure of the plan.

This brings us to Eck's action which ran parallel to that of Miltitz in which Luther as a theologian placed all his hopes. He finally wanted to appear before the great theological public and expound his concerns in a dispute with a prominent adversary such as Eck. We have already suggested that Karlstadt's unexpected theses against Eck's *Obelisci* were the point of departure for the entire enterprise. But it is significant that Eck conducted the preparatory discussion concerning place and time of the disputation with Luther, not with Karlstadt. The twelve that Eck published in December 1518 on penance, indulgence, the treasure of the Church, and purgatory are addressed to Karlstadt but are actually directed at Luther, especially the twelfth (later the thirteenth) on the authority of pope and Church which again outlines the framework within which Luther was to be finally unmasked. In spite of his agreement with Miltitz not to preach, write, or discuss, Luther promptly answered with counter theses and proclaimed that he would participate in what became the famous Leipzig disputation from June 27 to July 16, 1519, to which Duke George admitted him at the last hour and as a result of Beck's intervention.

Luther must have seen through the manipulation of his Ingolstadt colleague. But bored by Junker Karl's devout proposals, convinced of the correctness of his point of view, and obsessed by the idea of proving it, he overlooked the dangers and rushed passionately into the preparation for the *hastiludium* ("joust") in the Leipzig arena.

Particularly regarding the problem of papal authority and indirectly also the authority of the councils, Luther develops insights in the course of his hectic preparations by which he tries to verify the hitherto undisputed dogmatic propositions against the background of a very tempestuous history, an attempt that is far ahead of its time. In the course of this work, the papacy which jealousy protects and develops its power increasingly takes on the aspects of the Antichrist. Only someone with an intimate knowledge of the *Decretum Gratiani* and the papal "decretals" can judge what the intensive study of the newly opened sources must have meant for Luther's image of the pope. For what was he to think of a papacy that could see the spiritual predicament of the system of indulgences only from the point of view of its own prestige and tried to regulate by new decretals—such as the indulgence decretal of Leo X dated November 9, 1518—what could only be repressed and made more acute but never clarified by such a procedure. It is obvious that in this context the invocation of Scripture was the only defense against decrees, decretals, council resolutions, and theological propositions whose biblical grounding became an immense problem, and not only for Luther. It must also be conceded, however, that the scriptural principle that was thus being directed against the Church now assumed a significance it had not previously had for Luther and which it would not have attained without him.

A further comment on the Antichrist thesis that henceforth will orient Luther's quarrel with the papacy and which, especially in the final and crude polemical text, *Against the Roman Papacy, an Institution of the Devil* (1545), most Catholics find to be intolerably repugnant

Umb gelt ein fack vol ablaa.

Regnum.

Diaboli.

Schawet an das siben hewbtig tier  Bedeüt ir verfleische zung  Den doch gar nie erfüllen thetten
Gang eben der gstalt vnd manier  Das thier was aim pardel gleich  2 plet/pallium noch annatten
Wie Johannes gesehen hat  Bedeüt des Bapst mordische reich  Dann/opfer/peicht/stifft zü Gotsdienst
Ein tier an des meres gstat  Das auch hinricht durch tiranney  L and vnd leüt Künigreich rent vñ zinst
Das hat siben vngleicher haubt  Alles was im entgegen sey  Das es alles hat in sich verschlunden
Eben wie diß pabstier glaubt  Auch so hat das thier peren füß  Das thier entpfieng ain tödlich wunder
Die waren all gekrönt bedewt  Deüt das das Euangeli süß  Deüt das Doctor Martin hat gschriben
Die blattern der gaistlichen lewt  Ist von dem bastum vndertretten  Das bapstum tödlich wund gebieben
Das thier das het auch zehen hören  Verschart/verdeckt vñ zertretten  Mit dem otten des Herren mund
Deüt der gaistlig gwalt vñ rumoren  Das thier het auch ains löwen mund  Gott geb das es gar get zü grund
Das thier trüg Gottes lesterung  Bedeüt deß bapstum weiten schlund  Amen.

The seven-headed papal bull. Pamphlet against the traffic in indulgences.

and heretical. Without wishing to excuse a crudeness that soon went beyond all bounds, we should not become so indignant that we forget the theological significance this terrible accusation has for Luther. For him, "Antichrist" is no insult but denotes, in the sense of 2 Thessalonians 2:3–12, the "rebellion" that precedes the day of the Lord. The "man of lawlessness" and the "son of perdition" must be revealed who takes "his seat in the temple" to have himself worshiped as God. Luther takes this expression very seriously indeed, although some time passes until he becomes fully aware of all it entails. The following are the important insights here: the Antichrist and the rebellion he causes must become actual historical events, and the rebellion can occur only in God's temple, that is, within the "true Church." It does

not manifest itself in the "sects" and thus becomes the indirect eschatological sign of the "true Church" though that Church does not lose what makes it the Church as a result of his advent. The Antichrist therefore changes the structure of the Church only in the sense that he dethrones God and takes his place, and it is this that constitutes the horror of the rebellion. Applied to the pope, this means that it is not through his position of power but through its misuse that is directed against God, or because his vicarship thrusts God out of the way, that he is the Antichrist. The ultimate consequence that has governed Luther's thought from the very beginning although its full significance only dawned on him gradually is this: the coming of the Antichrist means that the end of time has arrived. Even the Reformation therefore cannot prevent the "rebellion." Only the day of the Lord or the "beloved Day of Judgment" as Luther hopefully calls it will bring salvation.

By way of anticipation, we have now also suggested what the Leipzig disputation will effect. While the electors choose the new emperor in Frankfurt, the Wittenbergians come to Leipzig where Eck, confident of victory, is already expecting his adversaries. Karlstadt, a short, ordinary-looking man, has a symbolic accident as they enter Leipzig: a wheel of his carriage breaks on the uneven pavement, the professor falls on the ground, and the manuscripts from which he intended to quote tumble on top of him. Luther asks himself whether he will be able to dispute with Eck or be confined to the role of attendant. After the solemn opening, Eck and Karlstadt enter the first round on the freedom of the will and grace. Luther meanwhile visits the town and enters a Dominican church: he is recognized and the celebrating friars scramble to protect the sanctuary from the heretic. Shortly thereafter, he hears that the dying Tetzel lies in one of the cells of the monastery. Luther writes him: "Don't blame yourself. You are not the father of the child that concerns us here."

On July 4, at seven o'clock in the morning, Eck finally encounters Luther with whom he actually wanted to dispute. The memoirs of Petrus Mosellanus, the Greek scholar and humanist who was living in Leipzig, contain a literary portrait of all three disputants: alongside the short, excitable Karlstadt, with his dark-brown face and weak memory, stands an ascetically slender Luther of medium height, intellectually nimble, polite, friendly, and even in good spirits though altogether too insolent and aggressive where his theology is at stake. There follows an obviously not altogether impartial portrait of Eck: tall and of square build, with a wide chest and a full, typically German, but rough voice and with the physiognomy of a butcher or mercenary rather than a theologian, and an intelligence, comprehension, and judgment that, had they been on a par with his phenomenal memory, would have made him one of nature's masterpieces.

Eck, the matador and passionate disputant does not succeed in teaching, let alone convincing, the Wittenberg friar. But he does goad Luther into making statements about the primacy of the pope, the capacity for error of councils as in the case of Hus, and Scripture as the sole source of faith with which the adversary is felled as easily as a stag which the duke presents to the "victor" as a trophy. The depressing result is that Luther's great hope is not fulfilled as might have been expected. The universities at Paris and Erfurt which had been selected as judges refrain because the threatening quarrel frightens them. Only the universities of Louvain and Cologne send two lame opinions months later which provoke the cutting answer from Luther that even those professors who conduct themselves as if they were infallible succumb to error. Only the humanists under the leadership of Erasmus and W. Pirckheimer from Nuremberg side with Luther after their own fashion. With malicious bons mots and sharpened pens, they turn the hated Eck's victor's image into caricature. For Luther, this applause comes from the wrong side and he feels that the pens are too pointed. For Eck, the attacks of the literati are a kind of calculated professional risk: someone who wishes to fight for truth in the "arena" of Church and history simply has to put up with a bad press now and again.

The modern judgment on the Leipzig disputation broadly supports Eck. For while the controversial theologians of both churches criticize his style and the calculated use of his dialectical method against Luther a glance at the end result shows that they really owe him thanks. The "Lutheran" side naturally considers Luther's critical comments on the papacy as genuinely "reformist" and is grateful to the disputant Eck for his help in bringing this matter to light at a critical juncture. The "Catholic" side is obliged to him for the opposite reasons and gives him credit for not having let himself be deterred by the lack of dogmatic clarity of the period as he showed that Luther did not want reform but was really launching an attack on the very structure of the Church.

There is not much hope that the pious and ecumenical front of one's colleagues will give way at this point. Nor does either side offer me the kind of promotion for which Eck proposed himself quite matter-of-factly when he placed himself at the disposal of the pope as inquisi-

With this caricature of the seven-headed Martin Luther, Johann Cochläus, in a polemical writing of 1529, attacks the contradictory statements of his opponent.

tor for the Saxon bishoprics and later as nuncio provided he receive an appropriate living in return. Yet I dare say that Luther's comments in Leipzig simply are not what, at the preliminary end of a depressing story filled with accidents, they have every appearance of being. It must be conceded, of course, that as provoked assertions and in the context of the situation described above, Luther's statements are not only misinterpretable, exaggerated, and onesided but clearly heretical in their tendency. But all these defects do not result from the theological approach but can be explained by historical accidents, as we have shown in the case of the Leipzig disputation.

This is confirmed by the fact that the "heretical" element in Luther as we observe it in a crescendo movement in the three great programmatic tracts of 1520 is never unambiguous or definitive, let alone clearly "un-Catholic." It can be shown further that the themes he dealt with in Leipzig or later—such as church office, the sacraments, the mass, or monasticism — could have been treated in a way that would have allowed for Luther's distinctive approach, yet been perfectly understandable as "Catholic."

This clearly applies not only to Luther but also to Eck and the other Catholic adversaries. It was more than simple passion that inspired Eck during the disputation and the prompt exploitation of its results. For we must assume that on the basis of Eck's dogmatically fixed and undeveloped doctrine of the Church it was quite simply a historical impossibility for him to understand the fundamental concerns behind the bold and equally immature and exaggerated pronouncements of the man from Wittenberg.

The entire further development is thus governed by a "historical necessity" which, in its human, all-too-human causes and the ambivalence of its motivations, never attained the stringency of "theological necessity," yet quite concretely seized and directed the life of the faith and the Church and of theological development.

If this is so, the further course of this sad story, from the writing of the bull threatening excommunication to the Diet of Worms and Luther's "kidnapping" to the Wartburg, can be condensed. We know the human qualities and weaknesses of the principal actors; we know the hopeless opposition between the two positions. A decision must be made, but that decision will decide nothing.

It is to the credit of the pope and the Curia that at the end of the political inactivity and of the emperor's election which did not turn out as they had hoped, they did not start running amok overnight, theologically speaking. Junker Karl is still active, and until the commission under the cardinals Accolti and Cajetan goes to work, more time passes. Although it becomes unmistakably clear that the honest elector of Saxony and his protegé now come into the line of fire, the reserved and seemingly arrogant Cajetan is too honest a Christian and too competent a theologian to lend his hand to an act of ostracism. He is exclusively concerned with the substance of the matter as he sees it, not the person whom he wishes to spare. He also knows that excessively pointed, misinterpretable propositions are not the same as heresy. Yet this honest man is unable to conclude the *causa Lutheri* to the greatest advantage of all concerned.

With Eck's arrival in Rome on March 25, the proceedings entered a new phase. Because of his experience in Leipzig and coming from Germany, Eck knows more clearly than his Roman colleagues that more than indulgences are involved. Toward the end of April, a new commission is formed of which not only the two cardinals but Eck also are members. A bull against Luther is to be discussed and to it, Eck contributes those forty-one propositions that are no longer to be condemned one by one but globally. On May 2, Eck reports on the bull to Leo X at Magliana, a castle where the pope was hunting boar and from where he had extended so paternal an invitation to Luther to visit Rome. As always when commissions make decisions, not everyone is in agreement with the bull threatening excommunication. Before the substance of the forty-one propositions is subjected to a critique, Cajetan objects to the wholesale condemnation and the canonists register their dissatisfaction with the procedure. It is probable that they did not make too much of their real doubt which concerned the relationship between pope and council. The bull thus contains a number of distinctions and uncertainties that either go unrecognized or are quickly forgotten if one simply listens to the bombastic trumpet solo of the *Exsurge Domine* ("Arise, O God, plead thy cause," Psalm 74:22) with which the Medici pope, a man who adored all beauty and art and who was not really at ease in the pontifical slippers of his blessed predecessor Gregory VII, called not only on God but on heaven and earth, and especially the emperor and the empire, for help against the "wild boar that wreaks havoc in the vineyard of the Lord," by which he assuredly was not referring to the wild boar hunt in Magliana, an activity he actually didn't much care for. M. Brecht is right when he calls attention to the distinctions and signs that one easily overlooks: the bull does not directly impose the ban and the unending list of canonical punishments, but Luther, the "notorious heretic," is given sixty days. The bull also distinguishes between person and doctrine and even between erroneous and non-erroneous books. There are additional indications whose actual significance can only be judged by those with a specialized knowledge of the papal chancery: the bull is dated June 15, and the signatures of the pope and the cardinals, which were so important to Eck and customary in the case of bulls, are missing. Instead of the appropriate seal-cord of hemp that protocol calls for, a multi-colored one is used; the proclamation date is July 24 when it is posted on the door of St. Peter's and in the papal chancery on the Campo dei Fiori.

As he had himself proposed, Eck and the humanist and director of the Vatican library Hieronymus Aleander were entrusted with the proclamation of the bull in Germany. Especially in the Saxon bishoprics, this did not turn into a victory procession for Eck, but even the

Caricature of Luther's opponents, among them Johannes Eck and Pope Leo X. Contemporary woodcut.

more successful Aleander ran into difficulties even in Mainz where the executioner refused to burn the books because he had doubts they had been properly condemned. Luther himself doubted for weeks that the bull was genuine—and *Exsurge Domine* would certainly not have been the first spurious bull in history. But finally, after Miltitz's last attempt, the letter to the pope, he disappointedly and angrily accepted what he could not change. Not without consideration for the elector who had told Aleander as late as November that he would resent attacks by Luther on the pope, there occurred, on December 10, the famous scene before the Elster gate: called on by Melanchthon, students burned the hated papal decretals and scholastic books such as the *Summa Angelica*, and Luther—hardly noticed by those present—himself threw the bull into the fire. Of course, this did not mean that the bull no longer existed. Even today, it moves the simple minds of those who understandably would like to make or correct history with "fire" if without stakes. But the bull *Exsurge Domine* is no juridical misjudgment which, like an unjustly pronounced and executed death sentence, must be revoked by the judge although even such an act does not return the innocently beheaded to life. The bull *Exsurge Domine*, being a theological and ecclesiastical judgment, cannot be so easily undone although this does not mean that the "highest judge" did not foresee a "revision" for such "contradictory judgments."

And this revision which precedes the final judgment sets in when those responsible for the bull before history begin to see the "contrariety" of their judgment. In the present case, it is none other than Johann Eck himself who, having learned something from his experiences as the nuncio of the bull, admits in a reform opinion for Adrian VI the shortcomings of the old bull and demands a new one: in the old bull, he writes, much had remained obscure and many of the condemned propositions had been so trivial that even the greatest scholars could not understand why they should have been condemned. The urgently proposed "new" judgment should therefore confine itself to the most important errors and refute them by full recourse to Holy Scripture.

It is a consolation that even the "passionate disputant" slowly rediscovered the capacity for instruction. Yet it would be going too far were one to assume that Eck had already understood Luther's "scriptural principle" and its underlying concern, the required changes being exclusively aimed at greater severity. But since it is true that "man proposes and God disposes," infinitely more happens here than the untiring defender of the "true faith" proposes.

A much greater consolation though very confusing at first glance is that Eck's truly plausible proposal was not heeded, however repeatedly and insistently he submitted it to Adrian VI's successors. Regretted not only by Eck but also by great modern theologians, the end result is that the representatives of the papacy leave their predecessor's bull untouched and leave it up to the army of theologians to regret or justify their unwillingness to exercise their highest teaching office. Indeed, those representatives make the ungrateful business of defense considerably more difficult for Eck's successors: even decades later, they condemn the zealous fathers of the Council of Trent, Luther, and his errors by name and proposition. Actually, and it is this fact that the greatest historian of the council sees as the "irony of history," the popes would have liked nothing better than to leave indulgence, purgatory, and the veneration of the saints alone since these problems had become so difficult and fateful for the Church, and because, being practical problems of the life of the Church, they had not yet become genuine problems for the theologians, or because they felt that the peculiarity of the problems constituted too much of a challenge. Massive pressure by the emperor was required before the fathers who were already sitting on their packed suitcases at least agreed to express themselves in three terse decrees, in the final session on December 3 and 4, 1563, on the fundamental questions which had given rise to the "Reformation" in the first place.

It is not easy to let oneself be consoled by the course of history. For what eventually becomes consolation seems at first, from a variety of points of view, a failure. Luther reproached the papacy and the Church throughout his life, saying that he had never been proven wrong in the question of indulgences, and that every exchange about this most difficult question had been denied him. Yet he would have been the first, he said, to acknowledge the "achievement" of a more humble papacy, had it admitted its failure. Luther certainly would not have hesitated to concede that among the forty-one condemned propositions, there were also some, like the thirty-first, "the just sins in every good deed," that, given its understanding of the faith, the old Church could not have accepted because they were incomprehensible to it although clarification would have been easy, had the other side entered into an exchange with Luther on the problem of love. This applies equally to Luther's misleading propositions on penitence, contrition, and the Eucharist, or on purgatory, indulgence, and the power of the pope. There can be no question that Luther would more readily have accepted a "revision" than did the successors on either side, although one must also grant that the perfectly legitimate defense of the "Catholic" or the "Reformed" has made a revision of the *Exsurge* considerably more difficult for them. Yet such a "revision" is under way in the living judgment of the Church, and one would not go too far were one to assert that it began when the inappropriateness and contradictoriness of the bull were first seen.

It was in fact this contradictoriness of the bull and of the entire procedure that defined the further course of negotiations. Having finally been proclaimed *haereticus vitandus* by the edict of excommunication *Decet Romanum Pontificem* on January 3, 1521—the date on which the friar who had been recognized as a "notorious heretic" for years was actually condemned is a purely theoretical matter—Luther should have been outlawed immediately according to prevailing secular and ecclesiastical law. For the implementation of the Church ban was the business of the emperor as the secular arm of the church. But it is legitimate to wonder why the emperor should have been less "ambivalent" than the pope and his judgment.

The emperor had important reasons not to make short shrift in Luther's case. Quite apart from the fact that the Germans almost unanimously backed Luther and opposed the Curia, a fact no one recognized and expressed more clearly than Aleander, the emperor also had to take the interests of the Diet into account. He could not overlook that in the course of time Luther had become something like the "mouthpiece" for all the complaints of the German empire, that he had committed himself by a solemnly sworn election capitulation to outlaw no one without a previous hearing, and that he had finally promised Frederick the Wise to give Luther a fair hearing at the Diet which up to this time the condemned man had been unable to obtain.

The *causa Lutheri* thus gave rise to waves of secret negotiations which in the mixed and contradictory quality of their goals shed a clear light on the entire situation. There is, most importantly, the elector's skilfully pursued plan to have the banned Luther appear before an objective tribunal of scholars. There is Aleander's heated protest which warns the emperor against making himself a higher judge than the pope but which also seeks to avoid all escalation of the nearly explosive tension in light of the fact that the imperial knighthood under Ulrich von Hutten and Franz von Sickingen threatened to intervene. And finally, there is the developing concept of an "imperial reform" which, seemingly mediating, enters into negotiations that are conducted by the emperor's confessor, the Franciscan Jean Glapion, and the chancellor Brück, a process that could hardly be to Aleander's liking. A plan is elaborated according to which negotiations with Luther about his books will not be conducted at the Diet but in a town near Worms. Even Franz von Sickingen's Ebernburg is seriously considered. The final result is that although important concessions to the papal side are made the emperor does not simply impose the ban. Instead, he summons Luther, sending along a safe conduct in which he addresses him as "honorable, dear and pious Martin," and asks that he give information about his books before the Diet. There is no mention of recantation.

On March 29, Kaspar Sturm, the imperial herald, himself highly critical of Rome, presented the summons to Luther in Wittenberg. As early as April 2, Luther set out on a journey which, because it could have been his last, initially proceeded like a triumphal procession. The town had presented him with a requisitioned dray equipped with a roof, and the university had allowed him expenses in the amount of twenty gulden. Although he had been expelled from the order, the monastery provided him with a companion as stipulated in its rules, the not terribly consequential Father Johann Fetzensteiner, and Luther even had his tonsure trimmed. Whereas his lectures obliged Melanchthon to stay behind, two other colleagues, Nikolaus von Amsdorf and a young nobleman from Pomerania, accompanied him. Pleasantly escorted by the herald, Luther journeyed through Germany's towns, where he was everywhere hospitably received—in Weimar, the elector's brother provided him

with additional funds—and gave sermons much of the time. In Erfurt especially, the humanists insisted on honoring Luther als the luminary of their university: Crotus Rubeanus, his former fellow student and now rector, set out to meet him with an escort of forty horsemen, and Helius Eobanus Hessus composed a long poem in his honor. But the most important tribute humanism pays Luther is that the jurist Justus Jonas, the favorite disciple of the great Erasmus, accompanies him on his difficult way to Worms. Luther's mood wavers between fear and defiant confidence. According to Cochlaeus's believable report, he caroused with friends in Frankfurt and, an Orpheus in his cowl, strummed the lute. But his popularity did not go to his head and he felt as skeptical about the fickle "rabble" as he did about the compliments of the humanists or the politically tempting offer of the knighthood of the empire. He even kept a cool head when, before having reached the goal of his journey, the emperor's confessor and a chamberlain try to detour him to the Ebernburg where the imperial reformers—with Martin Bucer, chaplain to von Sickingen, acting as mediator—intend to enter into secret negotiations with him, and where, under the protection of the powerful Franz von Sickingen, he would certainly have been safer than in Worms. But Luther refused to accede to this plan although he had no reason to question Glapion's honest intentions. Although the pronouncements he allegedly made on this journey are full of pathos, this odd friar was genuinely convinced of his mission and knew that Christ in whom he put his entire faith and love would protect him on his journey.

Although in negotiations with Glapion, the two nuncios had tried to arrange as inconspicuous an arrival as possible, a solemn reception which really should have been avoided awaited him. On the morning of April 16, trumpets announced Luther's arrival from the cathedral. Thousands went out to see the man no one knew what to make of—reformer and liberator of the Church or "wild boar" that had crashed into the vineyard of the Lord. Originally, it had been planned to have Luther stay in the emperor's palace because there any communication with the *haereticus vitandus* could easily have been prevented. But when practical reasons made this impossible and other difficulties militated against lodging him in the elector's inn, Luther was taken to the friendly Knights of Rhodes who had once kept Prince Dschem for Alexander VI. Under the generous supervision of the elector's advisors and the imperial marshal who were put under the same roof, communication with Luther was no longer a problem.

The next morning, the details of the procedure were

settled. Luther would be restricted to answering the questions addressed to him and not allowed to make additional statements. He would appear before the Diet, in the episcopal palace next door to the cathedral, at four o'clock in the afternoon. Accompanied by the marshal and the imperial herald and led like a thief through the garden of the Knights of Rhodes and down a few back streets to the rear entrance of the episcopal palace, Luther finally stood before his emperor and the estates of the empire. According to Aleander who was not present, the "fool" was laughing, and others report that he "looked merry." Unfamiliar with court etiquette, Luther must have tried to spot familiar faces and is even supposed to have spoken briefly with C. Peutinger from Augsburg. The marshal then admonished him not to speak until and unless a question was addressed to him.

The archbishop's chancellor, Johann von Eck, who functioned as the emperor's plaintiff and conducted the hearing was, for some, a welcome reminder of the negotiations that the archbishop of Trier had originally been meant to conduct. Others had no cause to suspect him and knew him from the recent book burning in Trier.

Facing the books that had been placed on a bench, the chancellor asked Luther in the name of the emperor and with reference to the summons whether he recognized the books as his, and whether he acknowledged them or wished to disavow parts of them. Although the questions allowed for a number of possible answers, Luther seemed frightened and confused. In a barely audible voice, he affirmed the first question and indicated briefly that he might have wirtten more. As he answers the second, he suddenly loses his nerve. Whether he wished to avow or disavow, this second and decisive question suddenly strikes Luther as involving ultimate matters and—to the disappointment of his friends and the amazement of his adversaries—he humbly requests time to reflect.

What the meaning of this request may have been is discussed to this very day, yet the answer does not strike me as excessively problematical. It may be assumed that Luther knew what had been agreed upon between Glapion and Brück regarding the hearing. Sophisticated "hermeneutic" scholars who existed even then would have recognized the "opening" even without stage directions. But Luther simply could not use the room he had to maneuver. "For whoever keeps the whole law but fails in one point has become guilty of all of it." This phrase from the Epistle of James that Luther will later call the "epistle of straw" was a handicap to him throughout his life. For someone who cannot detach himself from the maxim "everything or nothing" cannot "negotiate"

about "something" since he believes that in ultimate decisions about the truths of faith and salvation, it is always "everything" that is at stake. Among the ultimate things that made a decision for Luther more difficult during this fateful hour was also concern for the unity of the Church, a matter the chancellor of Trier did not have to remind him of. During the evening and the night, Luther apparently quickly overcame the temptation that was due to his ambivalence, and the consolation of his aristocratic visitors that he need not fear for his life or calls on him to persist probably did not help him much in his situation. For when, on the next day and at the same time, he again faced the emperor and had to answer the second question, he calmly and resolutely took the cross of the ambiguous situation upon himself. Again, he is unable to exploit the room for maneuver that he still has. But he also resists the temptation that threatens him both from within and without to conduct himself like the club-wielding, authority-crushing "German Hercules" whom Hans Holbein the Younger had presented to the public a short while before. Answering with a firm voice, he makes a three-fold distinction among his writings. He does not need to recant the first group which is devoted to his fundamental concerns because it is general and endorsed even by his adversaries. He cannot recant the writings in the second group, the polemics against the papacy, because the popes, invoking their "decretals," have acted against Scripture and the Church Fathers and made themselves the lords of Christendom. The third group includes those writings that are addressed to specific adversaries and with reference to which he concedes that stylistically, if not in their substance, they may have been more vehement than necessary, a statement which clearly shows that he cannot recant the substance of any of them.

He then discusses the danger to the unity of the Church and emphasizes that he also is concerned with this unity but that it is not possible to avoid destructive tension where the Word of God is concerned, for Christ had come not to bring peace but the sword. It is therefore not at the expense of the Word but only through the Word itself that the conflict can be settled.

It was very hot in the room and Luther perspired profusely but he insisted on also presenting his statement in Latin. In his answer, the chancellor praised the emperor's patience but rejected Luther's statement as insufficient. As is customary in such situations, he finally demanded an honest and simple answer to what was anything but a simple question. Luther cannot and will not be evasive but even at this point he does not become the defiant hero people prefer to see. He certainly never spoke the words "Here I stand, I cannot do otherwise." They are legend. In actuality, Luther simply invoked his "conscience," though a conscience that has nothing whatever in common with the autonomous conscience of today. For Luther emphasizes again that he is prepared to be refuted by clear scriptural testimony and plausible rational grounds. Even here, he does not radically reject pope and councils as authorities although he does state that he cannot believe them "alone" since it is a historical fact that they have erred and contradicted themselves in the past.

The effort before the Diet which had been initiated with so much trouble had failed. The emperor, just as the Church before him, could not act otherwise. But neither could Luther. Despite all that was done, the estates did not succeed in getting Luther to change his mind during the three-day period the emperor had granted. On the evening of April 25, the emperor informs Luther that, everything having failed, he now must, as the protector of the Church, take steps against him. It is clear that neither side can act otherwise, that neither side is concerned with Church politics, that both care about the Church and its reform. But despite the unavoidable decision, the situation continues ambiguous and contradictory. For all assertions to the contrary notwithstanding, nothing is really cleared up in Worms and nothing is less certain than the nonetheless allegedly certain thesis that the convictions about the nature of the Church were fundamentally different and irreconcilable.

The chiaroscuro that bathes all participants cannot be illuminated better than by pointing to the expectation that the Church had placed in the emperor in connection with the Worms hearing, an expectation he was doomed to be unable to meet. Aleander expects the emperor to clear up a situation that cannot be cleared up by the sword, yet at the same time thwarts such clarification when he calls it an intervention in the sphere of the pope's competency. This lack of clarity remains and feeds the reform of the Church. For without the emperor, no council would have been called, and without the emperor, the council would not have pronounced itself on indulgences, purgatory, and the veneration of saints. Yet in this paradoxical manner, he finally does serve the "revision" of a judgment that ultimately only the Church can make, and in this sense Aleander was proven right without understanding it.

It is one of the oddities of this story that the "Edict of Worms" that Aleander had prepared, that the emperor had signed after the termination of the Diet on May 26, 1521, and that had finally banned and outlawed an "ob-vious heretic" had a merely indirect effect. For the outlawed Luther had already left, but certainly not escaped from, Worms, on April 26, with his escort. True, he was not sure what would happen next but he could have confidence in his God and his elector. With traveling money from the elector's treasury, a safe conduct from Philip of Hesse, and a solemn farewell banquet, the "honest rascal" as Aleander called him sets out on a journey whose destination no one knows for sure. From Oppenheim on, the imperial herald and twenty horsemen, allegedly provided by Sickingen, escort him again. They travel via Frankfurt to Friedberg where he discharges the herald because he feels safe. He does not proceed directly from Eisenach to Gotha but, escorted only by Amsdorf and Petzensteiner, makes a detour to Möhra where he visits his relatives. As they set out from Möhra, it happens: on May 4, the small company is attacked by armed horsemen in a narrow passage near Altenstein castle. Amsdorf curses like a foot soldier, Petzensteiner saves himself by jumping into the bushes, and Luther has just time enough to pick up his New Testament and Hebrew Bible. Then, first on foot and later on horseback, they move by detours toward their secret destination. At eleven o'clock at night, Luther arrives at the safe Wartburg where, perfectly camouflaged as "Junker Jörg" and out of the public's eye, he will spend the following ten month praying, raging, and working. The elector was not only "wise" but also cunning when the situation called for it. The cleverly arranged maneuver succeeded, the witnesses kept silent, and the hoodwinked public soon spoke of a violation of the safe conduct that had cost Luther his life. Albrecht Dürer who was in the Netherlands at the time grieved for the dead Luther and the Bible that would fall silent now until God sent a new witness.

Frederick the Wise, his secretary and confidant Georg Spalatin, and the loyal castle captain all remain silent but do not know what will happen next.

We will conclude this chapter with an appreciation of the man who, like no other, documents the ambivalence of this time of turmoil and who, despite that fact, does not deserve to be criticized as an ambivalent human being or an ambivalent Christian. It cannot be denied that from the moment Luther came to be suspected of heresy, the elector took the public position that he would not tolerate any real heresy on the part of his professor and subject, and particularly no rebellion against the pope and the Church. But at the same time, he did everything in his power to defend Luther. During the first two "rounds," he did not find it difficult to maintain this position although both the pope and the Curia urged him at an early date to drop Luther. Medieval Christians were not prudish, the charge of "heresy" had lost much of its force from overuse, and double dealing in negotiations was considered a great art of the rulers on both sides. It can be taken for granted that chances of a "short trial" for witches, Jews and malefactors were immeasurably greater than for "notorious heretics." But it is also true that the elector must have taken the *causa Lutheri* quite seriously from the very beginning. For it was anything but natural that a personal encounter between the elector and the leading professor at his university and problem child should never have occurred. What can be explained with respect to Luther's first few years in Wittenberg on technical grounds and, in spite of all kindness, on the basis of the immense gap that existed between subject and prince must be seen, after 1518 at the latest, as deliberate, tactically motivated behavior on the part of the elector. Even though it was by no means rare that both found themselves at the same place at the same time, as in Altenburg, Wittenberg, and Worms, Frederick the Wise scrupulously avoided all personal contact. All communication was handled by the loyal secretary and chaplain of the elector and Luther's most intimate friend, Georg Spalatin, who for that reason deserves to be judged one of the few and extremely important key figures of this period, much more important than Philip Melanchthon who stood in the limelight.

If we inquire into the meaning of this behavior, the evident tactical motivation turns out to be merely a superficial explanation. It is obvious that it was only in this way that he could, by an unassailable pretext, counter the constantly recurring impression that both were conspiring jointly against Church and empire. That people accepted this pretext cannot be explained without the secret complicity of the emperor and the Church and presupposes the absolute integrity of his person and character. In contrast to quite a few other princes and electors of the period, Frederick the Wise pursued no personal interest of whatever kind in the *causa Lutheri.* His concern was neither the resolution of marriage problems as in Philip of Hesse's case, nor did he cast a greedy eye on the possessions of the Church, his university having been put on a sound financial footing by a very reasonable agreement of Church and state. His childish passion for collecting rare relics simply passed away.

To the extent that this can be judged, the elector's decision, although made under conditions that are not altogether transparent, was free of any moral "double dealing" which he knew to be a danger and sought to avoid. According to Luther, he made this serious charge

even against the great Erasmus who seemed to be his friend and on his side. The important passage from the *Table Talk* reads as follows: "Erasmus is an eel, only Christ can get a firm hold of him. He is a disingenuous person. When Duke Frederick the Wise asked him in Cologne why Luther was being condemned and how he had sinned, he answered: 'He sinned a great deal for he laid hands on the monks' stomach and on the popes' crown.' Frederick then said to Spalatin: 'What an odd fellow this is. One cannot tell where one stands with him.' Thus he caught him out in his malice ... May God stop him ... Those who don't hate Satan love your songs, Erasmus."

Free of such two-faced cunning, loyal toward emperor and pope, Frederick the Wise remained loyal to his modest and very pragmatic motto, *Tantum, quantum possum,* in the *causa Lutheri.* He did what he could and what his conscience let him. In his heart, he sided with Luther, yet remained wholly an elector of the "Holy Roman Empire" for which there can be only "one Church."

Thus it is precisely as one views the Wartburg situation that a profound inner kinship between the two dissimilar men becomes apparent. Generally believed dead, Luther works feverishly in his solitude, especially on the sample sermons, postils, and a translation of the New Testament. But as Junker Jörg who soon also roams the forests and the countryside, he seems to be moving in an ecclesiastical no-man's land. The old papal Church has expelled him and wants him dead whereas the "Church of the Reformation" is taking its first steps in Wittenberg and elsewhere without and against him. Yet paradoxically, he belongs to both churches, for he belongs to the Lord of the Church and, abandoning everything and ahead of everyone, he sets out in the faith of Abraham and his Church for the "Day of the Lord."

Frederick the Wise finds himself in a similar situation: in his heart and in his faith, he has long been traveling the road Luther is taking. But this does not prevent him from remaining in the train of the pilgrim Church, as it were. For in it, and in the belief that it also will set out, he wishes to serve as the rear guard of the man who is already on the way. We may also be certain that the elector was no less critical of the tempestuous beginnings of the Reformation in Wittenberg than Luther was himself even though he did not initially intervene in the course of things.

The "Lutherans," as the Christians from the Church of the gospel are soon called and call themselves to Luther's annoyance, are justifiably proud that toward the end of his life the elector openly subscribed to their

# ILLUSTRATION SEQUENCE IV

## PEASANTS' WAR—MARRIAGE—
## WORK FOR THE COMMUNITY
## 1522–1528

46   Martin Luther in the pulpit. Detail of the predella of the altarpiece in the town church in Wittenberg. Tradition reports that this masterpiece by Lucas Cranach the Elder was erected on April 24, 1547, the day of the Battle of Mühlberg in which Charles V defeated the troops of the Evangelical Schmalkaldic League. After his victory, on the Wednesday before Pentecost, the emperor marched into Wittenberg which had surrendered and visited Luther's grave in the castle church (cf. no. 24). When Charles V was called on to open the grave and to burn Luther's remains because he had been a heretic, he is reported to have answered: "I wage war against the living, not against the dead." But a Spanish officer from the emperor's retinue pierced the painting of the preaching Luther with his sword (at the neck and in the body), and shouted: "Even in death, this beast rages on." The holes made by the sword thrusts are visible still.

47   Ulrich (or Huldreich) Zwingli (1484–1531), the reformer of German-speaking Switzerland. Having been a priest at the cathedral in Zürich from 1519, he began to oppose the old Church in 1523 after he was won over to the idea of the Reformation by the reading of Luther's writings. A different conception of the Lord's Supper caused marked opposition to Luther.—Painting.

48   View of the choir of Zürich cathedral where Zwingli was a priest after 1519.

49   Peasants' War, the battle of Gaisbeuren (1525) near Ravensburg. Detail of the 1528 escutcheon of the town of Überlingen.—Überlingen, town hall.—The discontent of the German peasants about economic, social, and religious matters led to early unrest in 1493 for which the "Bundschuh" movement along the Upper Rhine and in Württemberg was responsible (1514). When the movement spread, Luther first wrote his *Admonition to Peace on the Twelve Articles of the Swabian Peasantry* (1525). He protested the false understanding of the gospel by the peasants who proposed making a law of it and transforming it into a social reality by the use of violence. Only after his appeal had found insufficient resonance did he write *Against the Robbing and Murdering Mobs of Peasants*, in May 1525. He then called on the princes to exercise their right to the sword and to put an end to the peasants' uprising.

50, 51   Martin Luther and Katharina von Bora, painting (1526) by Lucas Cranach the Elder, Wartburg.—Katharina von Bora (* 1499) became a Cistercian nun in Nimbschen convent in 1515. During the night before Easter night 1523, she secretly fled from the convent with eleven other nuns. Luther, who knew of and supported this escape, married Katharina on July 13, 1525.

52   Christ as teacher. Keystone in the choir vault of the parish church of St. Mary in Wittenberg (circa 1300).

HVLDRVOHVS ZVINGLIVS

NM PATRIÆ QVÆRO PER DOGMATA SANCTA SALVTEM

INGRATO PATRIÆ GÆSVS AB ENSE CADO

OBIIT ANO DNI M DXXXI OCDOB

ÆTRTIS SVÆ XLVIII

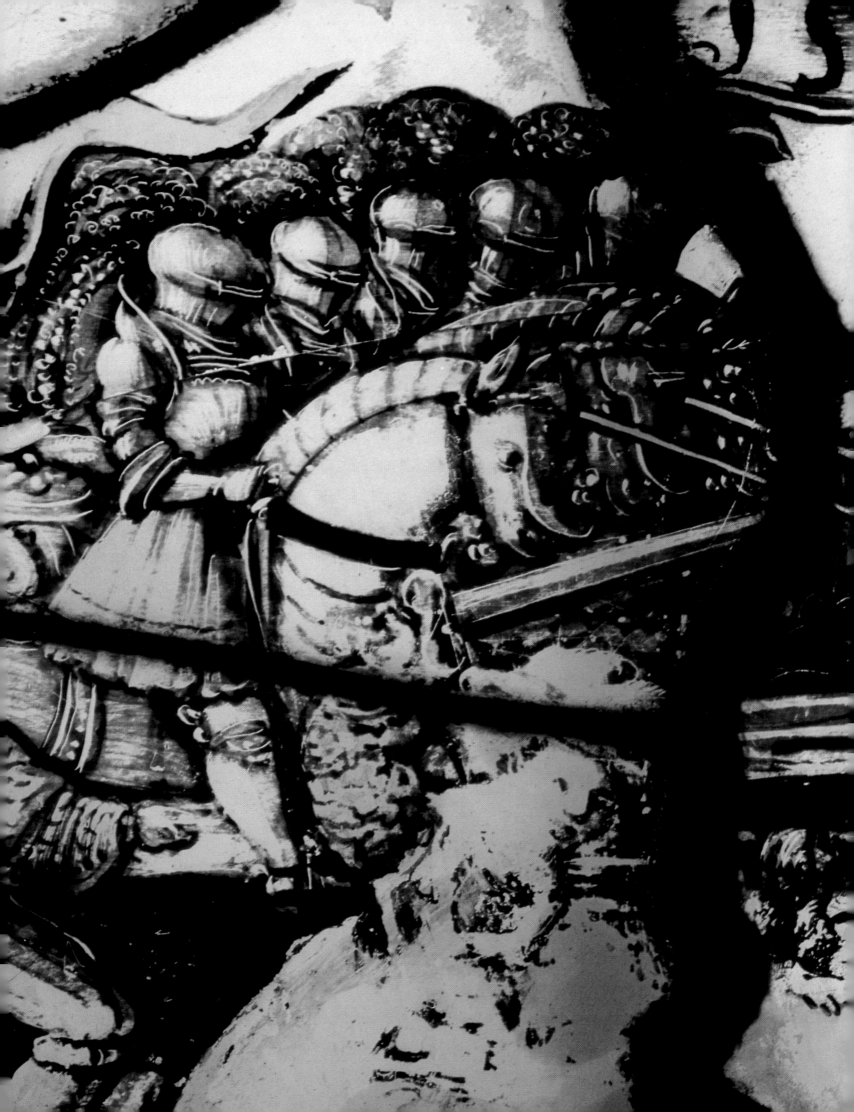

53   View into the choir of the parish church of St. Mary in Wittenberg with altarpiece by Lucas Cranach the Elder (cf. no. 46). This altar, like the other great Reformation altars of Cranach's, is a demonstration of Luther's opposition to the iconoclasm of Karlstadt. In his *Against the Heavenly Prophets in the Matter of Images and Sacraments* (1525), Luther defended Christian art. In connection with the biblical illustrations to which the iconoclasts did not object, Luther wrote: "They should not begrudge us our painting such images on the wall so that we might remember and understand better since on walls they do no more harm than in books. I wish to God I could persuade the princes and the wealthy to have the entire Bible painted on the walls of houses so that everyone might see them. That would be a Christian work."

54   Bronze baptismal font, created in the Vischer workshop in Nuremberg and located in the church of St. Mary in Wittenberg. Luther's children were baptized here.

55   The sacrament of baptism. Left panel of the altarpiece in the church of St. Mary in Wittenberg. Philip Melanchthon is represented as the baptizer; to his left stands Cranach with a towel. In the open book of the assistant, we read: "Who believes and is baptized will be saved, but who does not believe will be damned" (cf. nos. 53, 46). There are no records that indicate that Melanchthon, who was no ordained pastor, performed baptism himself. The painting is the iconographic illustration of the solemnly proclaimed right of laymen to perform emergency baptism.

56   The sacrament of the Lord's Supper. Center panel of the altarpiece in the town church. In the group of apostles among whom Christ is passing the bread to the traitor Judas, one can identify Luther as "Junker Jörg" to whom the cupbearer (Lucas Cranach the Younger?) is handing a goblet (front right).

57   The sacrament of confession. Right panel of the altarpiece in the town church. The confessor is the town pastor Johannes Bugenhagen who also confessed Luther. Bugenhagen carries the two keys that loosen the sincerely remorseful sinner and bind the impenitent one. The kneeling man demonstrates sincere penance whereas the impenitent lansquenet rushes off, his hands bound.

58   The congregation during the sermon. Detail of the predella of the town church altarpiece (cf. nos. 53, 46). The congregation, according to the Augsburg Confession, "is the gathering of all the faithful to whom the gospel is preached purely and the holy sacraments are administered in accordance with the gospel." Cranach also painted Luther's son Hänschen in this congregation. He is leaning against his mother's knee. The figure behind these two may be one of Luther's daughters.

59   The crucified Christ. Center section of the predella of the town church altarpiece. Luther is pointing to it (cf. no. 46) and the listening congregation is looking at it: "but we preach Christ crucified" (1 Cor. 1:23).

60   Doctor Martin Luther. Painting by Lucas Cranach the Elder (1528).— Weimar, State Collection in the castle.

creed and forsook everything that functioning as the rear guard had seemed to require up to that time. The first German-language service is held on April 9, 1525, in the elector's chapel in Lochau, in the presence of the already deathly ill Frederick. In his hour of death, he receives Holy Communion under both kinds and finally also has Luther called to his bedside. But does this mean that Frederick leaves the old Church whose awakening he had wished to hasten? Does he even finally "unreservedly adopt a new creed" as has been said? And does he die alone because Luther cannot hurry to his bedside because the distance is too great?

Here also, the real consolation of history is an altogether different one. However natural the self-confirmation that Lutheran Christians find here may be, the real consolation lies in the insight that it was precisely during this critical phase that there were leading Christians who, like the elector and his Junker Jörg, remained loyal to the Church.

Holy Communion under both kinds certainly was no betrayal of the old Church. Nor did Luther abandon his dying elector. For to console him, he wrote him that he would die with Christ and in the community of the saints who, through their justice, virtue, and love would intercede for his sins and his still imperfect love.

Concluding comment: someone who lives as Luther did, who risks his life and gives of himself to the point of total exhaustion, pays for such commitment with the health of both his body and his spirit. In the Wartburg, Luther was often ill and often fell into the most profound sadness which lay on his soul like a darkness. Those of our contemporaries who have visited psychiatrists know all about such matters. Something similar already existed in the Middle Ages which called it *melancholicus fluxus sanguinis.* Throughout his life, Luther had an exceptional magnetism for spiritually suffering individuals but no sophisticated name for his own suffering. He simply let himself fall into the deep hole, and when he came back out he was done with it and had suffered no harm. And he certainly wrecked no works of art and altars to rid himself of his aggressions. The man who had been so "modern" as to invoke his conscience in Worms remained in truth a medieval man. One should not try to deceive one's enlightened contemporaries: Luther not only believed in witches but in the devil as well. That he threw an inkbottle at him is not an established fact and is part of the legend. It is certain, however, that it was not just the power of prayer that protected him from the devil and the devil's mother-in-law. He did not put much trust in holy water but did turn his bare rear end toward him so that a cannonade of farts might drive the Prince of Darkness away. Of course, Luther not only grappled with hell at the Wartburg. He also remembered his adversaries on earth and his harassed friends Spalatin and Melanchthon, and some printing presses had their hands full publishing his polemical tracts and treatises such as the one against Hieronymus Emser, "the goat of Leipzig," or against the theologian J. Latomus of Louvain, and on monastic vows. What especially enraged Luther was that, "against his better knowledge and from pure greed," the cardinal archbishop of Mainz had opened an exhibition of his relics in Halle to see if the depressing game of indulgences for money could be played some more. Luther reacted promptly with a cutting tract, *Against the Idol at Halle.* But at the instigation of Wolfgang Capito who, in spite of a clearly reformist persuasion, had entered the service of the archbishop in late 1519, the elector and Spalatin prevented the publication of the pamphlet. Yet Luther saw to it that a vehement written protest was transmitted to Mainz which the cardinal answered immediately with an incomprehensibly humble apology. As one reads this document, one involuntarily rubs one's eyes, for after an introductory explanation the cardinal writes that the cause of the complaint has long since been dealt with and then continues: "And I will, so help me God, conduct myself as is proper for a devout spiritual prince, insofar as God will give me grace. For I can do nothing unaided and confess that I need God's grace, considering that I am a poor sinner who can sin and err and who sins and errs daily which I do not deny. I know full well that without God's grace, there is nothing good about me, and that I am as useless and stinking a piece of excrement as anyone else, and perhaps more." This incredible letter illustrates lightninglike the very peculiar situation in Mainz where it had all begun and where the mediating Capito, reformer in Strassburg after 1523, had assumed the role of "rear guard." After this, not much time passed until it became known that the man who was generally believed to be dead was very much alive indeed. While this does not mean that his hiding place was discovered, the "secret services" which already existed at that time now began their inquiries and thus made Luther's safety increasingly precarious.

Title page of the papal bull Exsurge Domine of 1520, which threatened Luther with the ban if he did not retract in sixty days.

Bulla contra errores
Martini Lutheri
z sequacium.

# IV

## 1. NEW "REFORMERS" AND "REVOLUTIONARIES" ENDANGER THE REFORM

Although he certainly did not take the "stinking piece of excrement" literally, Luther could consider the letter from Mainz as a kind of success. But from his beloved Wittenberg which many even today consider the "new Rome," very disquieting and then alarming news reached the Wartburg.

It all began with the tiresome question of celibacy, a kind of perennial problem in the life of the Church that was due for yet another eruption in the sixteenth century. Like most theologians today, Luther advocated a magnanimous solution. The case of his former student Bartholomaeus Bernhardi who, as provost of Kemberg, had married his own cook did not really present itself as a problem to him. But his magnanimity had its limits. What stand was one to take on the celibacy of monks which was based on a solemn vow to God? Luther became restless when, in the name of "evangelical freedom," monks suddenly started deserting their monasteries. His unease increased when his respected colleague Karlstadt—once again ahead of his time—suddenly became engaged to the young Anna von Mochau and promptly married her on January 19, 1522.

It is not at all remarkable and perfectly in keeping with our modern experience that, at about the same time, the reform of the liturgy which Luther planned to undertake after returning from the Wartburg became an urgent need. Again it was Karlstadt but also the Augustinian Gabriel Zwilling who forged ahead. They composed an "evangelical mass," did away with the abomination of private masses, and polemicized against the veneration of the sacrament outside of mass. Luther had become so restless that, at considerable risk, he traveled secretly to Wittenberg on December 2 to find out first hand what he could about this stormy development. And during the next few days, the first tumults did in fact occur: armed students and burghers drove the priests from their altars, mocked the monks in the Barfüsserkloster, and interfered with their private masses.

The elector who had earlier appointed a commission threatened punishment, but even he could not keep the pot from boiling over. Broad segments of the community backed the demand for "liturgical reform": free preaching of the gospel, the abolition of private masses, the lay chalice, and, to prove a superior morality, the closing of inns and whorehouses.

In spite of another prohibition by the authorities and in order to create a fait accompli before the elector could intervene, Karlstadt again took action: for New Year's Day, he announced the first "German mass"—it was actually celebrated at Christmas—with the words of consecration spoken out loud, without the Canon, ceremonies, and priestly vestments, without confession preceding the mass, and with communion under both kinds. The impression was enormous. At their chapter meeting on January 6, the congregation of German Augustinians left it up to the friars to decide whether to abandon the monastery. Those who remained were to earn their bread as preachers, teachers, or craftsmen. Begging was henceforth prohibited. On January 11, Zwilling gave the signal for the attack on images and side altars which were forcibly taken from the churches. A few days later, Karlstadt, who wished to avoid trouble, arranged for the official removal of the images by the magistrate.

But the pot kept boiling. For suddenly, the "Zwickau Prophets," the weavers Nikolaus Storch and Thomas Drechsel, together with Melanchthon's former disciple Markus Stübner, made their appearance in Wittenberg. Their concern is not the reform of the liturgy but the Holy Spirit who guides them directly by the "inner word," whereby they can readily do without the "outer word" and the sacraments but especially—and this has a familiar ring—infant baptism. They are terribly "moral" and "spiritual" and dream of hanging the priests and the godless so as to finally institute "God's Kingdom." Melanchthon, in whose house Stübner finds lodging, is disquieted but impressed by a doctrine that one cannot simply reject.

Although the Zwickau Prophets, being a wholly new and alien element, do not really fit into the concept of the "Wittenberg Reformation," they inspire Karlstadt, Zwilling and the zealous citizenry. Under Karlstadt's influence, the town council issues the "Order of the City of Wittenberg" which gives the initiative a quasi-communal and political basis. In addition to giving the above-mentioned programmatic points official sanction, the order combines the church revenues in a common social fund, the so-called "common chest."

The orthodox canons complained to the elector who had already received a decree from the Imperial Governing Council dated January 22, 1522, that ordered him to proceed with the competent bishops against the attempts at radical reform. But because no prompt intervention could be expected from the elector, and because the cathedral chapters, university, and magistrate were helpless in face of what was happening, Melanchthon and the council turned to Luther and requested that he return to Wittenberg.

The situation left Luther no choice. The elector seriously warned him not to come back because he could not protect him, but it is likely that he secretly awaited his return.

Luther's prompt decision is typical of his personality and his understanding of reform. It was characteristic of both the man and the Christian that every time he found himself in a life-threatening crisis, he confronted danger with poise, serenity, and total commitment, yet not without skill, reflection, and even reserve.

After some companionable tippling with the captain of the citadel the evening before, Luther set out on March 1, 1522, during a light rain.

At the very first stop, there occurred a delightful episode which we may be sure Luther enjoyed to the fullest, despite all his worries. While resting at the Black Bear inn in Jena, he makes the acquaintance of two Swiss students from St. Gallen who are on their way to Wittenberg to study theology. Still in his exceptionally becoming disguise as "Junker Jörg" with a real beard, jerkin, and sword, Luther strikes up an amusing conversation with them and invites them to his table. He wants to find out what the great Erasmus is up to in Basel, and the students are curious to learn whether they'll run into Luther in Wittenberg. Luther can assure them that they won't but there is Melanchthon from whom he urges them to learn Greek, although it would be even better if they started in on Hebrew at the same time, a piece of advice

the two may not have found to their liking. The episode ends with a marvelous discovery scene for which the garrulous innkeeper is responsible: he informs his solvent guest that the students take him for Ulrich von Hutten whereas he—the innkeeper—is absolutely certain that he can be none other than Doctor Luther. To which the mysterious knight answers jokingly that he will soon turn into a mockingbird.

At one of the following stops, Borna, there is more good beer for which the host, Michael von der Strassen, is famous throughout the land, but there is further bad news about Wittenberg and Luther must finally inform the elector of his decision. On March 5, he writes the letter to Frederick the Wise which scholarship justifiably regards as the most powerful he ever wrote and which documents impressively that, with all his respect and love for his prince, Luther was anything but a lackey. Substantially, Luther tells the worried elector that he is setting out on the dangerous journey to Wittenberg without counting on the protection of a prince with so little faith and that there is no reason for worry. For the protection under which he stands is so powerful that he could more easily protect the elector than the elector could protect him.

This is typical Luther, and besides he was right. In Wittenberg, where he arrived on the evening of March 6, he conducted himself much more intelligently and diplomatically than his character and his resoluteness would have led one to expect.

This is the first time, and at the very beginning of the actual Reformation, that Luther is dealing with "adversaries" from his own camp. He is guided by concern for the Church and the gospel. Arch conservative that he is, and instinctively opposed to all tumult and violent overthrow, he obeys both the will of the elector and the decree of the Imperial Governing Council.

He quite literally breaks the resistance of the citizens and the people by the power of the "word." From the first through the second Sunday of Lent, he spends every day in the pulpit of the parish church, his tonsure newly trimmed and wearing his monk's cowl, and preaches against all those who, without considering the weak, propose to make a new law out of the freedom according to the gospel. Except for private mass, everything the overly zealous reformers had abolished is reinstated. Even the service Luther will elaborate in 1523 will still contain a Latin mass although there is no mention of sacrifice.

The discussion with the originators of the Wittenberg reforms leads to major complications. Karlstadt vigorously resists the abolition of the "order" he has inspired and insults Luther, calling him "a neo-papist." Luther defends himself indirectly at first, then strikes back by openly attacking the "fanatics" (Schwärmer). In this process, slogans are first heard and limits are apparent that become typical of the Reformation.

It is worthwhile to reflect on the questions that arose here—their conditions, their developing differences, and their themes—related, in spite of all their differences, both from Luther's and from his adversaries' perspectives. For Luther, there unfolds here the wide field of a problematic whose extent he cannot immediately gauge, which his own mistakes helped create, and which cannot advance toward resolution without further mistakes—which will, indeed, ultimately prove irresolvable and which he must then accept as a misfortune.

He first discovers that his mysterious and painstaking effectiveness as "father in the faith" (he never referred to himself by that term, of course, however fond he may have been of identifying with Abraham and Paul) is matched by the not altogether fortunate impact of his works, which was much more immediate than could ever have been anticipated. By his carefully worked out biblical lectures, his unusually extensive activity as a preacher, his printed sermons, his devout writings and countless, very personal letters, his catechisms and hymns and his translation of the Bible, he became a "father in the faith" to many but this occurred in a process that is very difficult to describe. While at the Wartburg, he translated the New Testament in eleven weeks. The translation of the Old Testament, on which other experts and scholars collaborated, dragged on until 1534. While minor critical objections can be made to it, the Luther Bible, which made countless printers rich and never returned a penny to its author, is not only creative in terms of its language but, more importantly, a spiritual achievement. It is, quite literally, God's powerful and creative Word which comes to man through Luther's mouth and which, by its very nature, cannot remain without effect. No one, whether Protestant or Catholic, should dispute this, however critical one's attitude toward Luther may otherwise be.

But the impact of this work over time is a wholly different matter, for that is something which the author is no longer solely responsible for, nor is he in most cases its direct cause.

It is perfectly normal that others invoked Luther's work as they made his demands and concerns their own, or that they simply moved into the terrain Luther had staked out. Luther's call to "Christian freedom," his insistence that all who are baptized have fundamentally

Signatures of reformers on the Marburg Articles of 1529: Martinus Lutherus, Justus Jonas, Philippus Melanchthon, Andreas Osiander, Stephanus Agricola, Johannes Brenzius, Johannes Oecolampadius, Huldrychus Zwinglius, Martinus Bucerus, Caspar Hedio.

the same right, and his invocation of the "priesthood of all the faithful" a powerful though unfortunately not wholly unambiguous formulation which we find especially in the programmatic writings of 1520/21 against the tyranny of the pope undoubtedly point in this direction.

With reference to the Wittenberg unrest, this means that it was perfectly normal that during the time of his politically motivated absence, his Wittenberg friends should address themselves to the task of liturgical reform, for they believed they knew that, and how, Luther would take up this matter immediately upon his return. It is no surprising that the initiative here did not come from a professor like Karlstadt but from Gabriel Zwilling and his fellow friars in the Black Cloister for whom the reform of the liturgy, monasticism, and celibacy had suddenly become problems which no longer brooked delay. It is to Luther's merit that after his secret visit to Wittenberg, he did not insist on his exclusive ability, let alone right as "super-reformer," but that he initially wrote to Spalatin: "Everything I see and hear pleases me greatly. May God strengthen the spirit of those who are of good will."

He was actually angry with Spalatin who had withheld his tracts on monasticism and private masses for reasons of ecclesiastical politics. One cannot eternally dispute

Title page of a sermon on the Lord's Supper from 1520, before Luther developed his sharp polemic against the private mass and the sacrifice of the mass in general.

about God's Word and be indifferent to practical consequences. If nothing is to be changed in practice, then our teaching should not have been different either. Luther was also the first to feel this unrest that pushed him to action. It infected the normally cautious Melanchthon who impatiently stated in a disputation with Karlstadt in October 1521: "Someone has to make a start, otherwise nothing will happen." And here it is Karlstadt who affirms reform but rejects tumult, who denies transsubstantiation but demands the adoration of the sacramental bread, and is even willing, if necessary, to allow private mass where communion under both species depends on it.

It did not unsettle Luther that other Christians and "reformers" suddenly appeared and filled out the ecclesiastical space he had created in their own way.

Yet the dangers that attended such an "appropriation" of what were originally Luther's concerns is apparent. In the reform of the mass, Zwilling's enthusiasm but also Karlstadt's favorite idea of a "congregational Christianity" soon came to distort Luther's concerns. This applies even more to the new and autonomous initiatives that others deployed in Luther's historical sphere: the "Zwickau Prophets" who show up in Wittenberg soon prove to be "fanatics" and sectarians who, invoking the "spirit" and the "inner word," undermine the teaching of the gospel concerning the incarnate "outer word," the "alien and extraneous" grace and righteousness of Christ, the effective signs of the sacrament and the office of the Church, and who, with their rigorous insistence on the Kingdom of God—however justified their readiness to act may be—either end up in the desert of a self-chosen isolation or in the rebellion and violence the Anabaptists. I know that Luther's global and vituperative terms—"fanatic, iconoclast, agitator"—simplify and inadmissibly confound what could very well be distinguished by its descent from the Waldensians and Cathari. But traditions do not intermingle only in Luther but in history as well. Even the "Thomist" professor Karlstadt fell under the influence of the Zwickau Prophets, just as the altogether different Thomas Müntzer became involved in the Peasents' War via Zwickau, Bohemia, and Mühlhausen, and was finally executed after severe torture, although his activity as a fanatic preacher of the peasants had been episodic and of a mere three weeks' duration.

The course of the Reformation in southern Germany was similar and yet quite different. For here, very independent reformers such as Ulrich Zwingli, Johannes Oecolampadius, and Joachim Vaidan, and later, after

Zwingli's death, Heinrich Bullinger and Jean Calvin in Switzerland, or Wolfgang Capito and Martin Bucer from Strassburg who were more inclined toward compromise, each shouldered the great task in Luther's wake but in their own way. Luther also shaped the history of his influence by the paradoxical openness of his concerns and their increasing virulence in controversy and polemics.

This can be impressively illustrated by the unrest in Wittenberg, specifically over the proposed abolition of private mass. In November 1521, from the Wartburg, Luther had already demanded the immediate abolition of private mass in an aggressive tract, *De abroganda missa privata*, but its prompt publication had been prevented by Spalatin. What did this demand involve? Since nowadays, not even young Catholics know what this curious term refers to, a brief explanation is in order: private masses are not part of the worship of the community but are celebrated in the absence of a congregation by an individual priest at one of the many side altars, quietly and privately. The priest is assisted by a server or sacristan who may perform this function for several other celebrating priests at the same time. Decisive in the development of this form of mass after the tenth century were the countless ordained monks such as those at Cluny who not only manifested their spirituality in the celebration of private masses—a spirituality cut off from pastoral duties in the community—but who through the celebration of countless sacrifices of the mass, over and above the choir office, actually and "officially" strengthened the notion of monasticism as the "praying power" of the Church. Private masses soon became somewhat of a necessity as the growth of prayer associations and the resulting endowed masses for the dead led to such a number of promised masses that the obligation could only be discharged in this way. This was not only the beginning of the medieval system of endowments but also the beginning of a concept of priesthood which consciously omitted preaching and general pastoral duties and led to the rise of the so-called mass priests.

The removal of the side altars in Wittenberg and elsewhere was done with less harshness. We will also understand not only why Luther demanded the immediate abolition of private masses and the abuses they gave rise to but why his criticism now became more vehement as he also disputed the notion of the mass as a sacrifice. Theologically, both points are closely connected. For Luther believed he had understood the following ominous nexus: anyone who, remembering the "once and for all" character of Christ's sacrifice on the cross, makes a sacrifice anew, so that the indefinitely repeatable offering

Title page of Luther's sharpest and much criticized writing on the Peasant Revolt, Against the Robbing and Murdering Mobs of Peasants (1525).

of the sacrifice of the mass in return for a small stipend one may have its infinite fruit benefit certain of the living (to aid them in all that troubles them, from a toothache or syphilis to the urgently implored death of a bothersome fellow human being) or the dead, misuses not only the mass but avails himself of the sacrifice of the mass to justify the abuse. As the title of the German version of the tract, *Vom Missbrauch der Messe* ("On the Abuse of the Mass") clearly indicates, Luther's more virulent criticism does not directly address the sacrifice but merely a false notion of sacrifice as the basis for the entire abortive development. Yet this polemically pointed rejection

153

of what is in fact an untenable view of the mass as sacrifice had a negative effect on Luther's doctrine of the mass. For the inclusion of the Christian in Christ's sacrifice—a fundamental concern that Luther never surrendered—can now no longer be grounded in the original, properly understood sacrifice but occurs through the "Word" and without visible relation to the mass. Despite laudable liturgical reforms designed to make it more of a congregational service, the mass loses importance, because although respect for the sacrament of the altar increases, it becomes no more than communion, to be celebrated after the sermon. But because Luther unswervingly held to the true presence of the Lord under, in, and with the bread and the wine, and to the reintroduction of communion under both kinds, the reduction of the mass to mere remembrance which can be observed in Reformed churches did not take place.

Thus it came about that in the course of the intra-reformist differentiation of creeds, the real presence of the Lord in the sacrament became an article of faith over which, even after Luther's death, people and confessions will differ.

Making it clear for oneself why the other reformers disputed the real presence of the Lord in the Eucharist can be illuminating. Karlstadt, Luther's fellow Wittenberg reformer who acted so lucklessly in his shadow, was the first to let himself be sufficiently carried away to put forward this radical thesis. He certainly did not hold this view from malice and was not conscious of it at first. For in connection with the unrest at Wittenberg, he initially cared only about the liturgical reform of the "German mass," that is, a mass with the words of institution in German and communion under both kinds, where the dispensing with priestly vestments and the touching of the Eucharistic bread and the chalice by the laity were to make clear that there was no need of a special office for the celebration of mass because all are priests and celebrate the service as such. For Karlstadt, the reform of the external form of the mass was not a mere correction of ceremonies which might be assigned a subordinate place for the time being, as Luther held. From the very beginning, he therefore considered as sin communion under bread only, which Luther initially tolerated and whose validity he did not dispute. The question concerning the real presence of the Lord had not yet become a problem for Karlstadt during this phase, but in the course of time it necessarily became one where the distinction between mass and Christ's sacrifice on the cross or the adoration owed the Eucharistic forms was at stake. But when the question really arose for Karlstadt, he could give only a negative answer. For ultimately, he

knew of only two modes of Christ's presence—the historical bloody one on the cross and the "glorified one in the splendor of heaven" which Christ will abandon only at the end of time, when he comes to sit in judgment. A "third advent" or a spiritual and sacramental presence in the sense of the physical if unbloody presence of him who sacrificed himself for us on the cross under and in the forms of the Eucharist does not exist for Karlstadt. Because of this, Karlstadt, a realist who had originally belonged to the Thomist school of the *via antiqua,* must deny Christ's real presence in the sacrament. Perhaps excessively ridiculed by Luther, he explained the words of institution in the same childish and primitive way in which people, centuries earlier, had seriously asked, "what precisely does the mouse eat" when it nibbles at the consecrated host. When, at the last supper, Christ said to his apostles—and this is how Karlstadt deals with the difficulty—"this is my body," he did not point to the bread but to his own body. Thus we are to eat and drink from the chalice "in remembrance," in grateful recognition of the fact that he gave his body and shed his blood for us.

It was only gradually, and with complete openness only after he was driven from Electoral Saxony, that Karlstadt came to espouse this teaching. Despite their primitive theology, his writings found an unusually strong echo all over the land but especially in southern Germany and Switzerland. It was the first time Luther had to use the weapon of his against a "fanatic" from his own camp, indeed from among his closest fellow reformers. Henceforth, he will be obliged to do this time and again, and in always the same issue which naturally increasingly dampened his hope for a reformation within the Church. Compared to Karlstadt's childish and primitive approach, the reasons for the denial of the real presence by Zwingli and Oecolampadius become ever more sublime, learned, and persuasive. Soon, there are efforts at compromise that come via Strassburg and Bucer and impress even Melanchthon and, in a different way, the great Erasmus. Indeed, due to the promptings of the theologians of mediation and Protestant princes such as Philip of Hesse, negotiations and quasi-ecumenical attempts were made to arrive at an agreement that would satisfy all sides. But although Luther could not reject such efforts in principle, he remained skeptical about all efforts at mediation and unyielding on substantive issues. Although under the pressure of events he had himself set in motion, as it were, he made the attempt to combat his ever more powerful enemies by advancing theological proof of the real presence which was being disputed with so much scholarship. But the doctrine of ubiquity which he developed in this connection, according to which Christ, like the "omnipresent Lord," is simultaneously present everywhere in heaven and on earth, finally failed to bring the desired clarification and merely created new theological problems. Yet undeterred by all ultimately irresolvable questions, Luther held fast to the mystery of the real sacramental presence even when this led to accusation that he had relapsed into "papism." Luther was perfectly aware of this nexus.

In an important open letter "To the Christians in Strassburg," in which he attacks Karlstadt, he does not hesitate to say how considerable his own doubts about the real presence had originally been (circa 1520) and how much Karlstadt's argument would have delighted him at the time since it would not only have rid him of his own difficulties but enabled him to deal the papacy the greatest blow, for it would have given the mass the decisive push. But "being held captive" by the powerful text of Scripture, he could not abandon his position even when it benefited the papacy. This was Luther's line throughout his life. He also stuck to it when he made a demand that was usually relinquished and insisted that the celebration and administration of the Eucharist was the office of the Church so that Christians without an ordained priest must dispense with communion. And finally, he took the same line throughout his life and particulary in facing the danger of a definitive break with Melanchthon, when he obstinately rejected "ecumenical" recognition of the Holy Communion of other Reformed churches or the admission of Christians with different views to communion in his own Church.

The correctly understood history of the impact Luther had thus shows with great clarity how distanced and critical his attitude toward the historical Reformation ultimately was. It is true, of course, that he had a causal efficacy in this context, whether it be that in the heat of controversies he let himself be goaded into exaggerated theses as when he denied the sacrificial character of the mass, or formulated the ubiquity doctrine with its consequences, or onesidedly emphasized the priesthood of all the faithful; whether it be that his paradoxical statements on the freedom of the Christian, on justification through the "alien justice" of Christ, on "sinning boldly," or on the relationship between law and gospel were misunderstood and caused misinterpretations on the part of his followers. Wherever he could, Luther corrected the misinterpretations of his concerns as, for example, the peasants' call for unrestricted "freedom," the right certain laymen claimed to administer Holy Communion to their families, or the onesided proclamation of the gospel at the expense of the law.

Through his protest, his unyielding demands for corrections, and his intransigence in matters of truth, Luther not only involved himself in states of violent tension with most other reformers—quite apart from his animosity toward "papists" and "fanatics"—he also isolated himself to a considerable degree and allowed himself to be isolated where the development of a new ecclesiasticism or negotiations over ecclesiastical policy at the imperial level were involved. Since negotiations were not his strong suit, he participated only reluctantly and suspiciously in the intrareformist religious discussions as in Marburg (1529) or at the Wittenberg accord negotiations (1536). He did not join at all in discussion with representatives of the old Church, because an exchange of views with the "Antichrist" simply made no sense to him. Yet his relationship to the hopelessly decadent papal Church was closer, more positive, and more deeply rooted than that with "fanatics" and "sectarians," between whom and reformers such as Karlstadt, Müntzer, or Zwingli he hardly differentiated.

Luther's position along these lines is extremely difficult and necessarily becomes more so in the course of time, as his relations with Karlstadt show. As Luther confronts him, Thomas Müntzer, or others, he bears a responsibility which he knows he must fulfil but does not know. He will not be the "pope"; he does not see himself as "bishop"; he does not differ from the rest in being a "doctor of theology"; and they also invoke Scripture. In his defense of the real presence, Luther time and again must deal with the argument that this article of faith cannot be proven from Scripture, which means that he discover that the "scriptural principle" in this form is ill suited to protect the purity of the *Doctrina Evangelii* in every respect.

We may believe Luther nonetheless when he says that he did not really want to use force in his disputes with Karlstadt and other adversaries but that he ultimately trusted only the power of the word and of truth. He was perfectly serious when he wrote with reference to Karlstadt and Müntzer: "Let the spirits confront and strike one another... For we who carry the word of God should not fight with the first... Our function is to preach and to endure, not to strike with fists and to defend ourselves."

Yet finally the use of force against poor Karlstadt who certainly deserves our compassion became inevitable. It is no defense that it was the "secular power" of the elector or of the university that took steps against him. Luther discovered that even after the abolition of the tyranny of the pope and his decretals, the Church cannot be led without violence, the ban, dismissals, or even secular force.

Yet Karlstadt was anything but blameless in this development. It is true that the reproach of being "rebellious" does not apply to him. He had sought to avoid the destruction of images in Wittenberg by having the magistrate carry out the measures legally. And three days after the new order had gone into effect, he complained to the authorities that the images and side altars had still not been removed from the churches. Nor can it be shown that Karlstadt was involved in the uprising of the peasants. Yet he impressed those around him as a "fanatic." Quite apart from the theological difficulties and tensions, he irritated university and Church by an anti-intellectualism and social commitment which would certainly have earned him the sympathy of today's restless students. The formerly so proud prelate and university professor suddenly renounced his official garb and academic titles and went to live as "a new layman" in the parish of Orlamünde to whose revenues he was entitled as archdeacon of the All Saints collegiate chapter. He criticized the dogmatism of the new academic exegesis and emphasized the right and duty of the laity to read and interpret the Bible itself. In the midst of an active lay congregation, he carried through his reform of the liturgy and his idea of a "mature community" exercizing the "priesthood of all believers." In his view of community, a curious mysticism of "union with the divine will" combined with the practical social notion of communities established for a "better justice." His ideal takes on an even more aggressive quality by the sincerely meant nonviolence of all his undertakings.

When, in March 1524, the university recalled Karlstadt because it wanted him to resume his ecclesiastical and academic obligations, he reacted logically, radically, and yet impressively nonviolently, and was admired for it by his followers. Together with his congregation, he insisted on the right to choose priests of their own and thus put the Wittenbergians publicly in the wrong, for they were denying the "mature congregation" a right they demanded for themselves. Invoking his conscience, he then renounced his position as pastor and archdeacon and bought a small farm so that henceforth he might live honestly by the work of his hands. However unmodern Karlstadt may have been, this gesture shows a striking modernity. His story could take place today anywhere in the world, but unfortunately no university, no bishop, and no church today would refrain from taking steps against this "new layman" and "peasant."

The inevitable consequence was the inhuman expulsion of Karlstadt and his pitiable family from Electoral Saxony on September 18, 1524. He went to southern Germany and, via Strassburg and Basel, finally came to Rothenburg. Here he published five treatises on the Lord's Supper on communion which had an exceptional resonance and provoked Luther into taking a position against him. The outbreak of the Peasants' War increased the acrimony of the polemics. Many sided with Karlstadt, and even Melanchthon disapproved of the exceptional sharpness of Luther's attacks. Soon finding himself between the two sides in the Peasants' War, Karlstadt could not remain in Rothenburg. Even in his mother's home in Karlstadt, he found no rest. From Frankfurt, he finally turned to Luther, and his greatest enemy obtained the elector's permission for Karlstadt to return to Saxony. Karlstadt affirmed that he would no longer write, preach or teach. He had never participated in the unrest and regarding the Lord's Supper he had, apart from his willingness to be instructed, meant only to inquire rather than assert. Luther found this recantation acceptable, and with the elector's permission Karlstadt found lodgings in a village near Kemberg where he laboriously and under supervision earned a living for himself and his family, first as a farmer, then as a grocer. In the spring of 1529, he again shook off the restraint and escaped from his misery. In May 1530 he visited Zwingli in Zürich where he was employed first as a proofreader and then as a deacon. After Zwingli's death, he again lost everything until he found a final field of activity as preacher and professor in Basel (June 1534). Bullinger, Zwingli's successor, found Karlstadt "very easy to get along with, modest, humble, and unobjectionable in every way," and noted this with pleasure because it meant that Luther's inhuman misjudgment had finally been demonstrated. We should add that to earn his praise, Karlstadt had once again changed employment. In the service of the Swiss Reformed Church, he simply renounced expressing earlier personal convictions. Just as back in Wittenberg in 1518 he would have liked to dispute the great Master Eck on the indulgence problem before Luther did, so he now went back to writing disputation theses and presided as future masters and doctors, but no "laymen," obtained their degrees. He resumed his former titles and again wore professorial garb. On December 24, 1541, in Basel, death from the plague finally freed him from the self-imposed task always to be ahead of Luther, whether in marriage or the reform of the liturgy. I am not being ironic when I note that in death he finally succeeded. He preceded Luther in death and went to meet the universal judge who will judge both.

Meanwhile, Luther took care of the widow and son whose Christian baptism he had already seen to earlier though probably not altogether selflessly. Luther's belated and hardly very intense care for the survivors was probably insufficient to make up for the hardness he had been guilty of toward Karlstadt. This applies equally to his hardness toward Müntzer or the passionately reviled Zwingli, the peasants and the Jews, the pope and papists of all shades, but also to mediators like Bucer or his friends such as Johann Agricola and even Melanchthon. The acrimony and impulsiveness of his polemics deserve reproof and should not be dismissed by simply saying that Luther was no saint.

But at the level of moral criticism, Luther is not without excuse. For although it was certainly true that Karlstadt, his wife, and child were forced into a wretched existence for the sake of the freedom of his teaching, he was not blameless for his fate. Led astray by the spirit of the times, he always wanted more than he could achieve. As a learned professor of theology from the *via antiqua* school he could have lived peacefully in Cologne, Ingolstadt, or elsewhere. Even as layman or farmer, it is unlikely that much would have happened to him even in Electoral Saxony had he only wanted it. It must also be conceded that in spite of the sharpness of the disputes Luther treated his difficult colleague, teacher, and former fellow worker neither hatefully nor inhumanly. He did not avoid personal exchanges or refuse to mediate, nor did he turn Karlstadt's wife out of the house when she defended her husband. Even more, he received and played the host to his adversary even when Karlstadt, fleeing from the agents of the elector, knocked at the gate of the Black Cloister on Luther's wedding night. This gesture characterizes Luther the human being and sets him apart from the great Erasmus who mercilessly showed the deathly ill Ulrich von Hutten the door when he sought his protection, although he no longer had reason to fear contagion. Anyone who criticizes Luther's occasionally excessive severity in fighting his adversaries should also mention his unmatched readiness for conciliation.

But the judgment of historians and of church historians in particular is altogether different. It is simply false to assert that Karlstadt and all those for whom he stands in the present context had fundamentally the same right as Luther claimed for himself. The sole historical reality here, and therefore immune from the criticism that Luther is being inappropriately turned into a hero, is that he and his "adversaries" did not act at the same level. This applies not only to Karlstadt, Müntzer, and the "fa-

natics" but also to reformers such as Zwingli and even fellow reformers like Melanchthon, Spalatin, Jonas, or Johannes Brenz. This does not make Luther a Hercules or an incomparable "prophet," but makes a claim that corresponds perfectly with the position Luther, in spite of human weakness and sin, occupies in and for the Church, a position into which he grew or was led and which he has retained for Christianity even since his death. It is a fateful and unpleasant position, full of difficulties not only for its occupant but also for the person who tries to define it honestly and without hidden motives.

For, on the one hand, such a person must contradict the admiring judgment of those who see Luther's position as the result of an achievement that had the coherence of a work of genius. But in spite of his genius and his responsible and bold commitment, the truth is more complex and paradoxical and therefore ultimately more significant. Luther was no reformer with a fully elaborated concept. Time and again he compared himself to Paul whose fate he thought it was to give offense wherever he went simply because he wished to serve truth unreservedly. This was the reason he found himself on a path he had not chosen but along which Christians are led and which takes one where one does not wish to go.

One must also contradict the judgment of those who honestly and matter-of-factly take Luther for the reformer of the Church that bears his name to this day. Luther belongs to the *ecclesia apud nos,* of course, as it spread from Wittenberg throughout the world. But one cannot overlook the immense difficulties that Lutherans had then and have today when they are asked to define his significance for the "Lutheran Church" and their faith. At the present time, there is increasing reluctance to call him a "reformer" and that reluctance is indeed well founded. For while the "Reformation" lived off his intellectual impulses, it adopted neither his concerns nor his legacy. Especially at the end of the development, the history of Luther's impact in the Reformation presents itself as a "putting to use of remnants" which one invokes when it suits one's purposes.

Finally, one must contradict the seemingly unshakable judgment of "papists" and their successors who, especially during the most recent period, cling resolutely to their original condemnation and scold Luther as a "heretic" and a "divider of the Church." We have suggested that there is some truth in this. But it is fundamentally false that Luther had no message for the "old Church" or has none in a changed situation, and that he wanted a "new" one. Although his readiness to negotiate was nothing like Melanchthon's and Melanchthon's passionate efforts to prevent the splitting of the Church, Luther remains for the Roman Church the extremely bothersome but irreplaceable partner in a reform which he himself did not bring off but which no one acting without or against him has been able to carry out to this day.

*Summa summarum:* As at the Wartburg and yet quite differently, Luther again becomes "Junker Jörg" for all. Walking the path of Abraham, he becomes a stranger to all yet moves toward the goal on behalf of all.

ILLUSTRATION SEQUENCE V

"PROTESTANTS"—COLLOQUY OF MARBURG—
AUGSBURG CONFESSION—
REFORMATION ALTARPIECES—
RELIGIOUS PEACE OF NUREMBERG
1529–1532

61   The second Diet of Speyer in 1529 rescinded the temporary freedom of religion which the emperor, under the pressure of foreign policy problems, had been obliged to grant the estates. It also prohibited the further spread of the Reformation. The Evangelical estates protested against this decision which led to the designation "Protestants."—Record of the so-called "Reichstagsabschied" (decree of the Diet) of Speyer. Vienna, Haus-, Hof- und Staatsarchiv.

62   Landgrave Philip of Hesse (1504–1567) was one of the pioneers of the Reformation which he introduced in Hesse in 1526. Philip was a friend of the Swiss reformer Zwingli and attempted to eliminate the doctrinal differences between him and Luther in the Colloquy of Marburg. As the leader of the Schmalkaldic League (cf. no. 79), he became the emperor's prisoner (1547–1552) after losing the battle of Mühlberg.—Painting by Hans Crell (ascription). Stiftung Wartburg.

63   View of Marburg on the Lahn with the landgrave's castle and the church of St. Elisabeth. Mediated by the landgrave Philip of Hesse, the religious colloquy between Luther and Zwingli took place here between October 1 and 3, 1529, but differing views of the Lord's Supper prevented agreement. Whereas Zwingli interpreted Holy Communion as no more than a symbolic remembrance, Luther always upheld the real presence of the Lord in the bread and the wine. After the colloquy made the divergence between the two definitive, the fifteen Articles of Marburg were published. Fourteen of them expressed a common conviction, and it was only in the question of the Lord's Supper that agreement could not be reached.

64   Epitaph in the Wittenberg town church for Paul Eber, Old Testament professor at Wittenberg University and pastor at the castle church. Painted in 1569 by Lucas Cranach the Younger.—The painting shows the Parable of the Laborers in the Vineyard which is clearly being interpreted with reference to the Reformation. The upper part corresponds to Matthew 21:43: "Therefore I tell you, the kingdom of God will be taken away from you and given to a nation producing the fruits of it." Whereas the left part of the vineyard in which representatives of the Roman Church are working shows signs of neglect, the reformers are working in the right part of the vineyard. One can spot Luther with the rake. To his left, Paul Eber is trimming the vines. At the well are Melanchthon and Johannes Forster with a bucket, Johannes Bugenhagen with a hoe, and above them Caspar Cruciger and Justus Jonas who are placing supports under the vines. Georg Major and Paul Crell are busy above Luther. The paying of the workers in the vineyard who are represented by ecclesiastical dignitaries alludes to the final words of the parable: "So the last will be first, and the first last." A further allusion to events of the Reformation lies in the name of the donor Paul Eber ("boar"), for in Leo X's bull threatening excommunication, we read: "all the saints, including Peter and Paul, are being called on for help against the wild boar" (a reference to Martin Luther).

65/66   Martin Luther with rake, Philip Melanchthon at the well.
Two details from the epitaph of Paul Eber. The figures of Luther and Melanchthon correspond to Luther's comment, "I must root out the logs and trunks, cut away the thorns and hedges, and fill up the ponds. I am the rude forester who must break and dress a path. But Master Philip proceeds evenly and quietly, builds and plants, sows and waters with pleasure, as God abundantly gave him the talent to do" (Preface to Melanchthon's *Epistle to the Colossians*, 1529).

67   Coburg castle, whose oldest sections date back to the 12th and 13th centuries, was Luther's residence in 1530, during the Diet of Augsburg in which he could not participate because the Edict of Worms of 1521 had made him an outlaw.

68   Reformation altar by Lucas Cranach the Younger (1565) in the church of Kemberg, south of Wittenberg. When opened up, the great altarpiece shows the baptism of Christ and the resurrection on the wings, the Last Supper on the center panel, and, above it, the crucifixion and the ascension on the crown of the altar. Luther frequently gave sermons in Kemberg, for the pastor, Bartholomäus Bernhardi, had been his student and one of the earliest Wittenberg reformers. Like Luther, Melanchthon, and his son-in-law and successor, Matthias Wankel, he is shown among the reformers who are represented behind Christ's baptism on the left panel of the altar.

PHILIPPVS LANDT: GRAVE ZV
HESSĒ GRAVE ZV
ATZENELNBOGĒ
DIETZ ZIEGEN
HAIN VND NIDDA⟨

I·N·R·I

Johan
Chur
Sach

Georg Marg
Brandenburg

Ernst herzog zu
Braunschweig

Wolfgang furst zu
Anhaldt

Etlicher furtrefflicher Helden
der Augspurgischen Confessio
Keiser Carolo dem 5. übergeben
zubleit

PLVS VLTRA

Carolus V. Römischer Kaiser

Ferdinandus
Römischer König

Pfaltz
Abgesandter

Alexander Colbrecht D.
Rom. Kay. gehaim
Secretari

Alphonsus Waldesius D.
K. M. geheimer Secret.

Christian Bauwast Jac.
Rom. Kaiser. von Rath

Stadt
Nürnberg

Stadt
Reutlingen

Stadt
Welchkim

Stadt
Weÿssenburg

Stadt
Heilbrun

Stadt
Kempten

en und Stadt Behruaus welche sich
30. underschribe, und dem Großmechtigsten
standt Göttlicher genad steiff und vest darbej
vahr inen Gott helffe.

69  The gathering of the Evangelical estates at the Diet of Augsburg during which, on June 25, 1530, the Augsburg Confession was solemnly presented and read before the emperor and the empire. Philip Melanchthon had formulated the articles of the Confession because Luther, being an outlaw, could not be present. Luther commented: "I do not know what to improve or change nor would that be appropriate for I cannot step so lightly."

70  The Last Supper with the reformers as Christ's apostles. Altar painting for the castle church of St. Mary in Dessau, the last of the Reformation altars to be completed by Lucas Cranach the Younger, in 1565. The altarpiece, commissioned by Prince Joachim von Anhalt who, as the donor, is seen kneeling in the left foreground, shows on the left, next to Christ, his brother Georg, whom Luther had ordained in 1544 and of whom he had said: "Prince Georg is more pious than I am. If he should not enter heaven, I certainly won't." Next to him, we see Martin Luther, Johannes Bugenhagen, Justus Jonas, and Caspar Cruciger. To the right and next to Christ, seated, are Philip Melanchthon, followed by Johann Forster, Johann Pfeffinger, Georg Major, and Bartholomäus Bernhardi. In the background, standing, additional members of the house of Anhalt. In the right foreground, Lucas Cranach the Younger as cup bearer.

71  Christ as redeemer on the cross. Center section of the altarpiece in the town church of Sts. Peter and Paul in Weimar. The altar, donated by the elector Johann Friedrich who is shown with his wife and son on the inside panels, is the last work of the older Cranach and was completed by his son Lucas the Younger in 1555. The old painter can be seen standing next to John the Baptist and his friend Martin Luther to the right of the crucified Christ. Luther is pointing in the open Bible, to the last verse of chapter 4 of the Epistle to the Hebrews: "Let us then with confidence draw near to the throne of grace, that we may receive mercy and find grace to help in time of need." Above, we read: "The blood of Jesus his Son cleanses us from all sin" (1 John 1:7), and on the second page of the bible the following quotation from John 3:14–15: "And as Moses lifted up the serpent in the wilderness, even so must the Son of man be lifted up, that whoever believes in Him may have eternal life." These three passages aptly interpret the multiform theme of this altar: sin and redemption.

72  View across the old town and toward the citadel of Nuremberg. Here, Emperor Charles V had to conclude the Peace of Nuremberg because of the Turkish threat. Signed in 1532, it granted the members of the Evangelical Schmalkaldic League religious freedom until the council would be convoked.

73  Haiga Sophia in Constantinople, built in the 6th century by Emperor Justinian as the principal church of Christian Byzantium, was turned into a mosque after the Turkish conquest. During the same decade, the Turks conquered the Balkans and under Sulaymen I, advanced as far as Vienna in 1529. For the Reformation, the Turkish threat meant a time of calm development and consolidation during the fifteen years of the Nuremberg peace, and Luther said in one of his *Table Talks:* "The Turk is the salvation of the Evangelicals."

74  As the successor of his brother Frederick the Wise (cf. no. 40), the elector Johann (1468–1532) sided equally resolutely with Luther and the Reformation. He was a co-founder of the Schmalkaldic League (cf. no. 79) as whose leader his son Johann Friedrich (1503—1554) lost the electorate after being defeated by the troops of Emperor Charles V near Mühlberg.—Painting (circa 1515) by Lucas Cranach the Elder. Collection in Coburg Castle.

## 2. LUTHER SHOCKS
## THE PEASANTS BY HIS JUDGMENT
## AND THE DEVOUT BY HIS MARRIAGE

Nothing makes clearer how alien Luther can seem to us than his position on the Peasant's War which began in the spring of 1524 with the uprising of the Stühlingen peasants in the southern Black Forest and quickly spread into Swabia and Alsace, the Tirol and Carinthia, Franconia, Thuringia, and Saxony. Our contemporaries, attuned as they are to social issues, are especially offended by Luther's role here. Such a perspective makes it impossible to create understanding for Luther's position, and we must content ourselves with defending him against the most serious criticisms and present his concerns in their oddness but without distortion.

We may be certain that neither a questionable nor a political motive prompted Luther to adopt a position which is incomprehensible to many. He did not act as the princes' lackey or servant of established power, and was even less "the mindless, soft-living flesh in Wittenberg," the "father of obsequiousness," "sycophant," and "Doctor Liar" that his former admirer Thomas Müntzer, a man with an equal talent for trading insults and giving tit for tat, accused him of being. In his great "programmatic writings," he had made himself the speaker for a reform which, constant warnings against the "carnal" misunderstanding of the gospel notwithstanding, certainly did not exclude man's daily life, nor his longing for liberation from injustice and for the fulfilment of legitimate social desires.

There can be no doubt that Luther's reform contained very important suggestions for this-worldly reform and that therefore the peasants like the knights before them certainly did not lack justification in invoking Luther. Moreover, in his tract, *Von weltlicher Obrigkeit, wieweit man ihr Gehorsam schuldig sei* ("How Far Obedience to Secular Authority Must Go," 1523), he had resisted not only interference by the secular powers in the ecclesiastical sphere but had threatened divine wrath in severely criticizing tyranny, and the wilfulness and unlimited greed of princes in their dealing with peasants and burghers. In the middle of April 1525, the peasants turned directly to Luther. A delegation handed him the twelve articles with their demands. Everybody expected Luther to come down in favor of the peasants. The articles were so moderate, and this not just from today's point of view, that even Duke John who had taken over the business of government from the dying elector would have been willing to accept them. Why should Lu-

ther have objected that the peasants, invoking numerous biblical passages, demanded the free election of pastors, pure preaching, the use of the great tithe as salary for pastors (the original intent of that tax), the abolition of the lesser tithe, an end to serfdom, and the annulling of hunting and fishing privileges? Luther had a "fruitful talk" with the delegation, offered them food and drink, and promised that the would soon take a position. But the answer, *Ermahnung zum Frieden auf die zwölf Artikel der Bauernschaft in Schwaben,* in which he admonishes the peasants "not to misuse God's name," the manuscript of which was finished at the end April 1525, was the start of all the troubles that followed.

Sounding conciliatory, Luther nonetheless warns the peasants against confusing the two realms which would destroy secular authority and prevent the preaching of the gospel. How can the peasants invoke God's name and Christ's example if they go against Scripture by committing violence and refusing to obey authority? Luther reacts with particular annoyance to the demand that "servitude" be abolished "because Christ freed all of us." Anyone who argues like this understands "Christian freedom" carnally, according to him. For as a Christian, a serf certainly enjoys "Christian freedom." But those who wish "to make all equal" turn "Christ's spiritual realm" into a "secular and external one," and also threaten the order of the "secular realm" which is based on the "inequality" of people. Even the experience of injustice does not give the Christian the right to rebel against authority. But Luther also warns the lords emphatically not to abuse their power and admonishes them to stop "oppressing and taxing" the peasants.

In spite of all historical explanations—the serf of the Middle Ages was no slave and in Bavaria, for example, serfdom was not abolished until 1818, and in Russia not until 1863—and in spite of the modern insight that equal rights also create new dependencies and that one can even hang oneself on the "golden rope of freedom," Luther's fundamental thesis here makes excessive demands on our understanding. Even the significant observation that as theological postulates his demands do not preclude "social development" under "secular resonsibility" does not make our contemporaries more sympathetic.

But to the disappointment of the peasants and of modern Christians, things got even worse. For before the first tract which had been printed in May was published, Luther had written a second one in which, impressed no doubt by the unimaginable ferocity of the war and especially the atrocities committed by the peasants in Weinsberg, he turned indignantly and with great vehemence *Against the Robbing and Murderous Gangs of Peasants.*

Going beyond all permissible bounds, Luther now called on the princes to strike without pity. He takes the peasants for devils, their defeat for a divine service; they are to be slain like mad dogs.

Although the princes hardly needed Luther to encourage them, they carried out the slaughter with frightening savagery. As previously in Swabia, Württemberg, Franconia, and Hesse, Philip of Hesse and the dukes of Saxony and Braunschweig inflicted a crushing defeat on an army of eight thousand peasants near Frankenhausen on May 15, 1525. Thomas Müntzer who, confident of divine protection, had driven the fanaticized peasants into battle escaped into town but was discovered in his hiding place and executed a few days later after having been horribly tortured. All in all, one hundred thousand peasants were cruelly killed: shot, burned, beheaded, or blinded and maimed. The result was ghastly and can be excused neither by a conceivable motive nor the cruelty of medieval war.

In view of the horror of this, and of all later and all future wars, we do not propose to go searching for lame excuses for Luther. But we should realize that such an observation does not advance us any and that Luther's conduct affords no grounds for asserting that he was partly to blame for the awful end result. Although I do not consider speculation useless, I believe that it is idle to wonder whether the revolution of the peasants under Luther's leadership would have brought epochal social change. For the sake of the unpleasant truth, it must be noted that weighty theological reasons made it impossible for Luther to assume responsibility for a revolution. The catastrophe he foresaw for the peasants and which he surely did not want was, he felt, the lesser evil and the ineluctable punishment for their rebellion against God. All he can plead from a human moral point of view is this: his commitment was motivated by no opportunism of any kind. He did not make his decision in order to please the princes but because he considered rebellion unjust. And he made his decision although, along with the majority of his contemporaries, he was convinced that the revolution would be victorious which would have meant his certain death. In view of the situation, he therefore also had to acknowledge that without him the peasants' uprising would never had reached its terrible dimensions. In this sense, Luther assumed his guilt in 1533 when he said in a *Table Talk:* "Preachers are the greatest of all slayers. For they urge the authorities to execute their office strictly and punish the wicked. In the revolt I slew all the peasants; all their blood is on my head. But I pass it on to our Lord God, who commanded me to speak thus."

The talk is unusually harsh and Luther will have to take responsibility for it. But we note that in the tradition of the papal Church, in which the justice of the sword which is unacceptable to us is at home, a saint of the rank and quality of Bernard of Clairvaux said nearly the same thing when, faced with the horrible defeat that ended the crusade, he had to take responsibility for his advocacy of it before the European public.

What strikes most people as a horrible concurrence between the two cannot be explained away by saying that one copied the other but must have deeper reasons. If a more profound correspondence between the two men does exist, and if it also characterizes their relationship to the Church, there is especially one among an abundance of questions that should interest us here: Did Luther assent to a revolution against the Church, as many serious scholars assume, but reject such revolution with remorseless consistency in the case of the peasants? His position in the Peasants' War is not the last move that provides food for thought in this context. For right in the middle of that situation, this unusual man shocks us with the personal decision to celebrate his wedding with the former Cistercian nun Katharina von Bora, on June 13, 1525. Not only were enemies like Johannes Cochlaeus beyond themselves, even friends like Melanchthon were offended, and especially the "little man" who was burying and grieving over his dead during those days turned away from the celebrated "reformer" and "Hercules" to find a measure of fellowship among the fanatics and Anabaptists or just to stand aside suspiciously. The judgment that Luther gambled his immense prestige and lost is historically correct. The Reformation was no longer a popular movement. The authorities began taking up the cause of Luther and the princes' Reformation began. Instead of a congregational Christianity and the free election of pastors, we see the rise of the territorial and national church from which demanding and alert Christians suffer to this day.

From Luther's perspective, things look quite different. Leaving the Reformation aside for the moment, we will try to arrive at a somewhat better understanding of his late decision to marry.

The perfectly straightforward human point of view seems the most appropriate to begin with. Luther was forty-two and at the height of his powers, as his contemporaries liked to say. But it was certainly not virility that drove him into marriage, for his relationship to such "virility" was quite ambivalent, theologically speaking. And it would really be a pity were we to assume that Luther married his Kate to avoid whoring, as might be suggested by his interpretation, two years earlier, of 1 Corinthians 7, which he dedicated to the lusty Saxon marshal Hans von Löser at Pretzsch castle, a man who was very much in need of the *remedium concupiscentiae* ("remedy against lust") but found it quite difficult to overcome his male doubts about the obvious drawbacks of holy matrimony. Luther's exegesis of the problematical chapter allows one to see clearly that in 1523, he still felt deeply about the "fine thing," as he called it, that is, the heartfelt gift of chastity as the precondition of a valid vow, and that monastic celibacy therefore caused him no difficulties whatever.

The patience and indulgence he showed his numerous friends, colleagues and brothers who, like Karlstadt, Johann Bugenhagen, Justus Jonas, or Wenzeslaus Link, were suddenly in very much of a rush to extinguish the "burning fire" with the apostle Paul's permission also shows this inner freedom. Yet he does not seem to have been totally pleased with what was actually the exemplary decision of the German Augustinian congregation, on January 6, 1522, to leave it up to the friars whether or not to abandon the monastery. For when he heard that his old friend Johann Lang had left the Erfurt cloister, he answered rather bitterly on March 28, 1522: "I do believe that you had reasons for abandoning the monastery but I would have preferred seeing you rise above them."

And after a cutting remark about the very rapid progress of former Erfurt friars as pastors, who in all other respects had remained the same, he said: "I see that many of our friars quit the monastery for the same reason that once brought them there, their belly and their carnal freedom ... They are lazy people who only seek their own advantage. And so it is probably better that they should sin and degenerate outside the cowl rather than inside."

Luther was thus not nearly as happy about the development as one might be led to believe after reading his *On Monastic Vows* which, for all its severe criticism of monasticism, does not dispute that men are perfectly capable of observing vows. But in a human and Christian sense, this elitist point of view does not change the facts: while his friends concern themselves about their families and are taken care of by their wives, he sits, alone and deserted, in the tower of the Black Cloister, with much work and many failures, poor as a churchmouse and uncared for like a desert father.

If one wishes to criticize Luther's decision, this sad reality must be taken into account. And when one does one will modify one's critical judgment by first noting that it was not Luther who abandoned the monastery, as the mass of his fellow friars did before him and an entire army of monks and nuns did in the sixteenth century; it was rather that the monastery collapsed around him, as it were. Monasticism was losing its bloom and leaves, like trees in autumn. Of course, Luther bears a share of responsibility for this development, but as in the case of the Peasants' War, it is not his fault that monks, nuns, and priests misused the call to "freedom" nor is he the actual cause of this regrettable turn of events.

Luther did not abandon monasticism after he had allegedly recognized it as a typically "Catholic" miscarriage of life in the faith and because he thought it was irreconcilable with his "reformist discovery." He remained a monk longer than his fellows and would have continued unhesitatingly in a monasticism that fulfils its vow to God by the liberating tie of love without seeing itself as the indispensable path to salvation or raising itself above the rest of Christendom as a "state of perfection." But in an empty monastery, such a life became and still becomes impossible and meaningless in the course of time.

At just this time (and here, as is customary in marriage, accident played its mediating role), there lived in Nimschen convent near Grimma an apparently high-spirited group of twelve Cistercian nuns, who, lacking Luther's staying power and theological understanding, were affected by his critique of monasticism. The young nuns, who most assuredly had not yet died to the world and who, like the twenty-six-year-old Katharina von Bora, were by no means certain of their calling, had heard of the great Doctor Luther, studied his writings, and quickly found reason why, in their particular case, the omnipotent and fearsome God would mercifully exempt them from fulfilling their vows. After the early death of her mother, Katharina's father had quickly remarried and simply sent the unwanted daughter into the convent where her aunt Magdalena, for similar reasons, had earlier found a home. These aristocratic ladies, none of them over fifty and one the sister of Vicar General von Staupitz, had written to friends and relatives imploring their help in escaping as quickly as possible. The friends and relatives had then turned to Doctor Luther, and the Doctor, with his feel for real emergencies, had promptly taken the reluctant "brides of Christ" under his wing. For in 1523, when this story really begins, he was not yet the busy man he later became (that he was already thinking of unwashed dishes or the holes in his socks is not very likely, considering his basic talent for monasticism). I am distressed that for reasons of space I cannot tell the whole delightful story in all its relevant detail of how the then anything but "devout" Doctor Martin set about first kidnapping and then marrying off or finding homes for the difficult virgins, and

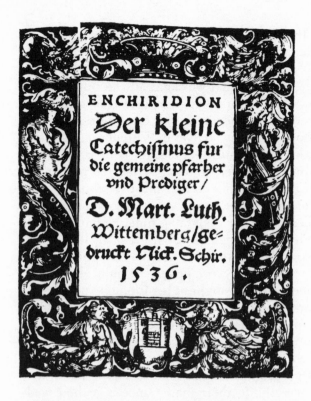

Title page and part title of Luther's Small Catechism, which was first published in 1529 and to which A Marriage Booklet and The Baptismal Booklet were appended. The Small Catechism belongs to the confessional writings of Lutheranism at the latest since the collection of the classical Lutheran formulae of faith in the Book of Concord of 1580.

how it happened that the one who insisted on becoming "his" finally led him where he had had no intention of going and made him a happy man. This long and uncommonly colorful story is so delightful because properly told and understood, it not only harms no one but is "ecumenically" liberating, for it makes all concerned laugh at themselves and gives them the hope of a "happy end" that need not be fought for.

The "Catholic" side will take delight in the clever and circumspect "Catholic" manner by which Luther, still in his dusty and worn Augustinian cowl, and his Lutherans resolved what was in fact a Catholic problem. Leonhard Koppe from Torgau, councilor and tradesman, a friend of Luther's and purveyor to the convent, took on the mortally dangerous and seemingly blasphemous part of the enterprise when, during the stillness of Easter eve, he kidnapped the virgins, hiding them in empty herring barrels and transporting them in his covered cart through Duke George's territory and on into Torgau in Electoral Saxony. There is no doubt in my mind that today it is precisely the "authentic brides of Christ" and all who have renounced marriage from love who keep their fingers crossed for their carnal sisters in those herring barrels. They breathe a sigh of relief and chime in as, in the light of Easter morning, a short distance this side of Torgau, the valiant Koppe and the jubilant women intone the Latin Easter sequence. On this occasion, one already notes the cultured alto voice of the young Katharina, a woman whose name always appears last on lists but who will soon prove to be "first."

The "Reformed" side will be delighted that she had nothing to do with Catholic "fraud" and "injustice" and that in Torgau, as the churchbells ring, the former Augustinian Gabriel Zwilling guarantees in her name, as it were, that right "order" will prevail during the following delicate scenes. Under his supervision for not all "fanatics"—and this is Luther's error—advocate the reintroduction of biblical polygamy, like the Anabaptists of Münster, the ladies of Torgau provide a change of clothing, and we may assume, considering the herring barrels, also a quick bath. But before the "unhaltered heavenly brides" have a chance to delight in typically Catholic joie de vivre and the vanity of fashion, the strict Pastor Zwilling returns and escorts the *rebellantes,* their heads modestly lowered, through the Nonnengasse to the Easter service in St. Marien where, in a mighty sermon, he makes clear to the congregation and the fleeing nuns what the flight from the "false" to the "true" Church means. Then decent Koppe takes over, for he has prepared a feast for the none too frightened ladies, and as they sit down to Easter lamb and abundant Torgau beer,

they taste the first pleasures of a new life whose table and holiday manners show no sign of any "reformation."

It is in the final act that we can really let ourselves go in ecumenically liberating laughter (the *risus pascalis*) at the "dumb devil." It begins as the three-horse carriage with the "honest virgins" arrives in Wittenberg on Easter Tuesday where the entire population is up and about. Koppe whom Luther celebrates as a "blessed robber," is the hero of the day, while Luther must set about matchmaking since only three of the twelve are taken back by their families. With the remaining nine, he had as many worries as debts, although he did not fear the latter inordinately, considering that he had vowed poverty and that even without the vow poverty would remain his faithful companion throughout his life. The other worries are more serious and not susceptible of a theological solution which Luther, undeterred, proposes to the public in writing in April 1523. But this does not get the virgins married. Luther then writes to Spalatin and any number of people; his friends lend a helping hand; and the ladies secretly do their share, since it is their weddings after all that are at stake. The situation is not altogether clear. Nikolaus von Amsdorf intends the oldest of the nine, his aunt, for Spalatin, but says nothing about other prospects. Yet such prospects certainly existed, especially for the younger nuns. The older ladies who know life begin thinking more and more about the Doctor. But when the honest virgins appear on the scene, they think of the devil. Thus Luther discovers that as "reformer" he cannot make matches as he wills. His worn cowl suddenly becomes a problem: if he is to continue wearing it, he needs a new one but a new one costs money, and at this moment he needs that for Katharina. He therefore does not have one tailored for himself and there is no one who will make him a present of one. But in his new role, he can no longer wear his dirty habit, although Katharina has nothing to do with that, of course. Where to lodge her for the moment is much less of a problem: he cannot bring her into the Black Cloister, although space there is abundant and the dirty dishes are piling up. But once the idea strikes him, it won't let go. But it is unnecessary to put her up there just now, for she is staying in Master Philip Reichenbach's house and then moves to Lucas Cranach's where there is a good deal of work to be done, with not only the famous studio but a printing shop, a pharmacy, and a busy inn to be seen to. Here Katharina can demonstrate that the role of "Martha" also offers opportunities for making oneself indispensable. No less a person than King Christian of Denmark, who was lodging at the Cranachs at the time, made Katharina a present of a golden ring, something Martin did not care for and a gesture that makes one wonder. Luther, every inch the reformer, holds back and insists that Hieronymus Baumgarten, the scion of a patrician family in Nuremberg, finally make up his mind to marry the "bride of Christ" who had been intended for him. But in Nuremberg they don't care for run-away nuns and the plan comes to nothing. But no one is sad in Wittenberg: certainly not Katharina, for she had known from the start that she didn't want to go to Nuremberg. Nor does the Doctor mind, for with the passage of time he has grown accustomed to the idea and is tired thinking in circles all of which lead back to Katharina. Still, nothing is resolved. Then, suddenly, something happens, and event follows event in rapid succession. And the terrible peasants' affair rather than impede developments actually hastens them. This is how Luther is, how he thinks and acts, eruptively and abruptly, as back in Stotternheim. Having hesitated for years, he will not wait one more day. He has a bad conscience neither about the order nor about the peasants and accepts a situation that not he but God created. He has nothing to hide for he does not "burn"; he loves his Kate and cannot be ashamed of it. Melanchthon is exasperated because he is thinking, and not without good reason, of the hue and cry of the papists and the peasants. But Luther cannot and will not be a hypocrite; the peasants actually lend urgency to the situation: he will marry his Kate "to spite the devil" and before they kill him, just as he still wants "to plant an apple tree before the Day of Judgment," an apocryphal phrase but one that characterizes him well. He knows he will not change the course of history but will not await the return of the Lord alone.

He thus takes the decisive step without any false pathos. On the evening of June 13, 1525, Johann Bugenhagen blesses the engagement in the Black Cloister with the faithful Justus Jonas, pastor of the castle church, Johann Apel, professor of canon law, and Lukas Cranach and his wife as witnesses. In great haste, Luther has a marriage bed made so that the nuptial ceremony can be appropriately carried out. Husband and wife climb into the bed and remain there for a moment hand in hand—Luther very serious, Katharina with a transfigured smile, and Jonas, who reported it all, with tears in his eyes. A few tears go along well with the laughter of this moving moment. For the marriage that is being blessed and witnessed here became one of the happiest in all of Christendom. It lies at the origin of the Protestant parsonage and serves as an example to this very day. As a love blessed by God, it also strengthens the love of those who renounce marriage for the same reason. Luther was as

capable of renunciation as he was of married love. We should not worry needlessly why he finally decided in favor of the latter. Nor should we be concerned for Katharina. For in her love of Luther, she made true and fulfilled what she had somewhat hastily promised Christ as a sixteen-year-old girl.

I can understand somewhat the annoyance of the young monk from Augsburg who recently wrote in his "Ninety-five Theses on the Luther Year": "Christ loved on the arms of the cross—not in the arms of a woman!" But I wonder if it might not help him in his bitterness if he considered that true love in the arms of the beloved can also take us into the arms of Christ. There is the vow, of course. But the addressee of that vow is not the Church but God who can permit us to substitute the lesser for the greater because He can bring it about that precisely by taking that way, we produce the "hundred-fold fruit" which is ultimately all that counts.

This renders irrelevant the question scholars frequently discuss. Whether Katharina was "beautiful" or not was simply something Luther did not ask himself. Catholics should give him credit for this as well. He lived in the conviction of the faith that "true" and "pure" love comes from God and makes the beloved beautiful, and that she does not love him merely because, and as long as, he is beautiful. Luther certainly loved his Kate deeply, even when she appeared as she does on the epitaph in Torgau, where she had fled with her children from the plague after the death of her beloved husband and lived on in poverty and misery till she died, on December 20, 1552, after much suffering from the consequences of an accident she had had along the way. But we should also rejoice with the couple that on the day their marriage began they looked to each other as Lukas Cranach has painted them for us. Why should we be more demanding than Tertullian who, even during a lifetime that was filled with tension, dared celebrate marriage as the "divine worship of the sexes"?

Luther did truly celebrate the feast of his love with his Kate, although certainly not with indifference to the sorrow of that terrible war "when rivers and brooks ran red with the blood of the peasants." It is very likely that Katharina suffered more from these conditions than her unyielding husband. Although from a noble family, she would surely have permitted a little more revolution if only because then her Martin would not have lost his heroic image.

It speaks for the couple's love that Luther did not melt like wax in the arms of his wife and that Kate submitted to her fate, although in all this-wordly matters she soon "wore the pants." This marriage is truly a great mystery:

Luther marries, yet in his commitment to others he remains what he always was. And the earthy and receptive Katharina develops the kind of devotion she had promised in Nimbschen but would probably not have attained.

Two days after the nuptial ceremony before a very small circle, the couple thus had every reason to invite the more extensive circle of friends to a "small merry wedding feast" in Wittenberg on June 27 so that the angels might laugh and the devils weep at so much undeserved happiness. The wedding bells chimed and Katharina had her great day. On the arm of her future husband and escorted by the students and professors of the university, she walks to the parish church to the sounds of the elector's band. In front of the festively decorated portal, they say their vows, *Tuus ego—Ego tua sum* and exchange rings to symbolize faithfulness until death. After the ceremony, the restive company moves to the Black Cloister for a joyful meal. From this day forward, the cloister revives because Duke George makes a present of it and all its privileges and land to the couple. Of the other presents, we will mention only these important ones: the magistrate had a huge barrel of "Einbeck beer" rolled into the cloister for since Luther must constantly do battle with the devil, he is always so thirsty that his wife will soon begin brewing her own beer in the old cloister brewery. Quite unexpectedly, there is a purse with twenty golden gulden from the archbishop of Mainz which he presents to his troublesome adversary without any derogatory comment. Luther is irritated and proposes to return the dubious gift by return mail. But already on this first day of their marriage, Katharina firmly contradicts him. She fears God, of course, but the "indulgence money" causes her no anxiety, and she is right. For her normally anxious husband will always need money for others but never demand payment for himself. O *admirabile commercium,* O "merry change and quarrel," about which the Doctor meditated so frequently and piously. There was no "quarrel" with the realistic Kate on this wedding day, but during the night she had to get out of bed to feed the not exactly likable Karlstadt the remains of the wedding feast. "How marvelous are God's ways with us poor sinners!"

# V

## 1. LUTHER AND
## THE FURTHER DEVELOPMENT
## OF THE WITTENBERG REFORMATION

Although the marriage does not constitute a break in Luther's spiritual development but rather a climax which had an unusually fruitful effect on his intellectual and theological creativity, it is yet an external and corollary sign of a change in his attitude toward the Reformation which was due to other causes. Here, also, one cannot speak of a break in his position and service in behalf of the Church, for he continued to be the "authority" from which everything of importance emanated. And however one might judge that authority, it had to be reckoned with whether one criticized, modified or rejected it. Yet typical shifts of the focal points in his life and activities occurred and in back of these lies that change, although personal reasons of course also played a role.

That Luther did not experience this transformation as something negative, as a decline, but rather as an upward movement he owed primarily to his Kate—abstracting, that is, from his unshakable faith and the qualities of his character. For the first time, at the age of forty-two, Luther had something like a private life which extended beyond the intimacy of the couple to the little community of the family which expanded in turn to include the circle of friends, table companions, disciples, and all those in need of such a community. Anyone who has brethren who at an advanced age have dared take the step from monastic or scholarly solitude into marriage knows the difficulties that make such a step a risky venture. In the case of Luther and his wife, there is no trace of problems. True, he must accustom himself to much that is new: the pigtails next to him in bed in the morning, Kate's intelligent questions when she sits next to him at the spinning wheel as he studies or when she develops a sudden interest in the Bible and he promises her fifty gulden (which he does not have) if she will finish it by Easter and which he never pays because she does not get beyond the fifth chapter of Genesis. Luther complains about his *"domina,"* his "rib" or "chain," his "prin-

cess of the pig market, Doctor Kate, female brewer and gardener and whatever else she may be," and is yet happy with her whom he loves more than himself and must not lose for anything in the world. Nothing she does disturbs him, not the whirl of rebuilding in the Black Cloister, not the confinements or the children—including nephews and nieces, there are twelve of them at times—not even the relatives. But neither does he allow himself to be bothered. He just growls when it all becomes too much, writes his books which don't earn him a penny, receives guests, celebrates festive occasions, and gives away whatever falls into his hands. But all the life around him cannot cover up the fact that a new and different phase has begun. Luther is about to concentrate on the internal task that confronts him. The advocacy of his reformist concerns in the outside world, vis-à-vis emperor and empire, the papal Church, the "fanatics," and other reformist churches, indeed the constitutional elaboration of the Church and its guidance by the Wittenberg reformation—all this he increasingly shares with or even leaves to others. While it is true with all his genius and originality he never rejected "teamwork," this was nonetheless a normal development which he initiated, welcomed, and permitted. Yet both to Luther and those whose activities now bring them into the foreground, the change mentioned above is clearly perceptible in all of this.

This is true even of a task Luther never surrendered, the mostly polemical discussions with his adversaries and the fight to keep his original concerns pure. Whether Luther attacks Karlstadt, Zwingli, Bucer, or the pope and the papists, his criticism is no longer accepted uncritically in all cases even if the doubts some have are usually not, or only cautiously, expressed. This is true even of the noticeably decreasing number of cases where all believe that Luther has to move into the front lines because everything is being threatened and only he can answer persuasively. This can be impressively documented by the great dispute with Erasmus which finally came in spite of the fact that those most directly involved did not really want it.

We have suggested repeatedly that Luther knew from

the beginning that this dispute was theologically necessary but that he kept avoiding it because he did not wish to jeopardize the victory and prestige of the Reformation by such an attack. The great Erasmus acted from similar motives. He also knew long since and more certainly with every passing day that an abyss divided him from Luther. But because he intensely disliked vulgar quarrels and did not wish to interfere with Luther's movement (in many of its critiques and formal approaches it agreed with his own concerns) and even supported him to a degree, he also had always shunned a clarifying discussion. But then things happened as they would. The public—the pope, the emperor, but especially Henry VIII of England and the learned world of the humanists—finally wanted to know precisely where the great Erasmus stood: Would he affirm the true teaching of the old Church which was admittedly in need of reform; would he uphold the peace and order of the old empire and especially man's inalienable dignity and freedom as preconditions of any moral order and all higher things; or would he side with the fanatical Wittenbergians and their radical, extreme, and subversive demands?

Erasmus was already at work when, in the spring of 1524, Luther politely but firmly advised him once again not to attack his teaching. The *Diatribe de libero arbitrio* ("Diatribe on Free Will") had been published in the fall. In it, Erasmus finally took a position with the calm, competence and superiority which he owed to his reputation and addressed himself, as Luther conceded, to the central question.

Luther was neither very much surprised nor intimidated. But for the first time, he surprised and disappointed his friends and the public because he did not strike back with his typical speed and sharpness. He put this very urgent matter aside and did not settle down to work until the end of September 1525. The manuscript was finished by November but not published until the end of December. Biographers have usually interpreted this uncharacteristic procedure as the reaction of a felt superiority. Luther had other tasks, after all. The dispute with Karlstadt had to be brought to a conclusion. More importantly, there was the horrible Peasants' War which preoccupied him. No one mentions Katharina. But such an explanation is not persuasive, and even Luther's immediate circle clearly had a different view. Melanchthon and his friends urged him finally to take a position. And on November 23, 1524, even the Strassburg reformers implored him for "Christ's sake" not to consider "flesh and blood," but to do what he can to defend the common cause because God speaks through him.

Why did Luther shun a task which only he could handle? He had lost none of his nervous energy and polemical vigor as his writings on the peasants show. And to bring up Katharina in this connection would be the height of bad taste.

This raises a question which it is better to leave unanswered because it admits of no unambiguous answer. Yet it is also an insistent one and must be asked. For as a question, it points to that "change" beyond which no answer can be given.

Similar considerations apply to an evaluation of the *De servo arbitrio* ("On the Bound Will") by which Luther answers Erasmus without noisy polemics but with unusual decisiveness. This tract belongs to the few works that Luther characterized as his best and we must take this estimate into account. But there is no overlooking the fact that to this very day, scholarly judgment is not unanimous. This applies equally to Erasmus' position. The controversial treatment of this extremely difficult problem cannot be set forth here in detail, and the problem itself certainly cannot be resolved. Yet I will try at least to characterize the controversy and the clashing positions in a few brief sentences.

In all disputes between fundamentally different points of view, one deals with fundamentally different presuppositions which are tantamount to prejudgments. If one decides for Luther's point of view as one studies the introduction—and that is my position—one has already decided against Erasmus.

Wherever ultimate questions of the faith are at stake —and the freedom of man with a view to salvation and therefore to God's prevenient grace is an example—the history of dogma provides no concrete starting point for an answer that would give equal weight to all aspects of the problem. For this reason, we should not demand too much from Luther and concede to him what we must concede to all, not excluding Erasmus and the teaching of the Church, who try to clarify this complex of questions in their own particular way.

This also means that we define a framework within which a clear position on Luther's fundamental concerns can be taken: Luther does not dispute what people have in mind when they talk about "freedom" among themselves, except that even in this sphere he does not except much from freedom, and this is something his contemporaries but more particularly ours who are so obsessed with freedom cannot forgive him once they understand what he meant. Nor does Luther deny the terrible fact that we turn to or from God in freedom, or the joyous fact that through, from, and in His incomprehensible grace, God makes us a gift of freedom and turns us into "collaborators" who are not pushed about like lifeless "pieces of wood" or "tree trunks." For Luther also, it is unreservedly true that "Heaven was not created for geese." But what he does dispute radically and with total consistency, and what Erasmus maintains or at least leaves open and suggests, is a "freedom" over which man disposes as man and which enables him to decide for the grace without which, even according to Erasmus, we cannot obtain salvation. What Luther rejects radically, then, is that man has a "freedom" that deprives God of His divinity, that it is ultimately up to man whether he is saved by grace or damned. Luther got this fundamental biblical and theological distinction not just from Paul but also set it forth irrefutably by invoking the Gospel of St. John: unaided man cannot bridge the abyss that lies between the "birth through blood and the will of the flesh" and the "rebirth through God." Nothing exists or mediates between nature and grace. Luther recognized the dangerous lack of clarity, the gray zone into which Erasmus' limping argument with its excessive concessions to human nature will lead us. With his approach, Erasmus remained far behind Scholasticism, and Luther recognized that as well.

Here we have the fundamental difference between Luther and Erasmus. Under the heading of "free will," it concerns the very image of God and man in the absence of a mediating alternative, that faith decide. If, because of Scripture and tradition, one sides with Luther on this point, one takes sides not only against Erasmus and the concerns of humanism but also offends against modern preoccupations and expectations in what is probably the most difficult complex of questions concerning faith. Within the horizon of this question, God is for Luther the all-powerful and mysterious One who makes Pharaoh's heart impenitent and in whose hands we are as potter's clay, without any right to ask why He made this one into a noble vase, the other into a chamber pot, why He chose Jacob and rejected Esau. Dark and terrible is the abyss of the *Deus ipse et in meiestate sua* (God Himself in His majesty) who wishes to be neither worshipped nor adored by us and who drives us into the arms of the *Deus praedicatus* (the proclaimed God) who saves us although He also remains the *Deus absconditus* (the hidden God).

With Luther, we fall silent before this ultimate mystery which even he could not formulate, let alone resolve, without chancing the most dangerous contradictions. We should note, however, that it is clearly this unfathomable and terrible God who drives Luther ever deeper into the arms of the "man on the cross" and thus decisively transforms his life, including his relationship to the Reformation.

Luther does not despair in the face of this paralyzing perspective. Like Jacob limping in fear of Esau, he uses all his strength, stakes everything on the expectation "of standing firm in the faith." And he cuts back on all world-shaking activities, which won't delay the "Day of the Lord" in any event.

This is the "turn" that becomes effective in his life although it cannot be further defined. Having grasped that, one will not misunderstand certain other aspects of that life, such as the fact, for example, that he suddenly spent so much time with his family, that (probably thinking of Frederick the Wise) he tried to fill Kate's stocking by working a lathe, and that when this attempt failed because he had not skill for it, he sometimes busied himself in his garden where he successfully and not without pride planted small apple trees, grew and harvested vegetables, and nonetheless espoused the right of birds because they, like the rest of suffering creation, were waiting for God finally and definitively to make man better with his "precious Last Day." Luther did not withdraw into private life and, more importantly, did not degenerate to a Sunday gardener, however. Apart from his enormous activity as preacher and lecturer, he devoted himself with much intensity to the further reform of the service and the teaching of the Church. In 1526, he continued the necessary reform of the liturgy with *The German Mass*, the *Pamphlet on Baptism*, new hymns and the transformation of the old choral into perfectly singable German church music. In 1529, he created the *Large* and the *Small Catechism for Ordinary Pastors and Preachers* through which he has remained the catechist for Evangelical-Lutheran Christianity to this day.

In another sphere which really fell under the purview of the bishop, Luther remained the competent "authority" although, strictly speaking, Johann Bugenhagen as the pastor of Wittenberg should have fulfilled this task. For on May 14, 1525, during the congregational service, Luther ordained Georg Rörer who had been called to assume the office of the Wittenberg archdeaconate. This was his first ordination and it took place without the pomp of the old ritual though not without the laying on of hands. It will be shown below that Luther did not understand this act as "evangelical investiture or introduction," as generations of Lutheran theologians thought, but as ordination according to the example and the precepts of the Apostles. As early as 1523, in response to an inquiry from the Bohemians, he had studied the question how one should install suitable Christians in Church office when papal bishops refused ordination and there was only the dubious possibility of having candidates ordained by subterfuge, which meant that willing Italian bishops assumed this task in exchange, for large sums of money. For many Christians but especially for many theologians of both creeds, Luther's answer was not what one might expect ("You are all priests; simply choose a pastor and install him"). Rather, he explained himself somewhat cumbersomely but with remarkable clarity: "If the Church as a creation of the Word needs the word to live, and if the Word falls silent without the office, then you have the right and the power of emergency ordination, just as you have it in the case of baptism which is necessary for salvation." Thinking of the future, Luther acted with this in mind in the case of deacon Rörer, although the hordes of ordained priests and monks who had gone over to the Reformation amply sufficed to fill all pastoral needs, and the Wittenbergians, especially Melanchthon but Luther as well, had not yet given up the hope that the connection with the old espicopate could be preserved or re-established.

This brings us to another task which was primarily assumed by the princes acting as "emergency bishops" and the ecclesiastical or secular visitors they appointed, the hiring of pastors according to canonical law not yet being far advanced. I am referring here to pastorates and parishes in the various districts which had already been neglected during Catholic times and which, under the conditions of the transition, naturally took on a special urgency. While Luther's involvement in this matter was only indirect and advisory, an important field of activity opened up for Melanchthon, Spalatin, Myconius, and other tested churchmen. Melanchthon wrote his *Instructions to the Visitors* which Luther revised and supplied with a preface and which first appeared in 1528.

But during this period, the incomprehensible God also did certain things that ultimately have a connection with the reform of His "pilgrim Church." Charles V had become too powerful for the popes, as Leo X had foreseen. To keep the protector of the Church from becoming more powerful still, Clement VII had hurriedly called on the Italian cities, especially the powerful city-states of Venice and Florence to join the anti-imperial League of Cognac. The presumptive emperor heard of this alliance and wasted little time. On his orders, the loyal, noble knight Georg von Frundsberg with his mercenaries and the duke of Bourbon with a Spanish army and additional mercenaries moved into Italy. The League could not prevent the imperial army from crossing the Po. Although the mercenaries mutinied against Frundsberg in Bologna

because they were not being paid and the "noble knight" suffered a stroke as a consequence, this sign did not prevent the imperial troops—for mercenaries know how mortal they are—from first attacking and then sacking the eternal city, and from committing unspeakable atrocities in the process. The horrible *Sacco di Roma* occurred on May 6, 1527. The Holy City was in flames and laid in ruins; the proud beauties of the city discovered, like poor nuns before them, what mercenaries mean by love, and the wealth of the churches, monasteries, and populace became the easy prey of the soldiers. Barely defended by his Swiss Guards, Clement VII escaped with difficulty across the Bridge of Sighs and into the secure Castel Sant'Angelo where—and this would hardly have happened otherwise—he began to reflect on the transitoriness of this life and the necessity of reform.

In quite different fashion, God made His presence felt in the Black Cloister in Wittenberg, two months later to the day. Luther felt unwell that morning and suddenly collapsed in the arms of his Kate and before the eyes of his friends. He reports that he heard the roaring of the sea and feared that would pull him into eternal night. Luther is not squeamish but takes the incident seriously. He has Bugenhagen called, confesses his sins, receives Communion, and prepares for death. But the attack passes as quickly as it had come. At noon, he goes to the inn to eat. Some distinguished gentlemen, come to Wittenberg to see him, are awaiting him there. Later, he and Kate visit Jonas and have their evening meal in his garden. Here, he loses consciousness a second time, is carried home, and put to bed. Again, he looks death in the eye and this time everyone notices that a particular fear seizes him: What will happen to his teaching if God calls him at this moment? Won't his enemies tell all sorts of stories and say that he finally "recanted" after all? How will his friends alter his teaching? Very briefly, he discusses this sudden fear with Kate and his friends. His physician, Dr. Schurff, the brother of the jurist and colleague of Luther, quickly controls the attack. The next morning, Luther already feels better but has not forgotten his fear, particularly as in late summer of the same year, the plague returns to Wittenberg once again. The university and Melanchthon are moved to Jena, and the elector insists that this time Luther go to a safe place. But as before, when he had been vicar provincial, Luther insists on remaining at his post in 1527. People may flee from the plague and death, as Luther expressly declares on this occasion, but that does not apply to those, like Luther who, hold office in the threatened town. This time he is not alone. His Kate who is already expecting another child (born promptly on June 7, 1526, and baptized by Rörer at four in the afternoon, and called Hänschen) stays with him which worries the doctor. And his friends and confessor Bugenhagen also moves into the Black Cloister with his family and belongings: "not so much on his account as on mine," Luther writes to Hausman, "so that he may keep me company in my solitude." Even in such situations, Luther talks of himself in a mildly ironic manner. For "solitude" was the last thing he could complain about. In the sermon on how to conduct oneself during times of plague, he had called on the cities to construct hospitals so that the burghers need not make their houses available for the ill. But Wittenberg did not build one, for it had Luther's Black Cloister which soon filled up with the sick and those seeking help.

But worry over the ill and the dying did not make him forget the fear for his teaching. The year of the plague, 1528, saw the publication of the *Confession Concerning Christ's Supper* in which he summarizes and attests to his faith. Although he was aware that as a single Christian he could not speak in the name of the Church, he did not hesitate to say that he wished to commit posterity to his confession. This personal confession is the overture to the elaboration of the creed by the Wittenbergians in which Luther played an active part as the Articles of Schwabach and Marburg show. But another work which he was writing concurrently is as important and revealing. This is the *Von der Wiedertaufe an zwei Pfarrherrn* ("Letter to Two Pastors on Rebaptism") in which he not only expounds his positions on rebaptism and the Anabaptists but also on the "Church of the Antichrist." However horrible its situation may be, the Church, even as Church of the Antichrist, remains the "true Church." Even more, the Antichrist proves it to be the Church of Christ, for he will not appear among the horde of sectarians. Everything Luther has comes from the "Church of the Antichrist." Yet the elaboration of the creed is a summarizing term for a process which, more than any other, makes visible the change that Luther undergoes. History provides the overture: although Clement VII had not forgotten the sack of Rome, he bowed to the inevitable. Since he had no weapons left with which to fight Charles V, he, like his predecessors before him, used the consecrated oil of investiture and coronation—not the "stinking chrism," as Luther liked to call it (centuries earlier, the original chrism had been replaced by the oil of catechumens)—whose particular charism it was to make one's political adversary the effective "protector of the Church" and the "patrimony of Peter." After this had been accomplished in Bologna, the emperor recalled the

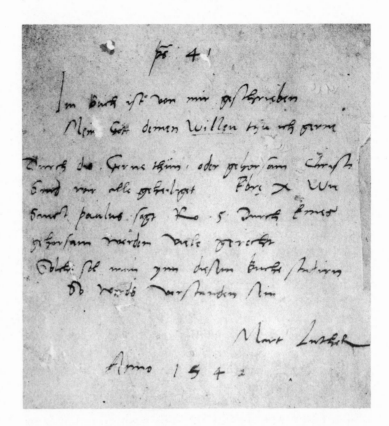

Luther's handwritten entry in the Bible printed by Lufft in 1541:

Ps. 41

In the book I have written,
My God, I gladly do thy will.
Through this doing gladly, or obedience to Christ,
we are all sanctified (Hebrews 10). As St.
Paul says in Romans 5: Through one man's obedience many are justified. Such things will one study in this book. Thus it will be understood.
Mart LutheR D.
Anno 1542

religious question he had neglected in Germany and which, in connection with the newly arising Turkish threat, had attained a new virulence. What no one had dared hope any longer could be read in the emperor's proclamation by which, even before the coronation, he summoned the princes and estates of the empire to the Diet of Augsburg on April 8, 1530. In addition to measures to deal with the Turkish danger, the Diet was at long last to attempt to heal the split in the faith and the Christian religion, renouncing all dispute and doing justice to both sides, so that "as they are and fight under one Christ, so they should also live under one Church and in unity." In Germany, especially in Electoral Saxony, people had faith in the proclamation because they wanted to have faith in it. The humanists were particularly hopeful, for *pax* and *concordia in dogmatibus* were not only their high and undoubtedly sacred aims but seemed assured and attainable as a matter of ecclesiastical politics because, at the emperor's court, humanists such as the chancellor Mecurio Gattinara and his men stood behind them. On the elector's order, the Wittenberg theologians worked out a draft for the Augsburg negotiations. Luther participated as an advisor but the so-called Articles of Torgau had been written by Melanchthon. The draft was both very simple and very optimistic: the reform of ecclesiastical usages will be defended before the emperor and empire, which is the reason the working paper is initially called *Apologia,* considering that in this sphere especially "many abuses" had caused strife. Should a justification of doctrine become necessary, one would fall back on the Articles of Schwabach. Luther had certain reservations about this conception but nothing is known of a veto against it.

Luther also obeyed the elector's order to accompany him at least as far as Coburg. The hesitation that is apparent here had clear legal and political motivations: being an outlaw, Luther could not simply present himself at the Diet. From the very beginning, it was clear that he would be excluded from the actual negotiations although he was wanted in an advisory capacity. Talks between the elector and Nuremberg led nowhere and Luther therefore could not accompany the delegation beyond Coburg castle.

On Sunday, April 3, 1530, Luther leaves Wittenberg with Melanchthon and Jonas and meets Spalatin and the elector's party in Torgau. In Saalfeld, Johann Agricola and Kaspar Aquila who are escorting the count of Mansfeld join the party which arrives in Coburg on April 15. While Luther preaches in the town church on the suffering and cross of Christ, the elector orders Melanchthon to work on the introduction to the *Apologia.* When it is determined that Luther may not even go as far as Nuremberg, he takes up residence, accompanied by Veit Dietrich, at Coburg castle in the early morning of Pentecost while the delegation sets out for Augsburg after the morning meal. Luther is in very bad humor which he tries to vent in the first few letters he writes from Coburg. He does not understand why he has to stay behind in the crows' nest and why, if he cannot go to Augsburg, he should not return to his Kate and his work. Very angrily, he writes Eobanus Hessus: "I am sending you 'four' very eloquent letters which I would have liked to accompany as a 'fifth' one. But someone said to me, 'Keep your mouth shut; you have an unpleasant voice.'" And in the afternoon, even before he has properly settled in, he writes a few cutting letters to his just departed friends, in the third of which he tells them that he knows perfectly well what will happen: as yet, his friends are nowhere near Augsburg and he has already arrived at "his Diet," the Diet of jackdaws, that is, who circle the castle in large flocks until they finally settle down to business on the opposite slope like "noblemen, with muffled croaks and incessant bows."

It thus appears that Luther thought very little or, more honestly, nothing at all of the negotiations in which the elector had placed considerable hopes and Melanchthon all of his. Although no one said so publicly—and this is still the case today—mistrust was mutual. The "leading intellects" of the Augsburg delegation, not including the excessively trusting Jonas and the faithful Spalatin, mistrusted Luther because they knew their own plans. Besides, it was so very easy to keep the "jewel of the Reformation" safe from harm in his Coburg solitude: no one could see Luther without electoral permission. Luther's secretary, Veit Dietrich, who was devoted to the reformer reported to Melanchthon who should have known how Luther was and what "devils" he was fighting at the moment. This perfect system had a single flaw which could not be completely eliminated: it was not really possible to forbid Luther all writing and his printers all printing so that, not being fully employed as advisor nor wholly content with that role, Luther soon had the somewhat outlandish notion to "admonish" the ecclesiastics assembled in Augsburg from his mountain in his own wilful way. His own "Diet" was not working out as well as he would have liked, of course, and Kate was dissatisfied because, of the many "golden gulden" the publishers earned from their author's books, not even a single "groschen" found its way into the family till. *O quae mutatio rerum!* Once again, Luther found himself in "Junker Jörg's" situation but no longer had the freedom of movement he had enjoyed at the Wartburg. But such is life in the Church: things inevitably become "public property," the author an "advisor" in negotiations about an important issue which has long since ceased being his. Melanchthon will have a similar experience with the Augsburg Confession: although he works on this important document during the following weeks only as an editor, he will deal with it at the Diet and during the next few years as if he were its author until his work becomes a creed and is expropriated so that he no longer has any say over its meaning.

ILLUSTRATION SEQUENCE VI

SCHMALKALDIC ARTICLES—
CALVIN'S REFORMATION—DEDICATION
OF A CHURCH IN TORGAU—
THE COUNTER-REFORMATION
IS FORMED—LUTHER'S DEATH
1533–1546

75　Martin Luther. Life-size portrait of the reformer by Lucas Cranach the Younger. 1575. Collections in Coburg Castle.

76　The Katharinenportal on the Luther house in Wittenberg was constructed in 1540 by Katharina von Bora and was a present to her husband. The Luther house was the former "Black Cloister" of which the elector made a free and unencumbered gift to Luther in 1532.

77　Luther's wife Katharina, unquestionably the ideal mate for the reformer, bore him three sons and three daughters and administered the liberal, large household so efficiently that Luther lovingly called her "my master Kate." Painting (1528) by Lucas Cranach the Elder. Weimar, State Collection in the castle (cf. no. 60).

78　Johannes Bugenhagen (1485–1558) belonged to Luther's inner circle and was his confessor. In 1523, he became town pastor in Wittenberg and professor at the University. His activity as reformer had the geographically most extensive and organizationally most enduring impact for he created the Evangelical church and school order for Pomerania, Braunschweig, Hamburg, and Lübeck among others. On February 22, 1546, he gave the funeral oration for Luther.— Detail of a baptism of Christ donated by Bugenhagen, by Lucas Cranach the Younger in the town church in Wittenberg.

79　View of Schmalkalden. Here, the Protestant princes and towns created the Schmalkaldic League to defend themselves against attacks on the Reformation by Charles V (1530). In 1535, the life of the league was extended by ten years. In 1536/37, Luther wrote the Articles of Schmalkalden which were intended as the basis for negotiations for a council to be held in Mantua. They are considered Luther's theological testament. While the defeat of the troops of the League in the battle at Mühlberg in 1547 put an end to the League, the Emperor failed in his fight against the Reformation because the resistance of the German princes was too great.

80　John Calvin (1509—1564) became a reformer in 1533. But in his *Institutes of the Christian Religion* (1536) which was accepted in Geneva as the constitution of both church and state, he deviated from Lutheran teaching. The Reformed Church as founded by Calvin became the driving force of world-wide Protestantism (Huguenots in France, Calvinists in the Netherlands, Puritans in England). Painting (16th cent.) in Geneva, Bibliothèque publique et universitaire.

81　Calvinist service in Lyon. The gospel is not just the message of the forgiveness of sin; as "law" it is also binding for the public order. The congregation which sees itself as God's nation has the right to resist an authority that no longer serves God's honor. This view underlies the political dynamic of the Calvinist Reformation.—Painting (16th cent.), Geneva, Bibliothèque publique et universitaire.

EMPLE DE LYON. NOMMÉ PARADIS.

· D · M · Lutherus ·

Pestis eram viuens moriens ero mors tua
Papa

+                                    +

+   Anno                    1 . 5 . 4~

                                      Ætatis suæ

                                      ~3 viuen

                                      in reden

                                      Et mort

                                      uæ

+                                      +

+                                      +

Obijt mortem 18 Februarij
in ... intra horam 2 et tercia
et uigesima 2 eiusdem mens..
Wittenbergæ in arce sepul..
ET MORTVVS ...

ORAVIT, DOCVIT, CHRISTVS, FIT VICTIMA, VICTOR

# Das newe Testament.
## auffs new zugericht.

# Doct: Mart: Luth:

## Witeberg.

Gedruckt durch Hans Lufft.

# 1 5 4 6.

82 Interior of the castle church in Torgau which was the first Evangelical church to be built and was consecrated by Luther on October 5, 1544. In his inaugural sermon, Luther defined the task of Evangelical churches: "that our good Lord may talk with us through His sacred Word, and that we in turn talk to Him through our prayers and songs of praise."

83 Martin Luther. Detail from painting no. 74.

84 Ignatius of Loyola hands Pope Paul III the rules governing his Society of Jesus which he placed under the direct supervision of the pope and which became one of the driving forces of the Catholic Counter-Reformation.—Painting (17th cent.) in the vestry of the church of Il Gesù in Rome.

85 Gathering of the participants at the Council of Trent which was in session three times between 1545 and 1563. It was the belated answer of the Catholic Church to a council Luther and others had requested repeatedly. The council laid the groundwork for the inner renewal of the Catholic Church but could no longer arrest the evolution of the Reformation.—Fresco by Cati (17th cent.) in the Altemps Chapel of the basilica of Santa Maria in Trastevere.

86 In 1518, Philip Melanchthon (1497–1560) became professor in Wittenberg and Luther's leading collaborator. With his *Loci Communes* (1521/22), he created the first Evangelical dogmatics, and with his *Instructions for Visitors* the basis for the internal structure of Lutheran churches and the training of Evangelical clergy. Melanchthon formulated the Augsburg Confession and had a share in the elaboration of the Articles of Schmalkalden and the various religious colloquies, as with Zwingli in Marburg.—Painting (1543) by Lucas Cranach the Elder, Florence, Uffizi Gallery.

87 The old Luther, lecturing. A drawing by Luther's student Reifenstein, made during his final lectures in 1545. The drawing is on the inside of a book by Melanchthon who also wrote the notes on Luther's deathday, his age, his place of burial in Wittenberg. The final words are confessional: ET MORTUUS VIVIT: Luther lives beyond his death.—Wittenberg, Lutherhalle.

88 Luther died on February 18, 1546, in Eisleben where he was born. The painter Lukas Furttenagel of Halle drew the reformer's face, marked by age and illness, as he lay on his deathbed. Berlin, Kupferstichkabinett.

89 Luther's grave under the pulpit of the Wittenberg castle church.

90 Luther and the Elector Johann Friedrich under the cross. Colored title page of the last edition of the New Testament to be reviewed by Luther (1546). Wittenberg, Lutherhalle.

Within certain limits, Luther's task as "advisor" was probably seriously intended and actually feasible. The question was whether he was really meant to participate in the negotiations and whether he would feel that he truly was a participant. For to merely play the role at the "Diet of the daws" that had been picked for him in Augsburg was impossible for Luther even if the elector tried to run the show himself.

At first, everything went well. As yet, there was nothing to "advise" since Master Philip had first to find his bearings in Augsburg where the situation looked quite different from what one had imagined at Torgau. None other than Johann Eck must be blamed for this since he proposed more to help truth prevail. In four hundred articles, he intended to show and refute before emperor and empire all the heresies Luther and his followers had committed. This meant that Melanchthon had to introduce the already prepared *Apologia* of the reforms with a summary of the most important doctrinal teachings. Work progressed rapidly, yet he had bad dreams: an evil spirit transformed him, the high-flying eagle, into an ordinary tomcat and put him into a bag to drown him. Luther did not forget this vision: toward the end of August, heedless of all dangers, he wanted to rush to Augsburg to free the "eagle" from his prison. What he could not know, was not meant to know, and never discovered was that Philip had found himself in the "bag" much earlier, although the end of August was the second time he got caught.

From the very start, Luther could not have been satisfied with what he heard. Only this explains the fact that he never became active as advisor. For when, on May 11, the elector sent him the quickly written document so that he might examine and revise it thoroughly, and Melanchthon wrote him with great urgency on the same day and for the same reason, he sent a brief answer of five lines on May 15: he liked the document as far as it went and felt that corrections or additions were neither necessary nor fitting since he could not step as lightly as Master Philip.

Although he tried very hard, Melanchthon could not wheedle him into making further statements on this the principal subject of the Diet. On May 20, he asked him again and then annoyed, stopped, and remained silent until June 13. This in turn annoyed the mistrustful Luther. After a strong warning, he angrily accepted "Junker Schweigler's" declaration of war and stopped writing letters as of June 7. He did not even open the imploring letters written with tears which Philip sent him after June 13 and especially during the critical phase of the document's public reading. The famous *Confessio Augustana,*

or Augsburg Confession, thus came into being without Luther's participation if not without his laconic assent. Not until two days after the solemn reading, on June 25, did a hailstorm descend on Melanchthon and the other friends from Coburg castle. One must read these splendid but terrible letters (misleadingly called *Trostbriefe,* "consolatory letters," by Luther scholars because they were requested to console the trembling Melanchthon) if one wishes to understand the profound difference between Luther and Melanchthon and his humanistically inclined friends.

However good the intention, however understandable such an effort on the part of the churches of the Reformation may have been, the crack that Luther's letters created could not be plastered over on this occasion. Even more, this crack would have widened into a definitive break, with consequences that are difficult to gauge, had Luther known of the political solitaire Melanchthon was playing, initially developed in conversations with the archbishop of Mainz in June and embarked on, immediately after the emperor's arrival, with the help of the Spanish secretary of state Juan Valdes, a confidant of Cardinal Gattinara who had died on the way to Augsburg. This sentence is enormously long because it tells a very sad story which occasionally surfaces in the scholarly literature but is then repressed or obscured again because it stains the memory of the "Augsburg confessor." The project that Master Philip tried to realize with Spanish help between June 15 and 21 was overwhelmingly simple: the Protestant princes and estates would renounce the solemn reading of their creed. In exchange, they would make known their demands, reduced to the lay chalice, the marriage of priests, and the mass in German, and the emperor and the cardinal legate Lorenzo Campeggio would see to the restoration of the unity of the Church.

This grandiosely simple plan came to nothing because the elector, represented by Chancellor Brück, did not give Melanchthon the requisite consent on June 21. But none of the princes criticized Melanchthon's independent initiative, nor did anyone object to Luther's being kept in ignorance of the entire matter. Melanchthon and his enlarged group of co-workers now had to finish the neglected Augsburg Confession without further delay. The task was barely completed before the solemn reading on June 25 in which the disappointed Melanchthon did not participate. In spite of everything, the valiant princes thus became the "confessors" of the true faith after all, and even Luther praised them for it.

But Melanchthon, who was supported only by Johannes Brenz, the Swabian reformer, recovered from a profound depression which the chief Nuremberg theologian, Andreas Osiander, so vividly described without knowing the details. Undisturbed by the harsh admonition from Coburg castle and again without Luther's knowledge though with the consent of the "confessor" princes, a trembling but intrepid Melanchthon began the second round of negotiations with Cardinal Campeggio, who allegedly loved him "like his own son" and also had a high regard for the still celibate Brenz (celibate although the widow he was to marry was already waiting for the wedding in Schwäbisch-Hall). For why should it be impossible to accomplish with the Confession what admittedly could have been more easily achieved without it?

The tenor of the famous letter which Melanchthon wrote to Campeggio in this matter (and which, having been circulated everywhere except at Coburg castle, caused unease even in Venice) was, from Melanchthon's point of view, fully justified by the Augsburg Confession as he understood it. (We must not blame the author for the missive's devout curial style.) The unreserved acknowledgment of the authority of the Roman Pontiff or the readiness of the Roman Church to content itself with a tacit, totally non-binding tolerance of Protestant demands, both of them elements that went beyond the Confession, will simply be toned down by later statements, or forgotten. But to the considerable disappointment of Melanchthon and his friends, and in spite of this extreme obligingness, the second attempt will also fail.

Luther, who sensed something but never heard about the decisive event, became increasingly impatient among his "daws": "Go home, go home, you confessors. I will canonize you if you finally break off these pointless negotiations." But when his own people publicly accused Melanchthon of having let himself be bribed with Roman funds, he stood like an angry bear in front of poor Philip.

In a paradoxical but ultimately credible way, Luther finally took a position on the Augsburg Confession: on the one hand, he straight forwardly faulted it for "stepping too lightly," but on the other, he celebrated it as the great, fundamental, and unifying confession. His first verdict shows that he never opposed it as such but simply objected to the aims and methods of negotiations that attempted not only to attain the impossible, that is, *concordia in dogmatibus* as distinct from an achievable "political peace," but which, in addition, jeopardized truth itself in that they proposed to reconcile "Belial and Christ," "Luther and the pope."

It can be seen that "negotiations" between Luther and the cardinal were an a priori impossibility. For negotiations (today we somewhat prematurely and globally call them "dialogue") make sense only where the two sides encounter each other as willing partners. But neither the cardinal nor the pope were willing and so the entire plan finally failed. Still Campeggio pretended to be ready to negotiate for some time, and Melanchthon made it all too easy for him to adopt that stance. Furthermore, one can exclude the notion that Philip would have proposed these concessions and the cardinal have accepted them had they simply contravened the gospel. For wouldn't the lay chalice and a married clergy have been a legitimate concession for preserving the unity of the Church? And wouldn't the recognition of the German mass have provided the opportunity of returning to a simple eucharistic celebration the full meaning of the Lord's Supper, which the Roman side had lost sight of?

Here lies the abiding rightness of the plan and also the reason why Melanchthon tried, with anxious singlemindedness but certainly innocent of any treacherous intent, to realize it without and even against Luther.

But it must also be noted that this "relative right" of Melanchthon's procedure can be justified neither factually nor objectively. Still less does it suffice to put Luther and his unyieldingness in the wrong. Quite the contrary is the case. From Luther Philip should have learned—and all of us can learn—how, in spite of all singlemindedness and passionate willingnes to reach an understanding, a negotiation does not deteriorate into a "horse trade" which, at the expense of truth, creates a unity that ultimately we have as little capacity to create as we do the justice through which we are justified before God. He could have learned from Luther how even seriously conducted negotiations can remain a genuine "dialogue" during which we do not simply talk at, and listen to, each other, but where, more importantly, the one is heard who alone speaks the liberating and unifying word of truth.

This is what Luther had in mind when he severely reproached Melanchthon's philosophy from Coburg castle and condemned the impious wilfulness of a negotiating style that takes things into its own hands as it seeks to push through its goals and thus strays from the path of faith. It is certainly true that Luther would never have initiated the kind of negotiation that Melanchthon conducted with Campeggio, but this does not mean that he was not ready for an exchange or that such an exchange would have been fruitless. His letter to the two Catholic pastors allows us to see clearly how, in an exchange between two hostile brothers where life and death are at stake, even the seemingly irreconcilable opposites "Luther or the pope" can be resolved.

It is also certain that what Melanchthon's negotiation lacked was faith and the radical willingness to subordinate all reason and will to obedience to Christ which ultimately leads us where we do not want to go.

Luther's harsh warning and his understanding of the true faith that was finally confessed in Augsburg after all are therefore fundamental preconditions for all who, on the basis of the Augsburg Confession, wish to carry out without ambigous reservations what Melanchthon negotiated and even what he was prepared to concede. If one follows Luther, one may negotiate like Melanchthon, for one will be immune to the temptation of a "home-made ecumenicity" which, because it makes the concessions expediency demands, destroys the very thing it seeks to bring about. Ecumenicity does not end but begins where, as in the demanding dialogue with Luther, we allow ourselves, on the basis of a shared faith, to be led into that "unity" which is never a matter of our choice.

## 2. THE FINAL YEARS AND ULTIMATE THINGS: "COME SOON, LORD JESUS!"

On October 13, 1530, Luther finally returned to his Kate and the children, his book and his Black Cloister. The "Diet of the daws" lay behind him, yet it had not been a waste of time: he had mourned his father, fought the devils in the air, emptied many a flask of wine, and prayed even more. Despite constant headaches—"my head is like a cathedral chapter"—he had worked like a man possessed. His hope was unbroken; he was in the midst of a new project, but knew more about the "change" and the conditions of the endtime which casts doubt on all our plans. Only one thing still counted, and that was that we "keep still" in our faith and await the " precious Last Day" with joy.

Because nothing of earthshaking importance will occur, we may call the fifteen years Luther still has left to live with his family and for Christianity the final ones, a period of literally ultimate things although penultimate ones occurred, of course, and life in the Black Cloister went on.

In June, 1531, Luther's mother followed his father. She had been privileged to witness the Doctor's life and activity in Wittenberg and to sing her grandchildren to sleep. Now, the son consoles the dying mother with the words of Christ: "Be of good cheer; I have overcome the world." And he also writes: "Everyone, my children and my Kate, are praying for you. Some are crying, some eat and say, grandmother is very ill. May God's grace be with us!"

During these final years, he spends more time teaching and training students. In 1531, he lectured once more on Galatians, his favorite epistle, his "Katharina von Bora," as he also called it. From 1535 to 1545, he lectured again on Genesis, the "histories of the fathers," and especially the story of Abraham which runs through his entire work like a red thread. In numerous important disputations in which he proved again that one can be both biblical theologian and scholastic, he tried to head off his fundamental concerns from developing misunderstandings. And he preached now and then as he always had and served piety through numerous writings.

The *Table Talk*—in which Luther comments on the events of the past, present, and future before friends, colleagues, students, and members of his household and which, as occasional speeches, deal now humorously, now angrily, sometimes crudely, not always correctly but usually relevantly and pointedly with topics from all spheres of life and knowledge—are not necessarily among the "ultimate things." Written down and supplemented by eager students—V. Dietrich, C. Cordatus, A. Lauterbach, G. Rörer, and J. Schlaginhaufen are some of the "stenographers"—entire collections came into being which naturally have a special interest for publishers and whose significance for Luther's biography would be even greater, were "truth" and "legend," the "authentic" and the "merely decorative" more easily distinguishable.

It seems plausible that Luther's "Domina Kate" or "kitchen-colonel," as he lovingly and caustically called her, naturally had mixed feelings about this favorite institution. It is not just that she became annoyed when the good food got cold because of all the talk, but rather on account of the constant ebb in family finances, she had to make sure willy-nilly that the number of table companions stayed within certain limits, and that the students lodging in the Black Cloister paid for their keep. Among her contemporaries and serious scholars, this has earned her the not exactly enviable reputation of having been "overly precise in her arithmetic," which was allegedly the reason why, sometime in 1534, a serious quarrel between her and Veit Dietrich developed and the vicar and his students left the Black Cloister and Wittenberg in October when Luther sided with his wife.

Although I cannot document my thesis with the nicety of those real scholars who hold to a particular image of Luther, I maintain with good reason and a little imagination that pretty much the opposite was the case. A wife who waits on her husband's table companions and perseveres like Kate and does not mutiny even when the Doctor calls his friends to one of his drinking bouts that rarely ended before midnight, a woman of whom her husband expects, and may expect, real miracles, is no miser even if she occasionally watches her pennies. That this happened particularly in the vicar's case had special, plausible reasons. For Dietrich was one of those men who earned a good deal of money from the publishers with Luther's golden words, yet the annoyed Kate never received so much as a single penny. Besides, the realistic and observant Domina probably came to recognize in the course of time what the excessively trusting Doctor had not even noticed in Coburg castle, and that is that the seemingly so devoted secretary and amanuensis was not nearly as loyal as he pretended in public. That the Doctor could pray earnestly and with all his heart Kate knew, and we know, without Dietrich's reports from Coburg. But that Luther occasionally quarrelled a little with his Kate we only know from Dietrich.

Much more painful for Luther were the deviations from the core of his doctrine of the law and the gospel that close and even very close friends were guilty of. There was the ever renewed dispute with Johannes Agricola who repeatedly quarreled, first with Luther and then with Melanchthon, because he disputed the permanent meaning of the law, holding that its demands were excessive as compared to the gospel. In spite of a close personal friendship which also included the two families, an unfortunate dispute arose which, with its polemics against the recalcitrant "Master Grickel," finally led to Agricola's expulsion from Wittenberg. Melanchthon conversely arrived at a doctrine that seemed to maintain —as Conrad Cordatus reported to Luther immediately after the lecture—that "good works" had to be considered a "necessary condition" of salvation. Luther was deeply disturbed that such a split in fundamental beliefs occurred even during his lifetime, and among his closest collaborators at that. In this case also, a quarrel developed and the peace-loving Master Philip suggested to his friends that he would not be sad to see the ties holding him in Wittenberg finally break, for he would prefer devoting the rest of his life to scholarship.

Resisting misunderstandings and making essential decisions about the future, Luther had to return to the question of church office. For after the failure of the Augsburg negotiations, it had to be accepted that "Catholic bishops" would not ordain pastors for Protestant congregations. At the same time, there was a marked decrease in the number of priests from the old Church aligning themselves with the Reformation. But everywhere, in cities like Augsburg and in the countryside as well, voices invoking the priesthood of all believers could now be heard that laid claim to the right of emergency baptism and emergency confession for all laymen, and also to the "freedom" of the head of household to administer communion to his family. Luther resolutely rejected all these demands and soon did so with considerable vigor. Without "ordained pastors," Christians, he stated, were like the Jews in Babylon and must do without the celebration of the Eucharist. Paradoxically, it became apparent that, for Luther, only ordained pastors had the power and the right to administer the sacrament of the altar to their congregations. Opposing the practice that began to prevail with the first *Church Orders* where ordination was replaced by the installation of the pastor chosen by the congregation, Luther stuck obstinately to the old order. In 1535, he created the first German ordination formulary according to which, once the examination had been concluded and a congregation had called them, the ordinands were ordained centrally, in Wittenberg. To justify ordination by the Wittenberg pastor. Luther invoked the example of Augustine who had first been "consecrated or ordained to preach" by his bishop Valerius and had "become a bishop himself" after Valerius' death and then went on to ordain a great number of "pastors or bishops" in his "pastorate." It is consistent with this that Luther later created an ordination rite for bishops, ordaining Nikolaus von Amsdorf bishop of Naumburg in 1542, and Prince Georg von Anhalt coadjutor bishop of Merseburg. Since both ordinands had already been ordained and Luther rejected " re-ordination" throughout his life, we may infer that, in practice, Luther did not object to the old-church distinction between presbyteral and episcopal ordination. Although Luther protested strongly against the claim to power on the part of the bishops of his time, his criticism fell silent whenever bishops made the pastoral office of Christ visible and effective through their ministry. Bestowed *ritu apostolico* and sanctioned *voce aspostilica*, the bishop's office was therefore hardly a human invention as far as Luther was concerned, however testily he may have reacted in all those cases where pope and bishop put forward the mandate of the Lord ("Feed my sheep," John 21: 16ff.) as their "divine right."

Luther's remarks regarding the impending council were of similar importance. It is not enough to point to the unquestionable ambivalence of the statements. For years, people had referred to this council because they felt it was their only salvation. Since they knew or thought they knew that the papacy would never assent to a council because it feared for its power, invocation of it gradually came to resemble a political veto that cost nothing but also produced no results. When news finally did become more definite and the possibility more likely, reactions were cautious and skeptical. One was aware of the dangers a council called and directed by the pope would have for one's own cause. Yet to refuse to attend was not a possible alternative. During the first phase, there was thus a good deal of jockeying as during the odd meeting between Luther and the papal legate Vergerio on November 6, 1535, in Wittenberg.

The situation became much more serious when Paul III finally did announce that the council would open in May 13, 1537, in Mantua. Now, the evangelical side had to take a position willy-nilly. In addition to the possibilities mentioned above, the elector considered a counter Council of Protestant estates and theologians. Because the problem was considerably more weighty than in Augsburg, the elector did not turn to Melanchthon but asked his chancellor to call on Luther himself. He was to determine which articles absolutely must be defended before the council and where room to maneuver without danger to one's conscience existed. The draft Luther was asked to prepare would be examined by other evangelical theologians and then given its final form. Luther completed his Articles of Schmalkalden in January 1537. They are clear, consistent, and uncompromising: there are, first, the doctrinal articles in which nothing can be yielded. And with a view to its character as a sacrifice and the abuses connected with this, the mass is rejected with uncommon severity whereas existing common elements go unmentioned.

The position on monasteries and the veneration of saints is more positive. Luther's rejection of the papacy is uncompromising, but he observes accurately that recognizing the papacy as an institution of "human law" would be of no service whatever to the papists. Yet this was precisely the concession Melanchthon was prepared to make as he attested in a special reservation he added to his signature.

The elector Johann Friedrich enthusiastically backed Luther's articles and wished to have them accepted at the meeting of the Schmalkaldic league in Schmalkalden on February 10. On February 7, the elector, accompanied by Luther, Melanchthon, Bugenhagen, and Spalatin arrives in Schmalkalden. While Luther assumes the duties of pastor as usual, Melanchthon joins up with Philip of Hesse and the Strassburgers and sabotages the acceptance of Luther's articles in order to avoid doctrinal disputes over the Eucharist among the Protestants. Compared with his position in Augsburg, this meant a one-hundred-and-eighty-degree change in Melanchthon's "coalition" and position. He thus prevented acceptance of Luther's articles as the "official confession" for years. But being the editor of the Augsburg Confession, he was now asked to supplement it by a tract On the Primacy and the Power of the Pope.

Luther, who had not attended the official negotiations because he was ill and suffering from kidney stones had become so sick in the meantime that one feared the worst. His face in tears, Melanchthon prays at the bedside of his hopelessly ill friend. This time also, there is no reason to doubt the sincerity of these tears, yet the scene illustrates the mystery of a friendship which cannot really be illuminated when one makes the distinction between person and issue.

As though by a miracle, Luther recovered. Dislodged by the shaking of the carriage which is to bring the dying man back home to his Kate, the stones pass through the ureter and Luther feels newborn. As when he was kidnapped to the Wartburg, people again believe he has died. At the urging of the princes, he must certify from Wittenberg by his signature and seal that his death is a favor he unfortunately cannot yet do the devil, the pope, and his enemies. God, he writes, had not wanted him yet, but the day would come when He would although at that moment, his enemies might wish that he were still among them.

In the summer of 1540, Melanchthon fell deathly ill and Luther knelt at his bedside to pray him back to life. In back of this event lay the saddening and disreputable marriage of Philip of Hesse. After the death of his father-in-law, Duke George of Saxony, in 1539, and just after contracting syphilis himself, the landgrave thought that the time had come to resolve the problem of his marriage to Christina of Saxony which, although allegedly unhappy, had yet produced a great many children. Because he was in love with a young woman from the country nobility whose mother insisted that the proprieties be observed, and because as the leading intellect of the Schmalkaldic League he was committed to Christian principle, only a theological and legal solution was possible. But what kind of solution was it to be—the unseemly idea of Abraham's bigamy was in the air from the beginning—and who would take responsibility for it? It was only natural for the landgrave to think immediately of the "mediators" Bucer and Melanchthon who had long been allied with him. And all three thought of Luther. In spite of what he may have been told about the troubled conscience of the landgrave, it is unpardonable that Luther allowed himself to be dragged into this affair. An opinion of the reformers enabled the landgrave to conclude a second marriage which, like the counsel of his confessor, was to be kept absolutely secret. Naturally, neither was, and Melanchthon was so foolish as to let himself be persuaded to attend the wedding. The scandal was real and made rather large waves. Luther felt deceived and probably had a bad conscience. Yet what was he to do? He stuck to the fiction that the confessor's counsel was being followed and lied his way out of the affair. He drank the barrel of wine the grateful Philip sent him but burned the accompanying letter. The world will perish in any event but certainly not just on account of his and the landgrave's sin.

Poor Melanchthon reacted quite differently. He was denounced and escaped into illness. On his way to the discussions in Hagenau, he collapsed in Weimar and slid into a serious depression. Luther heard of his friend's collapse and hurried to his side. Pressuring God with his prayers, he also forced Philip back into life and made him eat by threatening excommunication. When Philip felt better again, Luther wrote his "beloved virgin Kate:" "I am well, eating like a Bohemian and drinking like a German, thanks be to God, Amen. The reason is that Master Philip was really dead and rose from the dead like Lazarus."

Luther is clearly perfectly well again and everything he always was whenever he appears in public: drawing back like a hammer-thrower, he fights for and against everything that threatens him during these final years: *Against Usury, Against the Turk,* (1541), *Against Hans Worst,* (1541), *Against the Roman Papacy, an Institution of the Devil* (1545). Oddly enough, he no longer has any trouble with electoral censorship during these years. True, even now, the reformers do not proceed in a completely coordinated manner. Once again, it is Melanchthon who drafts a proposal for a "gentle Reformation" (1545) for his Wittenberg colleagues, and Luther signs although he is already strenuously at work on his "testament" against the "Antichrist" on the Roman throne, the illustrations for which are being provided by the concurrently published woodcuts of Cranach's ridiculing the pope, with a terse commentary in verse. We have repeatedly mentioned the theology of the "Antichrist." What remains to be discussed is the statement of the woodcuts which, to the present day, makes the hair of all peaceable, learned, and ecumenical viewers stand on end.

Since the publisher cannot grant me the space for detailed commentary, I will have to shock the reader by a brief one even if I run the risk that people will consider me neither peaceable, erudite, nor ecumenical. My comment is this: these woodcuts are unbelievably rude and therefore comprehensible only to mercenaries. Yet in spite of their foul-smelling and scatological pictorial language, they are not obscene—Luther himself objected to the breasts of the devil's grandmother from whose rear end the papacy and the cardinals are seen to fall—but, more importantly, expressions of very important concerns whose theological justification is not in doubt.

This even applies to a painting, unbearable in its medieval cruelty, that shows the hanging of the pope and his crew, for if the papacy's "anti-Christian" claim to power was blasphemy, then the execution including the torn-out and nailed-down tongues was the punishment provided for it. This is equally true of the seemingly horrible satire on John 21:18 in the text of the tract since for a papacy which, in true Petrine succession, does not content itself with the "shepherd's wages" by allowing the Lord to lead it where it does not wish to go, that path will necessarily take it to Ostia where Luther proposes to "bathe" the pope and his retinue in the Mediterranean until God's Church is rid of him. It also applies to those caricatures that impressively show the accursed quarrel for predominance in Church and empire between emperor and pope, the quarrel that gave birth to the papacy with its impious claim to power and destroyed the Christian Middle Ages because it was unwilling to accept the "crucifying" division of power of the two-power doctrine.

A final theme for which Luther has long since been publicly denounced and will unquestionably be denounced again in his jubilee year forms part of this eschatological thematic. I am thinking of the "Jewish question" regarding which our ever so peaceful public, ever so willing to make amends for the past, seems inclined to paint Luther and ultimately all his concerns in blood-red on the walls of houses as if he were the man without whom Hitler and his horrible final solution for the Jews would never have come about. Since the gentlemen who want to write history with the "paintbrush" understand little of real history, historical pointers won't do much good in this context. To mention, for example, that the exemplarily peaceful Erasmus wished even ghastlier things on the Jews, a fact that, oddly enough, no one cares to call attention to—cannot exculpate Luther. The same is true predecessors such as St. Bernard, and his contemporaries. It does not help Luther and does not ex-

MONSTRVM ROMAE INVENTVM MOR
TVVM IN TIBERI. ANNO 1496.

Was Gott selbst vom Bapstum hellt
Zeigt dis schrecklich bild hie gestellt:
Dafür jederman grawen sollt:
Wenn ers zu hertzen nemen wollt.
Mart: Luth: D.

DIGNA MERGES PAPAE SATANISSIMI
ET CARDINALIVM SVORVM.

Wenn zeitlich gestrafft solt werden:
Bapst vnd Cardinel auff Erden.
Ir lesterzung verdienet hett:
Wie jr recht gemalet steht.
Mart. Luth. D.

plain a great deal when other highly respected names are painted on the walls of houses below or above his.

I therefore content myself with the statement that it is very unjust to denounce Luther in this matter. I am also aware of the fact that the very summary proof which I will offer here will convince neither the public nor the people with the brush. But in the case of all those who do not consider themselves infallible, the following remarks should at least initiate a revision of the customary misjudgment.

(1) Luther's anti-Semitism had nothing whatever to do with any kind of racial theory. On the contrary, throughout his work, Luther rejects and combats any national theology that identifies the seed of Abraham with God's people. (2) Luther's position on the Jewish question cannot simply be inferred from his five works that deal with Jews but only from the place they have in his theology as a whole. From that perspective, the uncompromising harshness of the late writing on the Jews is neither a symptom of senility nor the expression of a hate neurosis but the result of the growing eschatological seriousness of the situation. Neither the murder of God for which the Jews are blamed, nor the crimes they are charged with, and certainly not the avarice for which they are forever criticized (and which bad Christians use as an excuse for not paying their debts), but only the "eschatological" intensification of the situation accounts for the uncompromising harshness. The Church can accept the fact that Jews will not convert. But what it cannot accept is Jewish missionary activity and the infiltra-

216

ORTVS ET ORIGO PAPAE.

Hie wird geborn der Widerchrist
Megera sein Seugamme ist:
Alecto sein Kindermeidlin
Tisiphone die gengelt jn.
Mart.Luth.D.

Three woodcut caricatures of the pope by Lucas Cranach with verses by Martin Luther. It is possible that Luther designed the illustrations as well. He certainly resisted the shamelessness and prurience of Cranach's scheme, as can be seen, for example, in a correction of the first illustration in the series. The following persons can be recognized hanging on the gallows: Cardinal Albrecht, archbishop of Mainz; Otto Truchsess von Waldburg, bishop of Augsburg; Johannes Cochläus; the pope (without a portrait likeness).

cannot call you, poor Judas, and the rest of the Jews enemies, for it our sin." Although this verse has not been explicitly ascribed to Luther, there are a number of statements that justify such an ascription (H. H. Oberman).

These few sentences will not get Luther out of the pillory that has already been prepared for him and his jubilee in Augsburg and wherever the respect one pays him is no more than "critical." Yet it seems to me that it is good to know that this time he is a scapegoat and is being pilloried for others' sins, which is not at all to say that he should not also atone for his own.

This brings me to a concluding thought which should fit in with this very wilful and narrative biography and causes me considerable difficulties for a variety of reasons. Instructive conclusions would be inappropriate and superfluous: the reader does not need our assistance to infer them from our portrayal. But a long farewell that would attest to my love for Luther as "father in the faith" could easily be misinterpreted as sentimentality and hagiography. I will therefore dispense with edifying conclusions, and especially with a detailed account of the truly Christian death that finally overtook him in the early morning hours of February 16, 1545, in Eisleben, where he had presumably come into this world sixty-three years earlier. His last words come from the Latin Compline of his monasticism: *In manus tuas commendo spiritum meum, redimisti me, Deus veritatis!* ("Into your hands, I commend my spirit. You have redeemed me, God of truth"). And later, a scrap of paper bearing this message in his handwriting is found: "The truth is, we are beggars."

I wish to take leave of the living Luther by presenting two snapshots that strike me as typical of his life in the face of death.

tion of the Church by the Sabbatarians. The fight against Jewry and its doctrines therefore necessarily becomes something like the fight against the "Turk" or the "Antichrist" though an effective defense against the latter does not exist. (3) But most decisive is the fact that, from his early to his late work, Luther never modified his theological interpretation of the "murder of God" which is normally the principal motive for Christian anti-Semitism and all persecution of the Jews. The Jews crucified Christ as representatives of Christianity and all humankind, yet God saves us by transforming the death of His son into the cause of our salvation. The same idea is expressed in a new verse of the Wittenberg songbook of 1544: "Our great sin and grievous misdeed have crucified Jesus, the true Son of God. But for that reason we

The first shows him on his last birthday in the bosom of family and friends, on November 10, 1545. He had wanted a final celebration with the kind of joie de vivre that is never irreconcilable with the thought of death. The elector had recently restocked the wine cellar, and in the kitchen of the Black Cloister Kate is busy preparing a hundred pounds of pike and sixty carp. The tables are buckling under the weight of steaming dishes. I would willingly trade one of the lesser polemical writing like the *Sententia ... de abolendo lupanari Hallensi* ("On Abolishing the Whorehouse in Halle") for Kate's pike soup recipe. The jug of golden Rhine wine or perhaps Franken wine is making the rounds, and the mood is the same as one would find at an unending banquet of a king. Two generations of reformers have come to celebrate: his friends Melanchthon and Bugenhagen have been given the best places, while Cruciger and Major sit further away. There is much talk until, as usual, the Doctor rises to give one of those great speeches whose conception will forever be a mystery—wild like a charging elephant that tramples everything in its path, yet also tender as an elephant's trunk which can pick a fragile butterfly from blooming roses without causing a single leaf to fall to the ground. Toward the end, there is an intimation of death and Luther speaks of it, roughly and unsentimentally, so that Kate will have reason to scold and need not weep, yet full of expectation and longing: "When I return from Eisleben, I'll lie down in my coffin and give the worms a fat doctor for their dinner. I am weary of the world and so depart all the more willingly, like a guest from a common inn."

The second snapshot comes from the "Great" Genesis commentary, the final lecture of which he gave November 17, 1545, and more specifically the preface which Luther had used as an introduction to the first volume of his works which, supervised by Veit Dietrich, had appeared in print a year earlier.

The unusual preface was written under the impression the reading of the Abraham story, which he loved more than anything, had made on Luther. Abraham died as a stranger in his own country but he died as the friend of God. Even during his pilgrimage, he lacked for nothing, not even the four hundred shekels of silver he needed to buy from the Hittite Ephron the cave of Machpelah near Mamre so that he might bury his Sarah there. When, years later, he died at a very advanced age and "tired of life," his sons bury him at the same place. The prologue begins with a short statement on the purpose of the lecture: from the very beginning, it had not been meant for publication. Rather, he gave it to serve the Wittenberg

school, his audience, and himself in order to practice the preaching of God's word and to avoid sitting about lazily in an otherwise useless old age. He thanks the *collectores* —K. Cruciger, G. Rörer, and V. Dietrich—for the trouble they took in going through the manuscript (what a pity the original text of the lecture has not come down to us) and also regrets the effort that was expanded on the improvement of his work. He cannot assert that he commented on Genesis; at most, he had intended to. Although this may be the usual "humble rhetoric" of all prefaces, the following explanation is literally true: " Everything is said *extemporaliter* and in very popular fashion, in my own natural diction, German and Latin intermingled, and much more wordy than I had intended."

But there is no need for big words. For it is Scripture, "the Scripture of the Holy Spirit" which he has tried to interpret. And who can do this after the Apostles? Then he quotes St. Gregory the Great on the Bible and expresses what he was privileged to discover throughout his life: "Scripture is like a huge stream along whose banks lambs scamper and in whose deep middle elephants bathe." With a view toward all who have interpreted Genesis before him, he says: Not he who has understood everything and made no mistake is the "best," but he who allows himself to be carried away by the "greatest love." In that sense, not even the "fathers" wrote the perfect commentary. "And how downright ridiculous are the modern exegetes who believe they are accomplishing great things when they paraphrase the subject matter of Scripture *pura latinitate* although they lack all intelligence and understanding and have as much talent for interpretation as donkeys for playing the lyre."

St. Jerome (whom Luther did not really respect) was therefore right when he said that everyone contributes what he can to the construction of "God's tent": "Some bring gold, silver, and precious stones, others only animal skins and goat hair, for the Lord needs everything for His 'tent.'" Luther permitted the publication of his lecture although—and here he is thinking of Christmas —he can offer the Lord no more than "the wretched hair of his goats." But then, looking forward to Christmas inadvertently turns into the eschatological longing for the return of the Lord who will perfect the work He has begun within us, who will hasten the great day of our redemption which we await with heads held high and with a "pure faith" and with a "good conscience"—even though love may be in need of perfection.

Thinking of Abraham and of Christmas, of his own death and the "precious Last Day," Luther ends with the final verses of the Book of Revelation: "'Come soon,

Lord Jesus!' (as the Spirit and the Bride prompt one another). And let everyone who loves you say, 'Come soon, Lord Jesus! Amen.'" How silly that expression was that for centuries we believed hit the nail on the head: "To lead a good life one must be Lutheran; to die a good death, Catholic." Anyone who follows Luther will live well and die even better, for at the end of the dark tunnel stands someone who loves us and to whom we can look forward. That is Luther's ecumenical legacy for which we should give him thanks.

# TIME CHART

| Year | Rulers, Popes, Contemporaries* | Luther | Reformation and Counter-Reformation |
|------|-------------------------------|--------|-------------------------------------|
| 1483 | Raphael (1483–1520) | Nov. 10: Martin Luther is born in Eisleben and is baptized the next day. | |
| 1484 | Pope Sixtus IV *(1471–84)*<br>Pope Innocent VIII *(1484–92)*<br>Elector Frederick the Wise of Saxony *(1486–1525)* | The Luther family moves to Mansfeld. | Dr. Johann Eck (1486–1543) |
| 1488 | Lorenzo de' Medici *(1449–92)*<br>Columbus's first expedition (1492)<br>Pope Alexander VI *(1492–1503)*<br>Emporer Maximilian I *(1493–1519)*<br>Paracelsus (1493–1541)<br>Hans Sachs (1494–1576) | L. attends the Latin school in Mansfeld. | Ulrich Zwingli (1488–1531)<br>Ignatius Loyola (1491–1551) |
| 1497 | Hans Holbein (1497–1543)<br>Vasco da Gama discovers a sea route to India (1497–99) | L. attends the school of the Brethren of the Common Life in Magdeburg. | Philip Melanchthon (1497–1560)<br>Savonarola hanged in Florence (1497) |
| 1498 | Sebastian Frank (1499–1543)<br>Benvenuto Cellini (1500–1571) | L. attends St. George's parish school in Eisenach. | |
| 1501 | Pope Julius II *(1503–13)*<br>Nostradamus (1503–66) | L. begins his studies at the University of Erfurt. | Founding of the University of Wittenberg |
| 1505 | | L. obtains the Master of Arts degree (Jan.) and begins the study of law (May).<br>July 2: the thunderstorm in Stotternheim; L. vows to become a monk.<br>July 17: L. becomes a novice in the monastery of the Augustinian Hermits (Friars) in Erfurt. | |
| 1506 | Christopher Columbus (1451–1506) | L. takes final vows (autumn). | |
| 1507 | | L. is ordained to priesthood (Apr. 3), celebrates his first mass in Erfurt (May 2), and begins the study of theology. | Pope Julius II proclaims an indulgence for the rebuilding of St. Peter's. |
| 1508 | | Vicar General Johannes von Staupitz appoints L. substitute lecturer on moral philosophy at the University of Wittenberg. | |
| 1509 | Henry VIII of England *(1509–47)*<br>Landgrave Philip of Hesse *(1509–67)* | L. obtains the Bachelor of Theology degree (Mar.) and returns to Erfurt. | John Calvin (1509–64) |

* The reigns of rulers and popes are given in italics.

| Year | Rulers, Popes, Contemporaries | Luther | Reformation and Counter-Reformation |
|---|---|---|---|
| 1510 | | L. journeys to Rome on affairs of his order (Nov.). | |
| 1511 | | L. returns to Erfurt (spring) and is appointed sub-prior of the Augustinian monastery in Wittenberg and takes over from Staupitz the chair of theology at the university. | |
| 1512 | | L. obtains the Doctorate in Theology (Oct. 19) and begins his lectures on Genesis. | Fifth Lateran Council (1512–17) |
| 1513 | Pope Leo X *(1513–21)* | L.'s "Tower experience" in the Wittenberg monastery (spring). L. begins his lectures on the Psalms. | Albrecht of Brandenburg, cardinal archbishop and elector of Mainz *(1514–45)* |
| 1515 | Francis I of France *(1515–47)* Teresa of Avila *(c. 1515–82)* | L. begins his lectures on the Epistle to the Romans. | |
| 1516 | Hieronymus Bosch (c. 1450–1516) | L. begins his lectures on the Epistle to the Galatians. | |
| 1517 | | Oct. 31: L. sends his 95 Theses against the indulgence preaching of Johann Tetzel to the archbishop of Mainz. | |
| 1518 | | L.'s *Sermon on Indulgence and Grace*, a popular account of his 95 Theses. Disputation at the chapter meeting of Augustinians in Heidelberg (Apr.). Beginning of the process against L. in Rome. Hearing in Augsburg before Cardinal Cajetan (Oct./Nov.). L. refuses to recant and appeals to a general council. Elector Frederick the Wise declines to surrender L. (Dec.). | |
| 1519 | Leonardo da Vinci (1452–1519) Emperor Charles V *(1519–48)* | Disputation between L. and Johannes Eck in Leipzig (July). | |
| 1520 | Sultan Sulayman I (1520–66) | The bull *Exsurge Domine* threates L. with excommunication (June). L. replies with his great programmatic writings: *To the Christian Nobility of the German Nation*, *The Babylonian Captivity of the Church*, and *The Freedom of a Christian Man*. L.'s writings are burned in Louvain, Liège, Cologne, and Mainz (Oct./Nov.). Dec. 10: L. burns *Exsurge Domine* before the Elster Gate in Wittenberg. | |

| Year | Rulers, Popes, Contemporaries | Luther | Reformation and Counter-Reformation |
|---|---|---|---|
| 1521 | Cortes conquers Mexico | L. is excommunicated by the bull *Decet Romanum Pontificem* (Jan. 3) and is summoned to the Diet of Worms (Mar.). April 16–18: L. is escorted to Worms by the Imperial Herald, defend his writings there, and refuses to recant. April 26: L. leaves Worms and is "kidnapped" to the Wartburg. The Edict of Worms puts L. under the imperial ban and prohibits his teachings (May). L. begins his translation of the New Testament while at the Wartburg (Dec. to Mar. 1, 1522). | Beginning of religious unrest in Wittenberg: abolition of private masses, reception of communion under both kinds (Karlstadt), destruction of religious images (autumn). |
| 1522 | Johann Reuchlin (1455–1522) Pope Adrian VI *(1522–23)* | L. leaves the Wartburg and returns to Wittenberg (Mar.). L.'s translation of the New Testament appears without mention of his name (Dec.). L. begins his translation of the Old Testament (completed in 1534) and writes *On Married Life*. | Zwingli initiates the Reformation in Zurich. |
| 1523 | Ulrich von Hutten (1488–1523) Pope Clement VII *(1523–34)* | Monks and nuns leave their monasteries. L. writes *On Secular Authority* (Mar.), the *Little Book on Baptism*, and begins to create his noble German hymns. | Admission of guilt by Pope Adrian VI at the Diet of Nuremberg |
| 1524 | | L. resumes his lectures in Wittenberg and lays aside his friar's habit (Oct.) | Thomas Müntzer writes against Luther. The Peasants' War (1524–25). Johannes von Staupitz (c. 1465 to 1524). |
| 1525 | Jakob Fugger (1459–1525) Elector John of Saxony *(1525–32)* Machiavelli (1469–1527) Albrecht Dürer (1471–1528) | L. writes *Against the Heavenly Prophets*. Traveling in areas of unrest, he preaches against the Peasants' Revolt (Apr./May), then writes *Against the Robbing and Murdering Mobs of Peasants*. June 13: L. marries the former Cistercian nun Katharina von Bora, writes *Bondage of the Will* against Erasmus. Beginning of the new church order in Saxony. | First Diet of Speyer (1526) Hesse becomes Evangelical. Brandenburg becomes Evangelical. |
| 1529 | | Oct. 1–4: the Colloquy of Marburg; no agreement reached with Zwingli on the Lord's Supper. L. writes the *Large Catechism*. | Second Diet of Speyer: the protest of the Evangelical estates against the abrogation of the resolutions of 1526 leads to their being called "Protestants." Sulayman besieges Vienna. |

| Year | Rulers, Popes, Contemporaries | Luther | Reformation and Counter-Reformation |
|---|---|---|---|
| 1530 | | Apr./Oct.: L. stays at Coburg Castle during the Diet of Augsburg. June 25: solemn reading of the Augsburg Confession. | |
| 1531 | Tilman Riemenschneider (1460 to 1531) | L. writes *Warning to the Dear German People.* | Separation of the English church from Rome |
| 1532 | Elector John Frederick of Saxony *(1532–47)* Orlando di Lasso (1532–94) Veit Stoss (1445–1533) | | Peace of Nuremberg occasioned by the Turkish threat |
| 1534 | Pope Paul III *(1534–49)* | First complete edition of Luther's biblical commentaries. | Württemberg becomes Evangelical. Anabaptists in Münster. |
| 1535 | Thomas More (1465–1536) | L. begins his last great lectures on Genesis. | |
| 1536 | Erasmus of Rotterdam (1478–1535) | L. draws up the Articles of Schmalkalden (Dec.). The *Table Talk* appears. | Denmark and Norway become Lutheran. |
| 1537 | Albrecht Altdorfer (1480–1538) | L.'s illness during his stay at Schmalkalden. | |
| 1539 | | L. writes *On the Councils and the Churches.* The first volume of Luther's Collected Works appears. | Saxony and Electoral Brandenburg become Evangelical. The Society of Jesus is approved by Pope Paul III. |
| 1541 | | | Calvin initiates the Reformation in Geneva. John Knox brings the Calvinist Reformation to Scotland. |
| 1543 | Copernicus (1473–1543) | L. writes *On the Jews and Their Lies.* | Braunschweig becomes Reformed (1542). |
| 1544 | | L. writes *Brief Confession on the Holy Sacrament.* In Torgau L. dedicates the first Evangelical church. | |
| 1545 | Hans Baldung-Grien (1480–1545) | L. writes *Against the Roman Papacy, an Institution of the Devil.* The first complete edition of Luther's Latin writing appears. | Opening of the Council of Trent (Dec.) |
| 1546 | | Feb. 18: L. dies in Eisleben. Feb. 22: L. is buried in the castle church of Wittenberg. | Electoral Palatinate becomes Evangelical. The Schmalkaldic War begins. |